To Ursala

REEL TALK

A CINEMOIR

Peace
& Prosperity

SPENCER MOON

REEL TALK

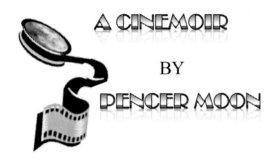

A CINEMOIR

BY

SPENCER MOON

©2011 by
Spencer Moon Publishing

Booklogix Publishing Services
Alpharetta, Georgia

Printed in the United States of America.

ISBN: 978-0-61556-815-7

Library of Congress Control Number: 2011960939

REEL TALK :

A CINEMOIR

OF IMAGES, PEOPLE AND IDEAS

TABLE OF CONTENTS

INTRODUCTION

August 1, 2010, 11pm, Atlanta, GA

I am a fountain of understanding with empathy for discovery who values the diversity of life. How I came to this vision is revealed through the pages of this book. Cinema and media have been a major influence on my life. I take the strands of these threads and weave the colorful story that is my life. At sixty-three (63) I've seen the new century arrive and am living in one of the most challenging times in our history. I feel secure that my story is one that is unique and common. The way in which my life tapestry is the fabric of my being is a story that bares scrutiny. I humbly invite your decision.

I am a book lover; I love them so much I have to write them.

I am a ratchet with life. I stand for going in the right direction with my writing and my life.

Ratchet – a tool used to allow effective motion in one direction.

ON CINEMOIR

This memoir is a montage of images,

people and ideas.

The result is a Cinemoir...

NOTE

* Indicates archived in the ***National Film Registry***. The **NFR** is "...meant to showcase the full range and diversity of the American film heritage...". This archive is preserved by the Library of Congress, in Washington, D.C. the NFR has made some of these films available in VHS.

In the over 560 films preserved in the Registry – newsreels; silent films; feature films Hollywood and independent; home movies; television movies; experimental; short subjects; documentaries; music videos preserved since 1989 almost fifty of these films feature the Black experience. The Asian, Hispanic, Middle Eastern, Native American, Pacific and Caribbean Islands experience combined include another dozen and a half films.

CHAPTER ONE

When I think about where I was born, it fills me with a multitude of images, people, and ideas. I was born May 11, 1948 in Talladega, Alabama. Talladega is a Muscogee (Creek) Native American word derived from Tvlvteke, which means "border town." Prior to Euro-American settlement in what is today Talladega County, it was the home of the Abihka tribe of the Creek Confederacy. Talladega County was established on December 18, 1832, from land ceded by the Creek Indians near the state's geographic center. The county seat was established at Talladega in 1834.

Talladega is home to Alabama's oldest (private) historically black liberal arts college, Talladega College, founded in 1867. Two former slaves, William Savery and Thomas Tarrant, both of Talladega, met in convention with a group of new freedmen in Mobile, Alabama. From this meeting came the commitment to build a lasting institution of higher learning for freed slaves.

On July 5, 1910 in front of six hundred reporters and twenty thousand spectators Jack Johnson a black man for the first time ever won the Heavyweight Championship defeating the "...great white hope...", Jim Jeffries, in fifteen rounds. Western Unions one million words transmitted on the event and the Newsreel* set off riots in many major American cities. Whites were angry, black people were celebrating Johnson's significant sports victory. Many people were hurt, black, as well as white and some killed. Professor William Pickens of Talladega College said of these events, "The fact of the fight will outdo a mountain peak of theory about the Negro as a physical man and as a man of self- control and courage." (1)

Talladega College is home for the Amistad Murals. The murals depict incidents in American history that led to the first civil rights case argued before the Supreme Court by former President John Quincy Adams. In this court case, former slaves led by a Mandi tribesman named Cinque and with the help of Quaker abolitionists won their freedom to return to Africa. The Supreme Court ruled in a seven to one majority, (a Justice had died prior to deliberations) in favor of freeing the Africans, based on the rule of law.

The murals of this historic event were painted by Hale Aspacio Woodruff. Woodruff studied with one the foremost muralists of the 20th century, Diego Rivera. Woodruff was commissioned in 1938 to paint the mural. The 1998 film **Amistad** chronicles the story of African slaves and their quest for and success in winning their rightful freedom. The images and ideas extolled in this film bear scrutiny.

The murals are now recognized as a national treasure. The murals were recently valued at $40 million dollars and will soon be restored. After restoration is complete, the murals will be displayed in Atlanta's High Museum and from there they will then be sent on a national tour that includes Chicago, Philadelphia, San Francisco, Los Angeles, New York, and Washington, D.C.

In the city of Talladega, there is a Moon Street, named in honor of my great uncle Henry T. Moon (1914-1973). 'HT', as everyone knew him, was an entrepreneur who owned the most popular barbeque and soul food place in town called **Moon's Café**. 'HT' worked initially at a local paper mill and had a small building built for his café. The cafe proved so popular he had to build a second larger building, which enabled him to quit his job to run his business full time. The secret formula for his barbeque sauce was only known by members of his immediate family. To date it is not known what was in the sauce that made it so special.

'HT' made white people go to the back door to get service from his café. Whites knew no matter whom they were, if they wanted to be served they came to the back door, even the local police if they wanted service. 'HT' was well known by everyone in Talladega. 'HT' was also known for being there when members of his community needed him most. This was during encounters between blacks and whites that needed someone of our community to represent our side and speak up on behalf of the brother or sister who found themselves on the wrong side of the white southern social mores. NASCAR has an annual race in Talladega.

My parents never married and separated soon after I was born, May 11, 1948. I weighed eleven pounds at birth. Dan Blocker the actor who was "Hoss" the middle brother of the Cartwright family on **Bonanza** fame was born in Alabama and he weighed 15 lbs. when he was born.

My father's name was Glasco Stewart McCann (1904-1969). There is a small town in Alabama called McCannsville; it is in Talladega County. My mother chose to give me her family name when I was born and moved back home to her parents' home. My mother, Florence Edna Moon, was from a family of nine, four boys and five girls. She was the third oldest female. I did meet, my father twice later in life, as a child and as an early teen. On both occasions, the memory is vague and it seems he spent most of his time with the adults and acknowledged he was there because of me but not much else. This is the image I remember.

A childhood story based on what my mother often told recounts my crawling phase as a child. Mom proclaimed that she told one of her younger sisters to watch me while she was busy doing household chores. When she looked up, I had crawled into the front of the farmyard of her father 'Big Daddy' Lloyd Moon (1902-1973) that contained vegetables and an old mule that pulled Big Daddy's plow.

I had found a seat in the middle of the vegetable patch and was eating hot peppers near the mule that pushed rather than kicked me out of his way. Mom came out and rescued me from the mule and the hot peppers. I was none the worse for my experience. My love of spicy foods today surely comes from that time.

I do recall later visiting 'Big Daddy' Lloyd and Lillian, his second wife, when I was about 10 years old. My mom's mother died giving birth to her last child and my mother's youngest brother, Edward. When I was a child, 'Big Daddy' showed more paternal love than from any male in my early life. Within a year of my birth, mom and I moved to Detroit, Michigan where her oldest sister Rosa (Moon) Boyd, had moved with her husband, Wilson and daughter Thelma Kay.

"...white supremacy was the central theme of southern history..." (2)

A film that is startling in its depiction of the Black experience of the South during my youth is **The Untold Story of Emmitt Louis Till** (2005), 70 min., b/w & color, documentary, produced and directed by Keith A. Beauchamp. Emmitt Louis Till (1941-1955) was a black boy from Chicago who went to visit family one summer in the South. It was his first trip and experience in the South. His Southern family lived in Mississippi.

Emmitt Till and two cousins went one hot summer day into town to buy candy and soda. They chose Bryant's Store, in the town of Money, Mississippi. Emmitt's' cousins went into the store and bought candy and soda and came out. Emmitt went into the store alone. Ms. Bryant later alleged that Emmitt said something lewd to her. When she and he came out of the store, Emmitt made a wolf whistle at her as she went and got in her car. His cousins were shocked and their expressions told Emmitt that he had done something wrong, even before they told him. Emmitt was not familiar with the social mores of the Deep South, in

1955. Three days went by and nothing happened. On the third night, several white men came with guns and took Emmitt from his family's bed and home. Emmitt was found three days later in the Tallahatchie River tied to an industrial fan.

Mamie Till-Mobley brought the body of her son home for burial. When she saw the condition of her sons' corpse, she wanted the nation to know what the price was for a wolf whistle by a mischievous but ultimately innocent teenager. She said, "I want the world to see this." The world did see with the assistance of the NAACP and the black press.

In 1955, at seven years of age, those images of Emmitt that I saw in **Jet Magazine** haunted me. His life was made sacred because the nation knew that despite the end of slavery, that in the 20th Century black people in 1955 could expect to be killed without justice being served by the rule of law. My mother confirmed to me this was why she left the South and moved to Detroit.

This film is a very sobering, and alarming look at American apartheid in the extreme. Despite two trials for two white men accused in Till's death, (one trial for murder and a second trial for kidnapping), no one was ever convicted for the death of Emmitt Till.

"...unearned suffering is redemptive."
Martin Luther King, Jr.

John Lewis, 5th district Georgia House of Representatives, Democrat sponsored this bill and it became law in 2007, *H.R. 923: Emmett Till Unsolved Civil Rights Crime Act.* This act is to provide for the investigation of certain unsolved civil rights crimes, and for other purposes.

Television was the major source of many of the first films I saw. Television took movies as a ready source for programs in the fifties. The Hollywood studios eventually saw television as another way to make money and not as direct competition and began the process of using their already existent resources, studios with production equipment. Television program production keeps many studio brand names alive today from that era: Warner Brothers, FOX, Metro-Goldwyn-Meyer, United Artists, Universal, and Paramount.

Most of the major motion picture production companies are now part of huge multinational business conglomerates. Films are more widely viewed today because of the digital age. Because of the digital age, there is more distribution and exhibition from the large studios. There is now a plethora of means to shoot and edit images, information, and ideas with sometimes nothing more than a cell phone in your hand.

I was conscious even as a youngster of the lack of black images on television at the time. The black images I saw were overwhelmingly demeaning and stereotypical. **Amos N'Andy** (1951-1953) came and went during my youth. "A square" was first a radio program in the thirties that featured white people imitating black people or what they thought black people sounded like. Radio made this too easy.

Eventually looking to spread the vermin and make money it was turned into a feature film titled **Check and Double Check** (1930) with the white radio actors Freeman Gosden and Charles Correll who portrayed the black characters Amos N'Andy on the radio but who were now in black face for the film.

The film also featured on screen performances by Duke Ellington and the Cotton Club Orchestra. They perform two original compositions, Old Man Blues and Ring Dem' Bells. Because of the seeming success of both the film and radio program, it was decided that for television it would be more

appropriate to hire black actors. What a favor. For those who have not seen the sickening images of **Amos N'Andy,** they stand as a pinnacle in media history for their sheer ignorance in portrait and visual rape of black people, using the instrument of television.

The irony is that **Spencer Williams** (1893-1969) who portrayed Andy Brown in the television series **Amos N' Andy Show** was a progenitor in American independent Black cinema aka *"race movies"* that were made in the early part of the 20th century from about 1910 until 1950. Before his arrival in Hollywood, Williams was a decorated World War I veteran. Willams worked for Broadway theater impresario Flo Ziegfeld. He studied acting with the great black comic artist Bert Williams. Of no relation to each other, Spencer Williams' film career follows the rise of studio production in Hollywood. Williams had a college education, which helped to open doors of opportunity for him in Hollywood. Williams' career in the Hollywood idiom included writing script continuity for a series of silent comedies shot in the South and produced by Paramount Studios featuring black actors. Williams was also involved in helping to set up and install some of the first sound recording equipment in Hollywood. From his experiences in the Hollywood idiom, Williams was poised to begin work when the race movie era arrived.

"Race movies" were written and produced, directed and distributed by blacks and starred all black casts. In addition to black entrepreneurs, many white independent filmmakers made race movies. The black experience in film and television in the U.S. has been and in many ways is still distorted, denied, denigrating, and dangerous. Newspaper accounts indicate that between 1910 and 1950 there were more than 150 production companies, black and white owned, producing race movies. Race movies were an alternative to Hollywood made films specifically

for the black audience. In addition, there were over 460 movie houses during this period that featured and exhibited race movies.

Race movies came about because of segregation and as a direct result of black and white filmmakers responding to D.W. Griffith's civil war chronicle made in 1915, **The Birth of a Nation***. It is a seminal film in American film history because it develops the cinematic grammar for American cinema as we know it with its editing, story construction and use of a live orchestra to accompany the film when it was first exhibited. However, the film glorified and chronicled the rise of the Ku Klux Klan after reconstruction.

In many ways, the film continues to be used as a tool for those who still hold less than generous beliefs of their fellow man. The cinematic images of black people using both black actors and white actors in black face make-up are a graduate level study of racist cinema. The stereotypes from that film created the lexicon of racist images that were so aptly described in Don Bogles' book on the subject of black images – **Toms, Coons, Mulattoes, Mammies, and Bucks.**

Race movies presented a variety of mostly positive images of the black experience. Black actors who made the transition from race movies to Hollywood films included Paul Robeson, Lena Horne, Bill Robinson, Robert Earl Jones (James Earls' dad) and Ethel Waters to name a few.

Spencer William's films of this period were a major influence on contemporary black filmmakers who as students studied race movies. Charles Burnett, Julie Dash, Reginald Hudlin, Melvin Van Peebles, John Singleton, and Spike Lee have all gone on record as having studied the films of Spencer Williams.

Williams wrote, produced, directed, and starred in **The Blood of Jesus** (1941)*, b/w, 56 min... The film depicts the

political, social, religious, and economic milieu of the black experience of that time. The story is about a man married to a woman with deeply religious beliefs, while, he is more of an agnostic. The husband accidentally shoots his wife with his rifle. In the film, we see his spirit is touched by angels of mercy and with his newfound faith along with prayer from his wife's pastor and their church members coupled with his religious conversion. The film has religious scenes that take place in the river where people are being baptized accompanied by a gospel choir. Later in the film Williams' use of an experimental montage of images to convey what heaven might look like are striking even in black and white. Williams captures a black American social realist perspective adroitly.

By 1950, the race movie era came to an end. Williams goes into semi-retirement in the Midwest and is working as a photographer when he reads a full-page ad in **Variety**, the bible of the film industry, asking for actors, specifically black actors of all types. That call was for the **Amos N' Andy Show**.

Another reason race movies vanished was after the Hollywood Antitrust Case of 1948, United States vs. Paramount Pictures, Inc. the court decision that forced the separation of ownership of motion picture exhibitors and motion picture production companies. Prior to this decision Hollywood studios had a monopoly on film production and distribution. Indirectly this also helped to expand opportunities in Hollywood studios for Black actors as a result.

Another black actor of note is **Hattie McDaniel** (1892-1952). Ms. McDaniel is the first black actor to win an Academy Award for **Gone with the Wind** (1939)*, for her role as Mammy, she won the award for Best Supporting Actor. Hattie McDaniel was also part of a group of black actors who in 1937 gathered in Hollywood to garner support from their members who were members of the Screen Actors Guild both black and white who

wanted to change the pervasive negative images and roles of black actors. The battle eventually had to deal with the business aspect of show business. Their choice was to both work in demeaning roles and try to do it with dignity or not work at all. McDaniel is famously quoted as saying, "I can be a maid for $7 a week or I can play a maid for $700 a week."

To learn more about her and other black female performers, read Donald Bogles' book titled **Brown Sugar: 100 Years of Black Female Superstars**. He turned his book into an excellent documentary series also titled **Brown Sugar** (1986). The series is four (4) one-hour programs co-produced by the Public Broadcasting System and narrated by Billy Dee Williams.

In the fifties, the African American presence on television was negligible except in stereotypical roles or as performers. Two black people were given the opportunity to be seen on a regular basis in the small media landscape of programs at that time and they were both unique artists in their own right. They both appeared in non-stereotyped performances.

Hazel Scott (1920-1981) was a musical prodigy. Once her family migrated to the U.S. from her homeland Trinidad, by age eight she was on a full Julliard School of Music scholarship. Her musical influences were the classics and Art Tatum, Teddy Wilson and Count Basie with whom she performed. In the nineteen thirties she was a regular guest on radio programs, she sang and performed in nightclubs and had performed at Carnegie Hall more than once. Her style fused classical music with jazz and created an unmistakably unique sound.

In 1950, the **DuMont** television network gave Ms. Scott a program on their network. Ms. Scott was an out spoken advocate for civil rights and opposed the "red scare" tactics of Senator Joseph McCarty and his House Un-American Activities Committee. When she was called to testify she refused as many

did to give names or be a friendly witness. Because of this even though she was the first woman of color to have her own television program the program was canceled. The program aired from July until September of 1950.

Ms. Scott later appeared in a handful of Hollywood films usually as a musical interlude in the films. She continued to perform in clubs and in Europe. She was married to one of New York's most known black congressman of the 20th Century Adam Clayton Powell, Jr. and they had one child, Adam Clayton Powell III. Ms. Scott continued to record, perform in her own inimitable fashion, and performed until shortly before she succumbed to cancer.

The other forgotten black pioneer in early television is **Nat "King" Cole** (1919-1965). Nat Cole for many years led a jazz trio that featured his unique piano styling and his accompaniment a guitar and bass. Because of their exceptional artistry, his trio made a very good living. One night while in a club performing, a very drunk customer asked him to sing the song "Sweet Lorraine". The owner not wanting one of his best customers to be upset insisted that Cole sing the song to make the customer happy.

Cole complained, "...I don't sing very well..." Fortunately, for us it opened the door to a completely new career for Cole as one of the leading vocalists of his time. Cole's success was amplified when he was given the opportunity to perform his vocal styling on **NBC** for fifteen minutes once a week in 1956. Eventually the program expanded to thirty minutes. His style, grace, and demeanor made Cole one of the first black artists to cross over and win white audiences with his appeal and sound. Cole has a unique phrasing and timing in his vocal style. No less an artist than Frank Sinatra described Cole's voice as having "...true tonality and substance..."

The program ran from 1956-1957; he was seen in sixty-eight programs. His guests were the most popular performers and artists of that time. They included: Ella Fitzgerald; Mel Torme; Oscar Peterson; Harry Belafonte; Eartha Kitt; Mahalia Jackson: Tony Bennet; Johnny Mercer; Stan Kenton; Pearl Bailey; Cab Calloway; Frankie Lane and many other artists.

Eventually **NBC**, which had paid for the production of the program, could not get sponsors. Part of the fears and complaints was from southern audiences seeing Cole touching and being close to the white guests. Eartha Kitt, when asked many years later about Cole and his program on which she had appeared, she was very frank. She said, "It was too early for a black man to be seen as intelligent." Cole himself pulled the plug on the show, discontinued production, and said, "Madison Avenue is afraid of the dark."

My first experience of cinema was when I was six. Then it was called "the movies". I accompanied my mom and her girlfriend Vairee, who were among the millions of women world-wide who wanted to see Marlon Brando in **The Wild One** (1953). We went to the Dexter Theater on Dexter Avenue in Detroit. I was impressed at how big everything and everybody looked to me. We got refreshments and then found seats and once the movie began, I was over whelmed by the sheer size of the images in front of me. Brando worked his magic on my Mom and her best girlfriend. I on the other hand could not get over how visceral was the experience of the movie theater with the sound and pictures and all those people in this big auditorium. It was very different from our school auditorium where we could hear the noisy projector as we were compelled to watch science movies en masse. We sat through **The Wild One** and I mostly consumed popcorn, soda, and candy. The second film came after a break for me to visit the lavatory from the soda. The second film was a

horror film I remember, the title escapes me but it made me scared and mom saw that and we left before it was half over. I remember Vairee made fun of me on the way home she stuck her tongue out at me and called me a "...fraiddy cat..."

Marlon Brando (1924-2004) achieved immortality through his life and his films. Brando was a man of deep convictions his talent shown brilliantly for many years. However, it was his social conscience that led him to take up the struggle of civil and human rights in America. America was not ready to let him stop being an actor and become a political activist. He was not the first in Hollywood by any means, John Garfield, fought for civil rights in the forties, Paul Robeson fought for human rights in the thirties. There were many other actors who fought for their social and civil beliefs besides those mentioned.

Brando was one of the first actors of the Beat generation to show that acting and social activism were not exclusive. Brando was there lending his support for Dr. Martin Luther King, Jr., in his work for civil rights for black people. He marched and spoke at the March on Washington in August of 1963. A famous photo of the event shows Brando with his arm around James Baldwin (1924 - 1987). Baldwin was a prolific, brilliant, eloquent, and openly gay black author at a time when people still did not want to understand or accept openly gay individuals. Brando was also a supporter of Native American causes. He donated money and his influence and access to resources to both these very important causes. He was very visible and vocal in his activism.

Brando's Hollywood star was shattered the night Sasheen Littlefeather an Apache Native American actress, arrived at the Academy Award ceremony in buckskins, beads and moccasins. Brando had called her and asked her to appear in his place should he win an award. She rejected the Academy Award for Best Actor on Brando's' behalf.

She gave a short speech seen on national television at the Academy Award broadcast decrying the negative images of its' native people in Hollywood films and America's treatment of its indigenous people. Later she read a more detailed message on Brando's behalf, to the gathering of international press that expressed his support of the then ongoing struggle of Native Americans at the Pine Ridge Reservation in South Dakota. The siege was led by the American Indian Movement (AIM). AIM is a group of native people who had been influenced by the activism of the Black Panther Party and the philosophy of Malcolm X. They advocated radical social change for native people *"by any means necessary"*. Their seventy-one day siege that ended with several deaths caused by agents of the federal government, opened the door for a resurgence of indigenous peoples standing up for their human rights, language and spiritual practices. After Brando's' political stand, a poll of Americans taken after the Academy Awards showed support for Brando's' position. Brando had won his second Academy Award for Best Actor that year, 1972, as Don Vito Corleone in **The Godfather***.

Growing up in Detroit, Michigan, it is just across the river from Windsor, Ontario, Canada. I remember local Canadian television station **CKLW-TV**, channel 9. It was Windsor's' first television station and came on the air in 1954. Channel 9 was an affiliate of the **Canadian Broadcasting Company**. In terms of programming the station looked more American than Canadian. One of their local programs featured the same movie five nights a week. It was called the **Million Dollar Movie**. The film was introduced by a studio host. They ran the same movie five nights a week, so I began at an early age to study film, watching the same film many times.

I realize now that I had myopic vision because I was sitting right under our 24-inch black and white screen. I still recall my mother saying, *"Spencer sit back son, you're sitting too close."* Five

minutes later when my Mom was gone or occupied, I was right under the screen looking up at it as you would in a movie theater. One film that I saw on the **Million Dollar Movie** was **Go for Broke** (1951), 92 min., b/w, written and directed by Robert Pirosh. Pirosh was nominated for an Academy Award for Best Writing, Story & Screenplay. The film starred Van Johnson, Lane Nakano, George Miki, Akira Fukunaga, Ken K. Okamoto, Henry Oyasato, Harry Hamada, and Henry Nakamura.

This film was a recounting of the World War II regiment of Japanese Americans who fought heroically in Europe in the war. This group the 442nd Regiment was one of the most highly decorated units of the war. Members of the 442nd also starred in the film as well. Seeing Japanese Americans as heroes was an important idea for me, then as now.

Japanese Americans that lived on the west coast and in other parts of the country were rounded up and put in camps until the war was over. Many of the volunteers for the 442nd came from these camps. Japanese Americans received $1.2 billion dollars in reparations from the American government because of the loss of their homes and businesses while in these American internment camps.

My home life was stable but... Mom lived with this man from the time I was three until I was a teen. His name was Ike. He worked for Dexter Chevrolet in Detroit. He was many years older than my mother was. Mom worked initially and I was left home with Ike's, mom. Because I was introverted and an only child, I would sit in a chair in Ike's mom's space upstairs part of the big two-story brick house with full basement we all shared. I would sit in this chair all day and play on the arm of the chair with a little toy car and never get out of the chair except when I would be feed or go the lavatory. I would go back to the chair and stay there until my mother arrived later in the day from work. When

she found out that was what I was doing every day she worked, she became worried and stopped working, to be with me.

As I approached school age, my mother set about teaching me the alphabet. Her own education stopped in her high school years when I was born. I had difficulty learning the alphabet so she spanked me because that was what her parents did to her, spanked her. I know in hindsight that it seems a little cruel. I did learn my alphabet by the time I reached kindergarten. The spanking seared the significance and importance of knowledge in me. My mother knew knowledge would be my salvation and her redemption.

Ferndale, Michigan is a near suburb of Detroit and this is where I grew up. I attended Ulysses S. Grant Elementary School. I recall that my early years were an assortment of positive and negative images. Making friends became more difficult because by the time I was nine my myopic vision was diagnosed and I began wearing glasses. Kids with glasses tended to be picked on more. Glasses made athletic and physical activities even more challenging.

It was not until I reached third grade that I had a real buddy. His name was Donald. We played and talked and when given the opportunity in class would spend our time drawing cars with skirts. You know skirts that cover the outside of the back wheel well and match the color of the car or not. Later under Donald's influence, I learned the meaning of the word intimate. One of Donald's uncles had used the word in conversation over a weekend. When Donald came to school that Monday and used the word, the boys were thrilled to learn its meaning. Unfortunately, by weeks end we were saying in-to-me and having somehow lost the pronunciation and creating a child's version of an adult word. I was crestfallen when the next year Donald and his family moved from our area and my buddy was gone.

The bad memories include being picked on by a kid who I learned later had spent time in a juvenile institution. His name was Arthur Brown. He was bigger and at least a year older than we were but was in the fourth grade with us. His favorite taunt was to have the music teacher when we would do a class sing-a-along lead us in the song "Shine on Harvest Moon". I of course hated this, but he loved making me squirm in anguish as he sang the lyrics louder than any one. It was not until almost a year later when I decided to sing the song with as much vigor as he did that this torment stopped. A fond memory includes the annual fundraiser a teacher/student basketball game.

The teachers names who were going to play were announced on the public address system giving them names like "Crazy Legs" Hale, "Big Chief" Nance for our Native American gym teacher and other zany names for the teachers who participated, which when announced brought gales of laughter in classes of the respective teachers.

The event was held after school in the gymnasium. Hot dogs, popcorn, and soda were sold and all the money went to things like band uniforms and extra sports equipment and other things our Board of Education could not afford. The game was popular and fun. The students loved competing and the students always won. Right!

Another fond memory was the father/son night at school. This included a meal, we dressed up, and the program always included a talent show featuring students. I have mixed emotions about this memory. Ike, my mom's lover was my surrogate father. I was always confused about the question when asked at the event by fellow students, "Is that your father Spencer?" I usually replied, "He's my step-father", but I always felt embarrassed and tried to have as good a time as possible under the circumstances.

Ike was stern but my mother never let him spank me. He might give me a gruff talking to which made me cry, but the physical discipline which was part of my life until I was fifteen was always delivered by my mother. Ike was more distant than close. He and his family were all very musical. They all played piano very well. I remember that some weekends he would leave to go play in local clubs. My mother said his musical ability and sophistication compared to her rural background was part of what drew her to him. His mother played piano in church for many years. There was an upright piano downstairs where mom, Ike, and I lived. Upstairs there was a baby grand piano.

Their nephew Claude who stayed upstairs with Ike's mom when he was not traveling or staying with his friends played and practiced on the baby grand when he was home. Claude played piano full-time professionally. Sometimes he would have a drummer and a bass player come to the house and they would practice. Occasionally he would have a full combo with horns at his practices. Playing piano for the vocalist Dakota Staton was his best gig. I remember it was a big deal with the family when he got this job.

There was a period when I tried to learn how to play the piano. I gave up despite having so many people in my immediate home that played piano very well. A music teacher later, gave me a clarinet. I think I lasted about a month with that. A year or so later I achieved better success with drums. I became first chair drummer in the school and at one point we had uniforms and our marching band was in local parades. One Christmas I received a toy saxophone. I took the little music book which came with the toy sax and learned the Marines marching song. That tune was one of several songs in the booklet. I later transposed the tune for piano. Ike's mom heard me play that tune one day on piano and insisted that I perform that tune on

piano in our local Methodist church during a talent showcase, very odd. I have a great love of live and recorded music, which has become the soundtrack of my life. It certainly comes of all that musical exposure. I never successfully mastered playing an instrument.

My life as an only child revolved around other kids in the neighborhood and television. Two of my favorite television programs included **The Adventures of Rin-Tin-Tin** (1954-1959), a program about boy and his dog in the old west and **Circus Boy** (1956-58) this was about a boy with a traveling circus in the old west. These were all very thrilling images for me at the time.

My mother often had to make me go out and play when television programs I liked were on. Mother and Ike were together for my formative years. By my early teen years, 6th grade, my life changed dramatically. Ike liked to drink. He lost his job of many years and proceeded to drink more.

He even began to sell 'corn' liquor, homemade alcohol to a steady stream of customers who came to the house. He had set up the basement as his personal parlor and bar. My mother had already begun the process of ending their relationship. Eventually we moved out and moved into a small basement apartment in Detroit.

I now had to commute by bus to school in Ferndale from Detroit. Before the move, I only had a two-block walk to school. Now two buses were required to get to school and the ride took more than an hour. Therefore, I got money to buy lunch in a local drug store that had a lunch counter that was fifteen minutes from school. Our school did not serve meals to students except on special occasions or events.

Occasionally I would see some of the school teaching staff having lunch at the same counter. I felt more adult having to commute, buy lunch, and get home safely by myself five days a

week. Also occasionally, a teacher who lived near us once the teaching staff found out I was commuting to school offered a ride home on bad weather days. This went on until the end of the school year and the end of the sixth grade.

The plan worked out by mom and her sister, Aunt Rosa, who now lived in walking distance from us, was that I was going to go to summer school in Detroit. I would take some classes move ahead half a grade, make new friends, and start junior high school, that fall, already completing half of my 7th grade in Detroit, at Durfee Junior High. It was during this time that we lived in a small one-bedroom apartment. I slept on our living room couch. Eventually mom met a man named Howard Finley whom she decided to marry.

I was not happy. I was thirteen going on fourteen, my hormones were raging, and now I was going to have a real father. I was not happy because Howard was less educated than my mother was and to me it showed in his demeanor, his manner, and the way he spoke. What began after mom married Howard Finley was a war between he and I that lasted for several years. I realize now that everything my mother did she did for me so we could survive. As a child, you do not see or understand these things.

My teen years were traumatic for me. We did find a flat big enough for the three of us and my life with a stepfather began. The initial debate was about changing my name to my step fathers which I refused to do. This was part of what widened the gulf that existed between us for many years.

Someone who was there for me though, throughout my life, was my mom's sister's husband, my uncle Wilson Boyd. My best, most interesting conversations with another family member and a man were always with Uncle Wilson. He only had a high school degree. But he kept studying, and continued taking classes and

tests. I watched him take himself from janitor for the Detroit Street Railways, which when he began had streetcars and buses, to boiler operator for the City of Detroit for gymnasiums and pools, to eventually with his hard work and continuing education, was promoted to air pollution inspector for the City of Detroit. He made a wonderful home for my moms' sister Aunt Rosa and their daughter Thelma. He was very hard working he read widely and always challenged my belief systems and made me proud of my burgeoning intellect. This has had a lasting impact on my life.

As time passed during my teen years, my ambition was to survive adolescence, get a drivers' license and graduate from high school. I knew men and women had sex but that was about it. I had overheard my mother and her lover, and later my first stepfather making love on more than one occasion while growing up.

I discovered the mechanics of sex with the help of a book in my aunt and uncle's house one day when I was alone in their living room and opened one of their encyclopedias and discovered diagrams with complete explanations of the sexual parts and the sexual act. Since my mother never bothered to explain any of this to me, it was revelatory. I felt not only more informed about sexuality but more adult as well for my discovery.

High school was mostly unmemorable. There were very few high points. One I do remember was being enrolled in an English class where we were required to read one book a week, write about it, and discuss it in class. We also were given a new vocabulary list every week that we had to make into an original essay. I received an A on one of my essays and the teacher read it in class.

My love of reading despite my early trauma learning the alphabet was stoked by comic books and MAD magazine. On more than one occasion, someone commented to my mother about my growing comic book collection. My moms' reply was, "*At least he's reading....*" Comic books stirred my imagination, vocabulary, and reading skills. In high school, I was too shy and too hip I thought to go on a date on the bus. On more than one occasion, I let my stepfather take me to pick up my date, drop us off, and pick us up at the end of it. Even though my stepfather Howard was always kind to me, I still held out hope he and mom would split up. It never happened.

I waited until I got my driver's license at seventeen and asked the vice president of my high school graduating class, Charlene Brown, out to dinner and a movie. We both graduated from Central High School, class of January 1966. I was ranked 20th in a class of about 160 students.

The movie we saw was **The Agony and The Ecstasy** (1965), the film starred Charlton Heston as Michaelangelo and Rex Harrison as Pope Julius II. My favorite part of the entire film was the opening sequence where there was a great deal of time spent showing us the legacy of Michelangelo's work up close in 70mm. Those huge images were spectacular. I felt a special inspiration seeing the work of this extraordinary artist. Charlene and I however went out no more than a few times.

My first serious romantic interest was a girl named Geraldine. "Deenee", is what her family of six siblings including an older sister and four brothers, called her. She had a brother nicknamed Butch, his real name was Gerald. He and Geraldine were fraternal twins. Butch was like me. He was quiet, and he liked listening to jazz albums and wore glasses, once we met through being introduced by my family he and I became fast friends. I would go to his house to hang out listen to music and talk. I do remember he and I occasionally would go to a movie. Butch and "Deenee" were my age, which was seventeen.

I see now what she saw in me, reasonably intelligent, shy and not aggressive, but respectful. All in all a good date because I spent money and used my parent's car, once I had my drivers' license. One of my favorite date movies with her was **Dr. Zhivago** (1965). This film was another 70mm epic. The music was very evocative and *"Lara's theme"* from the film still is a tune I can hum when I concentrate. The story of love, lost and regained set against the Russian revolution is an epic and extraordinary one and it is still a great film.

What I saw in Deenee was a very attractive young woman who liked me enough to go out on more than one occasion, come to my house on occasion, talk, and listen to music. I spent the better part of several years taking her out to movies, the Ice Capades, concerts, and dinner and never doing anything other than holding her hand and kissing her politely on the cheek.

Later, after we had stopped dating for some time, I did meet one of her later boyfriends at a party given by her brother Butch, who by then was in his own apartment. Her new boyfriend danced the *'Funky penguin'* better than I did and he seemed older and more experienced. I will always have a spot in my heart for this girl. She helped me figure out how to enjoy myself with women and get over being shy.

To get from high school to college I needed to get a job and save some money. A family friend Gloria Gardner helped to got me a job in a warehouse, where she worked doing data entry. My job consisted of running a machine that stuffed computer generated invoices into envelopes. I then ran them through another machine that put postage on them. Then through another machine that tied the bundles together and dropped

them into bags that someone took to the post office. This was the first time I had worked forty hours a week and also the first time I had worked in an interracial environment.

I made friends with some of the white guys, and eventually one of the guys and I went to the movies. I remember we saw Peter Fonda and Nancy Sinatra in **The Wild Angels** (1966). Fonda leads a chapter of Hells Angels with Sinatra as his love interest. The most memorable aspect of this Roger Corman directed film for me was the music. The music was written by Mick Curb and Dave Allan. At my first opportunity, I bought the sound track to the film.

At the warehouse, I asked one of the white girls out and it turned into a joke because no one in the plant thought that I was serious. The women both black and white socialized at work but went their separate ways after work. I came to realize in this environment in 1966 interracial dating was not considered appropriate by management.

Jump cut to fall 1966 I'm enrolled in Wayne State University, Monteith College which was endowed by a Ford Foundation Grant. Its purpose was to provide general education in an innovative way. The school was named for John Monteith (1788-1868). The University of Michigan owed its birth to Mr. Monteith, who had the office of president and no less than six professorships conferred upon him. He was also an uncompromising anti-slavery champion.

Monteith College was an experimental college developed by the Wayne State University, College of Liberal Arts. Monteith College promoted student skills by library research assignments integrated with interdisciplinary general education courses. The program featured the same large auditorium setting for lectures, which had large groups of students in attendance but the

discussion groups were smaller with no more than a dozen people.

After I was accepted to WSU and was enrolled in Monteith, the faculty of Monteith did all they could in the smaller discussion groups to help incoming freshmen make the adjustment to college. One of my discussion professors invited the class to attend a jazz concert at the Detroit Institute of Arts, which was very near the WSU/Monteith campus.

This was a unique experience for me because it was my first jazz concert and the person we saw was **Rufus Harley** (1936-2006) who was playing saxophone, flute and bagpipes with a trio of piano, bass and drums. Yes, bagpipes! Harley like millions of Americans watched the funeral of John F. Kennedy on television and was compelled by the sound of the Black Watch of the Royal Highlanders Regiment, the Scottish infantry bagpipe corps that marched with the late President's funeral cortege. Harley was so enthralled by their unique sound that he tried first to recreate the sound using woodwinds. Unsatisfied with his efforts he bought his first bagpipe in 1964. Harley even wrote a tune titled '*A tribute to courage' (JFK).*

By the time I saw him in 1966, he had mastered the instrument and had an album released with him playing sax, flute, and jazz bagpipes on a major record label. The concert was memorable and his extraordinary performance and the images and sounds are a lasting experience for me. I later bought his album at my local record store. I was also discovering the joys of meeting a multicultural mix of people on a social and intellectual level.

One day while reading the campus newspaper, I saw an ad for a part-time job. The ad said it would be good job for a college student. When I realized that the ad was for the local movie house two blocks from where I lived, I was very excited. I called and the

person who answered said that the position had not been filled. I made an appointment and the next day went for my interview.

I went for my interview in a sport coat and tie at my mother's insistence. I rang the doorbell, as I was instructed, on the door near the theater. When I went up the stairs to the office just above the theater, I discovered that there was a full apartment and office above the theater. The person who interviewed me was white man named Terry Kelley. He said he was the assistant general manager for the Studio Theaters. He was very congenial and said he liked my name, which helped put me at ease. Before I left he introduced me to his wife Victoria who popped in for a minute. After we talked about duties and pay, I shook his hand. He asked me when I could start and within the week, I began working. I started working initially as a parking lot attendant.

Eventually I was promoted to usher and then finally to assistant manager. Later I worked as assistant manager at two of the local art house chain of four cinemas in Detroit and its near suburbs, called the Studio Theaters- Studio North, Studio Eight, Studio New Center & Studio One, where I began. Their specialty was exhibiting foreign language films and some American films. The average size of the auditoriums was less than eight hundred seats for some. I learned to appreciate cinema as art. During my tenure with the theaters, I saw cinema from all over the world. I continued to spar emotionally with my stepfather. I moved out of my parent's home in 1967.

CHAPTER TWO

My mom and my Aunt Rosa found a room right across the street from Aunt Rosa in one of her neighbor's homes. Ms. Smith, Rosa's neighbor was happy to have a roomer and the extra money. An arrangement was made so I had dinner with my Aunt Rosa and her family nights and my other meals I prepared in Ms. Smiths' kitchen. So now for the first time I was spending time with my favorite relatives every day. It was nice to be part of a surrogate family. I always exhibited my best behavior with these relatives; they always seem to inspire the best in me. My Uncle Wilson and I always got into interesting political and social discussions around the dinner table. I was working and going to college. My study and love of cinema thrived while I worked part-time for the Studio One Theater to earn money to pay for college and rent.

Blow-Up (1966), 111 min., color, directed by Michelangelo Antonioni, written by Antonioni and Tonnino Guerra based on a short story by Julio Cortazar and Edward Bond. This film for me exemplified the state of mind in which I found myself. I could not reconcile my emotional conflict with a step-father who I really did not understand. The central character of this Italian masterpiece is a professional photographer, who one day near dusk strolls through a park with camera in hand and he sees, he thinks two lovers in an embrace. When he takes his pictures into his lab to develop them, he is not sure exactly what he has captured lovers, or something more sinister. His blow-ups reveal the lovers doing quite what he is not sure. Antonioni manages from this point on to immerse you in a mystery. There are no

easy answers in life experience is the best teacher. Antonioni captured for me, my own state of mind. I had to look closer at my own pre-conceived beliefs about people. I had to come to understand that everyone is human no matter the sex or race until they prove to be other than what they seem.

It was a big deal when my mother learned that most of my close friends now were white. I remember her saying on more than one occasion, "...just be careful..." I was never quite sure what she thought. Later as she came to trust me and meet my friends she said, "...you have some really nice friends." In this film the photographer spends his time trying to meet the woman in his photographs and his friends and relations send him on a journey that has him questioning just what does he see sometimes with his camera. Antonioni is having us look at ourselves looking at his film, life, people, relationships, and the world of that time. We were in the height of the Cold War. Here today gone tomorrow, in a cloud of radioactive fire.

1967 was an important year for the city of Detroit. I was rooming in the area that was very near the inner city Detroit. I awoke one Sunday and thought, "What is that noise?" I did not know there was a parade or celebration going on, when I came out of my room Ms. Smith informed me that, "Them niggas' is rioting." July 23rd marked the beginning of five days and nights of civil disorder, rebellion, riots, uprising, pick a description, in Detroit. Twenty-two million dollars in damage was incurred because of the violence and destruction and forty-three people died. The incident was set in motion by a police raid on a local illegal after hour's establishment, called a "blind pig". The under lying causes of the post-raid incidents include police brutality, persistent poverty, lack of political representation for Black people, and the war in Vietnam, where black men died in disproportionate numbers.

While I was in college, I had a deferment after registering for the draft. I was called to take a physical and later received my status card that had 1Y on it. I did not do anything other than take the physical. I was not accepted and turned into cannon fodder for what we all know now was a wholly unjustified war.

The riots effect on me was the Studio One Theater along with all other public establishments were ordered to close from dusk to dawn. So I went to work at the theater, we ran one screening of the movie and closed after the first show. I had to get home and be in my house before dark. At this time without a car, taking the bus to and from work made this quite an adventure. After a few nights, ALL movie theaters in Detroit were closed because they did not want gatherings of people.

In my neighborhood once safely home I remember seeing caravans of local and state police vehicles, eight or ten cars in a row passing through the area just before dusk with four people in each car and all but the driver wielding rifles and shotguns which they deliberately held out the window of the cars to impress upon anyone who saw them what they intended for those who broke the curfew. They did this every night of the curfew. I believe that the current struggles that the city of Detroit, aside from the stupidity and greed of the automakers, can be directly traced to this event. It began the "white flight" to the suburbs, it opened the door to a city that was fairly integrated to creating a city that became even more homogenous and divided racially. Sure Detroit began to elect black politicians but the last several generations of them have spent as much time in the courts or headlines for their rape of the city's financial resources both overtly and covertly. I do not have an answer but it saddens me.

A former NBA star and successful businessman Dave Bing is someone who cares Detroit has been recently elected to the office of Mayor on a slate of change and progress. This is happening despite the major decline of the auto industry in Detroit and Michigan. Currently Michigan, like the nation has significant unemployment, fifteen percent. Detroit has nearly a twenty-nine percent unemployment rate. There are increased foreclosures on homes, which is a by-product of the unemployment. Currently the city has twice as much land as it uses because of shrinking population.

Living Cities, a philanthropic collaborative of 22 of the world's largest foundations and financial institutions, is investing with local groups nation-wide on strategies to help low-income residents. Nineteen urban centers competed for the money. Five urban areas won including Detroit, which should receive about nineteen million dollars. The hope is this money will help to generate additional funds for the future. Their goal with the money is to concentrate population to revitalize neighborhoods.

The **ABC** television network premiered in Fall of 2010 a new series called **Detroit 187**. The title was derived from the California penal code for murder, 187. In Michigan, the designation for homicide is actually 750.316. Go figure?! The program is being championed as a series about homicide detectives in Detroit; in the vein of **NYPD Blue,** a successful series also about homicide detectives. I have to ask myself as a former Detroiter, Why? What really is the cost to the image of the city? Does the city need jobs so desperately that it is willing to let the location shooting which I'm sure adds to their troubled economy, perpetuate an already troubled city with another negative image of its city and its people?

I spoke first to a long time Detroit friend about the show and its impact on jobs for folks. He works sometimes as a cinematographer on films and commercials as well as being an excellent photographer. He said he had not personally gotten

any work on the program but he knew people who had. He saw nothing wrong with the program or image it projected. I spoke to relatives who were visiting from Detroit recently and they said they saw it as negative and it looked like a "bootleg" program from the way it is shot and produced.

Television that is part of the solution is a program on **NBC** titled **School Pride**. This is a reality program. In August of 2010, the program producers and crew managed to get 1,792 people to volunteer to help repair the Communications and Media Arts High School in Detroit. The donations necessary to repair the fifty-two year old building were supplied by Fortune 500 companies. The series is designed to deal with education and schools in real basic effective ways.

The good things about Detroit are institutions like the Detroit Institute of Arts, which contains the fifth largest fine art collection in the United States. The Detroit Children's Museum the third oldest children's museum in the country and the Detroit Historical Museum established in 1928 one of America's oldest and largest museums dedicated to metropolitan history are important institutions for people young and old.

A recent community based group called the **Detroit Black Community Food Security Network** and another group called **Feedom Freedom Growers** are creating agriculture projects helping to create other important food focused groups like the **Detroit Food Policy Council** and the **Ujimaa Food Coop** all designed to grow food, supply low cost healthy food through cooperative buying power. These groups are self-generated, self-sustained financially with only a recent grant from **Kellogg's**.

Another wonderful aspect of Detroit was the local musicians and clubs where some of the worlds' best music thrived. Some of these local musicians became the house band for Motown

Records during its heyday and reign as one of the preeminent black owned and operated companies in Michigan and the world during that time. The Motown Records house band came to be known affectionately as "the Funk Brothers." Besides the lyrics, there was the very danceable music, that all came to be known as the "Sound of Young America", in the late sixties and early seventies, which was performed by an assortment of more than a dozen Detroit musicians.

Standing in the Shadows of Motown (2002), color, 110 min., directed by Paul Justman. This film is inspired by the book In *The Shadows of Motown: The Life and Music of Legendary Bassists James Jamerson* by Allan Slutsky. This documentary tells a story that most people are unaware of. It is the story of the Funk Brothers. The DVD has interviews with the surviving members and a bonus disc, which features jam sessions, biographies, and discographies of the Funk Brothers. It is not for nothing that Motown Records from this period in American musical history lives in the hearts and minds of America still to this day. The highlight of the double disc DVD set is the concert tribute to the Funk Brothers in which surviving members perform and today's artists sing the Motown hits from their glory years. The artists who perform include Joan Osborne, Bootsy Collins, Ben Harper, Montell Jordan, Chaka Khan, Gerald Levert, Meshell Ndegeocello, and Tom Scott. If you can find it, get *The Best of The Funk Brothers* part of the 20th Century Masters Millennium collection on CD.

A film with the revolutionary fervor that was missing in greater abundance in the auto plants is **Finally Got the News** (1970). This film focuses on the League of Revolutionary Black Workers in the Detroit area auto plants and their efforts to organize the workers to a more politically active social consciousness. The film examines the U.S. auto industry and its

effects on Detroit but especially the Black blue collar workers. The image of life in the plants is grim and prophetic. We learn the reason for the revolutionary element, its cause, and seeds of emergence. We see the black workers political consciousness aroused. It is the tip of the iceberg.

The film documents that the vast majority of the snipers caught by the police in the Detroit insurrection of 1967 were Appalachian whites. The people who were leading the Detroit insurrection were workers, black and white. This is "... the only radical film of the sixties which was made under the direct control of the revolutionary working class with the specific purpose of radicalizing other black workers." (3)

There are two very important music documentaries from this period. **Monterey Pop** (1969), 79 min., color, directed by D.A. Pennebacker, producers John Phillips & Lou Adler. This is the original pop music festival, produced by John Phillips and Lou Adler. The film was shot in 16mm. This film played to great success at the Studio Theater while I was working there. John Phillips a member of the group The Mamas and the Poppas decides that he wanted to produce a pop music festival. With the assistance of his manager (Adler), and others he pulls it off. This is a milestone in music and cinema history.

Woodstock (1970), 225 min., color film, directed by Michael Wadleigh. This is the - Dawning of the Age of Aquarius. The Woodstock Music Festival: three days of peace and music, became a turning point in American socio-political culture. "..when half a million kids get together to have three days of peace and music and have nothing but peace and music I say God Bless 'em...", announced to the crowd by Max Yasgur, on whose farm the event was held.

The actual event cost $8 per day or $24 for a three day ticket. 186,000 tickets were actually sold. 250,000 people were in the area and never made it to the festival. 400,000 is the estimated number of people who actually made it to the festival. Because of the sheer number of people, the New York state throughway was closed. The event was scheduled for three days in 1969, Friday August 15th to Sunday August 17th, but the last act, Jimi Hendrix played on Monday morning. 320,000 left before they saw Hendrix.

There were some excellent music documentaries from this time that did not receive nearly the exhibition or receive the attention as the two previously mentioned films. **Soul to Soul** (1971), 95 min., color, directed by Denis Sanders. Almost on the other side of the world in Ghana, Africa in March of 1971 a music festival featuring Black and Hispanic artists were creating what is now called an 'African Woodstock'. 100,000 plus Africans came to hear this American soul music coming home to its African soul.

The artists who made this historic journey were Wilson Pickett; Ike and Tina Turner; Les McCann & Eddie Harris; Santana; The Staple Singers; Voices of East Harlem. Roberta Flack was in the festival but declined being included in the film. We follow artists across the Atlantic as they talk about their expectations and concerns being the first trip to *"...Africa, the motherland..."* for all of these artists.

The journey and their arrival being greeted by great ceremony are chronicled. Their interactions with the African people they meet at meals and in special performances by African artists given just for them, are shown. Some of the Americans join in the spirited dancing with a troupe of African men and women in tribal costume honoring their guests.

One very special interaction captured in the film is with an African musician named Amowah. We learn that he traveled hundreds of miles, by thumb and foot, to meet and interact with these artists, when he heard they were coming. His solo performance with a large seed filled gourd making sounds and dancing unlike any of the artists, nor any other dancing we have seen in the film is remarkable.

The twelve-hour length performance of the African and American artists at the music festival is condensed, but all the footage seen in this documentary is uniformly excellent. The DVD has contemporary interviews with Les McCann; Mavis Staples; Ike Turner; and Kevin Griffin, who was eleven years old as a member of the Voices of East Harlem, when the film was made. Now in the supplemental interviews he tells about this great adventure with the maturity of an adult.

There is a second disc of music, re-mastered for this double disc-set. This CD features music by Wilson Pickett; Ike & Tina Turner; The Staple Singers; Les McCann & Eddie Harris; Voices of East Harlem and Earl Thomas.

Wattstax (1972), 103 min., color film directed by Mel Stuart. This is 'the black Woodstock'. 100,000 people in Los Angeles see a litany of black artists from the popular soul music label Stax Records, Stax was the southern counterpoint to Motown Records. The artists captured in truly special performances include soul and blues artists Isaac Hayes; The Staples Singers; Luther Ingram; Johnnie Taylor; Kim Weston; Little Milton; the Rance Allen Group; The Emotions; Carla Thomas; Rufus Thomas; Albert King and comedian Richard Pryor. History in the making captured for posterity. The power of music is undeniable. The DVD has an assortment of commentaries on the film and the actual event from musician/ rap impresario Chuck D; historian Rob Bowman;

Isaac Hayes; the director Mel Stuart and Al Bell a Stax Records executive and the producer of the film.

Part of the challenge for me in watching films from outside the U.S. was learning to understand the overall structural differences and reading sub-titles for non-English language films. Foreign films have an intrinsically different pacing. The story telling technique of a particular film comes from the directors choices based on their individual cinematic skill. Not having been exposed to non-American cinema, I learned to expand my own understanding and try to be more open to the differences in foreign films vs. American films.

Many people hate sub-titles. I do not mind them but having recently watched a dubbed foreign language film I had not seen in a while it did help in terms of following the story in English. But the film purist in me prefers to see the work as the director presented it in their language with only the added distraction of subtitles for those who need it.

"Jean Luc-Godard once described the difference between cinema and television as the difference between raising your eyes to the movie screen and lowering them to the television screen." (4)

Jean-Luc Godard comes from a group that emerged in the nineteen fifties and labeled themselves as the Nouvelle Vague or New Wave. This group consisted of film critics who had worked on the leading French cinema magazine, Cahiers du Cinema and included other French filmmakers, Francois Truffaut, Louis Malle, Eric Rohmer, Claude Chabrol, Jacques Rivette and others who had worked on the Cahiers with its founders Andre Bazin and Jacques Doniol-Valcroze. This group of filmmakers began with short films and eventually began to make feature films. By 1962, the magazine devoted an entire issue to this group and listed

over a hundred new directors who were working in France. Jean Luc-Godard was born in 1930. Godard's background includes having grown up in Switzerland and France. He studied ethnology at the Sorbonne and worked in French media including the Cahiers du Cinema. Later he emerged as one of cinema's most singular voices as part of the French New Wave of filmmakers.

Weekend (1967), color, 105 min. written and directed by Jean-Luc Godard. It was one of those films that I recall because it ran for some time in the Studio One theater where I worked. Godard's intellect then seemed light years from my own still burgeoning intellect, at nineteen, when this film opened. His ideas and images were overwhelming. The film contains the many elements of Godard's cinema, the absurd, politics, philosophy, poetry, and anti-cinema, i.e., deconstruction. Godard says in this film, *"...the bourgeois society is so sick nothing done in bad taste or vulgarity even disparages it even a little..."*

Now when I look at this film I have a greater appreciation for the mastery of his craft. In 1967, even with numerous viewings it was like watching a mystery. Between learning to read sub-titles and then understanding what action related to the dialogue and Godard's jarring juxtaposition of ideas, the film baffled me. There are moments in this film where the characters say things like, *"What a rotten film, all we meet are crazy people..."* which is true. We see a French couple who set off on a weekend holiday to meet friends and family outside the big city and it turns into something akin to Alice in Wonderland. They meet a variety of characters that seem to be set loose from an asylum who are fully costumed for another time, place, or film entirely. Godard, a student of cinema history has scenes where characters communicate over CB radios and use the names of classic cinema to exchange ideas.

"Battleship Potemkin calling The Searchers", films directed by Sergei Eisenstein and John Ford respectively, two major filmmakers. Later the CB callers invoke two more films and their renowned directors. *"Johnny Guitar calling Gosta Berlin",* Nicholas Ray and Maurice Stiller are the respective directors of these cult film classics. This film is a mad fantasy/allegory of life and living as Godard sees it. Prepare to be assaulted on every level by this work of French new wave cinema. The film ends with the parting shot and comment, *"fin de cinema",* the end of cinema, certainly, as we've known it. For me now more than ever this is a good thing. More young filmmakers need to study cinema closely and this is as good a place to begin as any.

I moved from the room in Ms. Smiths' house to sharing a house with other Studio Theater employees. The 945 Hancock Street house originally was owned and run by a fraternity. The fraternity guys found and moved into a better house further from campus so they rented out the Hancock street house. Their only caveat was to continue to be able during the week to park in the back of the house, which could hold about eight cars. Eventually when they saw who was living in the house they stopped parking in back of the house. I remember initially when there were parties in the house about half the people who showed up were crew cut white fraternity types. Eventually that stopped as well.

The house consisted of people who can be described as longhaired freaks. I moved into the house in 1968 it was a house with other college students. The people who ran the house and the majority of my roommates were white. I was one of two black people who moved into the house the other black person was a woman. Hancock House was a large eight bedroom duplex three blocks from Wayne State University's campus. Most of the people who lived in the house worked in the movie theaters and

our bond of friendship and work brought many of us that much closer together.

One summer night we were sitting around on the front stoop of the Hancock House, drinking cheap wine, and complaining about the hot Detroit night even after the sun had gone done. This led some of us to say, "... let's get in the pool..." which was virtually in our back yard. There was an alley, a small parking lot, and another street to cross and there sat Stone Park. This City of Detroit Parks & Recreation community park which consisted of a playground and a public swimming pool open "only" during the day. We decided to cool off in the pool. Along the way, we met an interracial couple who had the same thought we did and joined us. We could not have been in the pool more than ten minutes.

Two security guards broke up our party as we scrambled to get out of the pool too late. One of them had radioed the Detroit Police saying, "an officer was shot..." The result was six police cars converged on the pool. We were arrested for trespassing, because so many police cars responded and the security guards pressing charges we were hauled off to jail in four separate cars. Those taken to jail and charged included the five men and a woman from the Hancock House. A few of our friends and the girlfriend of Rob, we learned his name as we all sat in jail, got away. We made one call and got one of our housemates to go to one of the Studio Theaters and get money from petty cash and bail us out. It cost us each one hundred dollars, to make bail.

That weekend we had a party and Rob who was white and his girlfriend Deidre who was black came. We toasted more than once to our fortunes and freedom. Over the next two weeks while we awaited trial one of our roommates who was always well connected for beautiful women, tickets to concerts, free albums, other free stuff in general, found us a lawyer who looked like members of our group. Our lawyer William G. Segesta was wearing a three-piece suit, with a briefcase in hand and he wore glasses and had long hair. We were all dressed neat and conservative as per his pre-trial instructions. Our lawyer helped us get our story together. We told the judge that we just wanted to cool off. The security guards did not have a consistent story. We got off with time served and the bail money was our fine. We called ourselves the *Stone Park Six*. The irony is I had a summer job as a City of Detroit Parks & Recreation employee. I was the night watchman and clerk at a boat launch dock on the Detroit River run by Parks & Recreation. My hours were midnight to eight in the morning, five nights a week.

If I had four people before I left, it was a busy night. When we were being booked, the police got a chuckle out of that fact. In 1965 our lawyer W.G. Segesta along with the support of 70 other law students from Wayne State University, founded the Free Legal Aid Clinic (FLAC) with contributions from private donors. FLAC was originally established after the Michigan Supreme Court adopted a court rule allowing law students to represent indigent people in a clinical setting under the supervision of an attorney. The on-going purpose of FLAC is to offer legal assistance to indigent clients while providing practical experience to law students.

The following summer, my summer job during the day was working at that same Stone Park pool as a Locker Room Attendant, for Parks & Rec. putting people's clothes in a wire basket and giving them a bracelet with the number that matched their basket. After we closed for the day, I worked with the lifeguards and we hosed the showers and dressing area and scrubbed the place with disinfectant. Needless to say, there was some irony here. I think I got in the pool maybe once that whole

summer. I spent most of that summer catching up on my reading.

American independent filmmakers produced some important breakthroughs. **Faces** (1968), written, produced, directed and edited by John Cassavetes, (1929-1989). The film starred Gena Rowland, Seymour Cassel and many actors who were friends and part of Cassavetes self-styled repertory company. Cassavetes used an improvisational style for the story and interplay of the characters in this film.

Faces, is an adult drama that delves deep into the inner workings of marriage and the challenges of interpersonal relationships. It is an emotionally charged film from beginning to end. There are no easy or pat answers. Cassavetes makes you think as much as he allows you to be a voyeur to people in conflict.

When the film opened at the Studio North cinema, Seymour Cassel was present to introduce the film and answer questions. It was clear he found the experience wanting because he seemed more pleased smoking a cigarette in the lobby than being on display for an audience that in some ways had no clue what actors do to give credible performances, like those in this film. Cassel received an Academy Award Nomination for his work in this film.

Cassevetes directorial debut film **Shadows** (1959)*, 81 min., b/w was also very improvisational. That film dealt with a trio of young black people who are siblings. Leila (Leila Goldoni) is so light skinned as to be able to pass for white if she chose. Her older brother Hugh (Hugh Hurd) is very dark and a younger brother Ben (Ben Carruthers) who was also light complexion and could pass for white if he wanted. Not unlike the families of black people all over America then as now. A commentary about racial mixing that has been a part of the American poli-socio-psycho-sexual mores since the days of slavery. This film makes a poignant observation about the color caste, racial mixing, and the Beat era.

Easy Rider *, 94 mins., color., written by Dennis Hopper, Terry Southern and Peter Fonda, produced by Fonda, directed by Hopper. Fonda and Hopper also star with Jack Nicolson in the supporting role that made him a star. The film cost nearly four-hundred thousand dollars and grossed over fourteen million dollars opened in 1969 at the Studio New Center in Detroit. The film received two Academy Award nominations, Best Original Screenplay and Best Supporting Actor for Nicholson. It was also a Winner of Best Film by a New Director at the Cannes Film Festival. This film's impact on me could not have been more profound.

Hopper and Fonda were both well-known and much seen young Hollywood actors, Hopper appeared in an assortment of A list Hollywood films. Fonda was part of Hollywood royalty because his father Henry and sister Jane had created this lineage of family actors. Hopper and Fonda were insiders moving to the outside with this film and its production, as well as producing a vision that would be seen by a wide audience. I saw the characters of Captain America and Billy, played by Fonda and Hopper as embodiments of the notion of American youth finding itself in turbulent social and political times.

I had read *On the Road* by Jack Kerouc, which chronicles the nineteen-fifties vision of trying to find America in a car with his friend Neal Cassidy, much like Hopper and Fonda were doing in this film, except on motorcycles. The film redefined culture. It came out of the Pop Art revolution and the post Summer of Love, America. It is a western metaphor with Wyatt aka Captain America and Billy in this film are characters perhaps from a John

Ford western traveling territory not seen by Wyatt Earp or Billy the Kid. It is a motorcycle movie with a message. It is not Brando's **The Wild One** (1953) or Roger Corman's **The Wild Angels** (1967) which presented fantasy outlaws. The struggle of young people in 1969 is exemplified in some ways by Wyatt and Billy. They are hippies who took the profit from a big drug sale of cocaine purchased in Mexico and sold in Los Angeles and set about to find America with their ill-gotten gain. They are at once romantic, naive, venal, silly, troubled, out of touch and in touch both at the same time are Fonda and Hopper in their respective roles.

Along the way, they meet George Hansen played by Jack Nicholson after they are arrested for disturbing the peace of a southern town. Their adventure from this point forward is surely a cautionary tale with as many lows as highs. This film presented the smoking of marijuana as if it were the most ordinary thing in the world, like having a drink of alcohol. Nicholson plays the ACLU alcoholic lawyer Henson, who delivers the most important lines in the film.

At one point when the trio sits around a campfire after they have joined up and talk about America, he says, "They'll talk to ya and talk to ya and talk to ya about individual freedom. But they see a free individual, it's gonna scare 'em. I mean, it's real hard to be free when you are bought and sold in the marketplace." These words so very much exemplify America in 1969. Nicholson received his first Academy Award Nomination for Best Supporting Actor in this film. Fonda, Hooper, and Terry Southern received an Academy Award Nomination for Best Writing, Story, and Screenplay Based on Material Not Previously Published or Produced.

The film conveys the perspective of young people who were striving for the promise of our constitution. We saw that the older generation that did not want to acknowledge the fallacy of some of the decisions that were being made affecting young people lives like the war in Vietnam. As we know now the Vietnam War was a mistake. I saw people who came out of the movie theater that were clearly moved and stunned by this attempt to speak to America of that time. It is a landmark independent film of its time. It opened the door to a frank discussion of drugs and consciousness altering as a part of the American socio-political scene and emblematic of a true "counter culture".

The film was the first independently made film distributed by a major Hollywood studio, Columbia Pictures. Laslo Kovacs, the cinematographer for the film captures the wide-open vistas of the road as assiduously as he does the nuances of the films performances by its myriad of characters along the way in this road adventure.

The music that was used for the soundtrack was supplied by groups and performers from the then free-form radio music soundtrack for America of that time. The artists whose songs and performances were used included The Band, Roger McGuinn, Bob Dylan, Jimi Hendrix Experience, Byrds, Holy Modal Rounders, Fraternity of Man, Electric Prunes, Electric Flag, and Steppenwolf. The music was as much a character as any of the actors and it is used as a wonderful narrative device. The film soundtrack became a popular purchase when it was released. The DVD has a documentary on the making of the film.

Living in the Hancock Street House over the course of time, I met a variety of people because we were so close to the WSU campus. The house came to be known as the Hancock House. We tried sharing food and chores like cleaning the house communally. That turned out to be directly proportional to the level of commitment people were willing to make. So, it was like

a graph it had its ups and downs. For the life of me, I cannot ever remember there being big fights among the people in the house rarely even a loud disagreement.

During the my tenure working for the Studio Theaters, I was seeing films sometime four or five nights a week at work in the theater. Many a night off, I spent going to other theaters that were part of the chain because that meant free admission and inexpensive dates. It is during this period that I grew to understand, like and love the passion of Jean-Luc-Godard, Francois Truffaut, Ingmar Bergman, Akira Kurosawa, Satyajit Ray, Federico Fellini, Michelangelo Antonioni and Luis Bunuel to name a few. My American cinema education from films screened at the theater and films screened on my own included dozens of American filmmakers but my favorites were the mavericks like Robert Altman, John Cassavetes, Sidney Lumet, Elia Kazan, Sam Fuller, and Stanley Kubrick.

While a student at Monteith, I took a class in the WSU Speech Department, which included cinema and broadcasting. The class was *History and Appreciation of Motion Pictures*. The course was about the similarities and differences between cinema and other art forms; the motion picture as a modern visual art; we saw films representative of important periods of advancement.

The early films of the USSR now Russian Republic are films that were shown and made a deep impression on me because of their great cinematic skill and great humanity. **Sergei Eisenstein** grew up in an upper middle-class background. He spoke Russian, German, English, and French. Early influences included the cinema of George Melies, the circus, and drawing which led to enrollment in both schools of fine art and later engineering. His work led him to delve deeper and deeper into the fundamentals of creative art. While in the army in 1920, he led his first theatrical groups. In 1924, Eisenstein expanded his theatrical vision and made a short film using actors from his group of associates **Even a Wise Man Stumbles**. The film we saw in my film class was Battleship Potemkin (1925). In 1924, he met Eduard Tisse a cameraman with which he collaborated on his first feature length film **Strike**. This film recreates historic events of the burgeoning system of communism. One of my favorite films of Eisenstein's is **October** aka **Ten Days That Shook the World** (1927), 104 min. b/w, silent. script by Grigori Alexandrov and Sergei Eisenstein some parts based on American journalist John Reeds book *Ten Days That Shook the World*, directed by Eisentein & Alexandrov, cinematography by Eduard Tisse, music Dmitri Shostakovich. Starring Vasili Nikandrov, N.Popov, Nikolai Podvolasky, Boris Livanov.

This is the restored version supervised by Grigori Alexandrov with music and added sound effects for the 50th Anniversary of the Russian Revolution. This film recreates the social, political milieu of 1917 Russia in her shift from monarchy to communism. The scenes and story are stunning in their rendering of events that make this film look and feel like we are watching newsreel footage of the actual events. After destroying the royal ruling class of the 19th Century, the socialist revolution died before the 20th Century was over. In the 21st Century, Russia is a burgeoning capitalist country. It is now part of the world capitalist system.

This film has a certain edge of having recreated effectively the movement of a nation and its people. The people are the ones who must survive whether yoked by monarchy or repressed by a corrupt social system. The people make themselves survive in a new economic model that often forgets it is the people who make any of these economic models succeed or fail. Eisenstein's films are filled with the touches of a singular director.

Denis Arkadevich Kaufman aka **Dziga Vetrtov** (1896-1954) was born in Poland. His family fled to Moscow in 1915 to flee the German invasion. His early influences were in writing. He wrote poetry, satires, essays, and science fiction. He used the pseudonym Dziga Verto that loosely translated means "spinning top". Verto was a man in motion. He began to study medicine in 1917. Under the tutelage of science, he began a series of experiments with sound and recording equipment. Thus, he had his need for scientific control and artistic impulse fulfilled.

His opportunity to continue his montage experiments in sound using the medium of film came in 1918. He was primarily a newsreel filmmaker in 1919 during the Russian Revolution. In 1922, he created the Kino-Pravda a film version of the well-known Soviet newspaper Pravda. By 1926, he had made his first film-poem **A sixth of the World**. During his early film work, his two primary collaborators were his wife Yelizaveta Svilova as editor and his brother Mikhail as cameraman.

This trio made **Man with a movie camera** (1929), 68 min., b/w, documentary. This is an unusual newsreel that documents the cities of Kiev, Moscow, and Odessa. We follow the people, places, and life of these cities. This film is compelling because of the techniques and effects created in the film. The filmmakers use a plethora of cinematic techniques; slow motion effects, superimpositions; repetitive images; the rhythm of the editing are among the many other cinematic techniques that makes this an exemplary film. Now with music added it becomes more luxuriant as a wonderful cinema experiment that worked. The images and shadows of these people from the last Century will forever be in our eyes in these images that live vibrantly in this film.

Alexander Dovzhenko (1894-1956) was Ukranian born with mixed Cossack heritage grew up in a farm community in

Sosnitas. His early life was influenced by the death of twelve brothers and sisters all dying before reaching an age at which they could work. His films reflect the cycles of life, a love of nature, and empathy for the rugged agrarian life. After the 1917 Russian Revolution, he worked first in the Red Army, then as a diplomat for the Ukraine Republic, then an illustrator and political cartoonist. Eventually while designing film posters he met people in the Ukranian film industry. When given the opportunity to direct films he first made comedic films but his first work to show his true vision was in 1928 for the film **Zvenigora**. It was a mixture of legend and history remembering a thousand years of Ukranian peasant life.

Dovzhenko strengths are in his images that evoke lyric poetry nowhere is this better illustrated than in the film **Earth** aka **Zemla** (1930), 75 min., b/w, drama. Written and directed by Alexander Dovzhenko. We see an agrarian society in the cycles of love, labor, loss and a passion for life. This then is an eternal look at the life of those who labor with the soil for their daily bread.

My life was a mixed review of school, work, and new roommates in a new house. I had stopped working for the theaters and started working for a bookstore and I started in earnest on learning more about cinema and filmmaking. The Commonwealth Street house included some of the last tenants of the Hancock House including yours truly. I was the only Black person in this house, which had five bedrooms. I had an upstairs bedroom. The only couple in our now smaller household got the downstairs bedroom.

The other residents were three single men. Mike and I worked in a local bookstore called Bookworld his girlfriend Sylvia still went to school at Wayne State University. Doug worked at a supermarket as a stockman on the other side of town. Dale was an entrepreneur and worked part-time still at the Studio

Theaters which is where we met and worked for his family part-time selling real estate. A friend from Monteith College, Rick who is Lebanese was the other member of our house.

Rick was a musician with a band and that was how I met him at one of his club gigs. Rick was one of the co-leaders in a band called *Justice Colt.* The band was named after a local kids television program that ran old Hollywood western films and had a local actor dressed as a cowboy who hosted he called himself, Justice Colt. My friends and I from the Hancock House saw his band in the basement of the local Unitarian church, which was turned into a non-alcoholic club. We were the loudest and most enthusiastic people in the audience we liked what we heard a lot.

Their music was progressive music. Guitars and drums with electric piano and horns, Rick played electric keyboards and wrote music for the group. After the show, he came down to meet us because of our enthusiasm.

Terry who had hired me for the Studio Theaters had made films and wanted to create a film group, which we did together in meetings at the Commonwealth House. Initial meetings included other people with production skills and productions under their belt. Later we began to meet on the east side of Detroit in a big four-bedroom home in a posh but transitioning neighborhood called Indian Village. This part of town was in transition with the influx of long hairs integrating and sharing houses.

The renters of the Iroquois Street house in Indian village were people who worked for a local rock radio station, **WABX-FM**. This group consisted of three single women and a couple. The group was all white; the couple was the only two who did not work at the station. **WABX** was an influential free-form radio station in Detroit from 1960 to 1984. Free form radio is a radio

station programming format, in which the disc jockey is given total control over what music to play, regardless of music genre or commercial interests.

Free form radio stands in contrast to today's commercial radio stations, in which disk jockeys have little or no influence over programming structure or play lists. Free form stations played rock music and other musical idioms. George Harrison of The Beatles took up learning to play the sitar and studied with India's most well-known musician, Ravi Shankar. After that, free-form radio stations even played Shankars' music.

Free-form radio introduced me to not only rock and roll some of which I loved and still treasure in CD form now, but blues, jazz, new age, Latin and serial music. My musical palette had been broadened considerably. My musical horizons would forever be open to music that became an integral part of the relationship I had at the time with the people I lived with. We spent many an hour when not either studying, working or going to class, listening to the latest music from John Coltrane, The Beatles, Muddy Waters, Taj Mahal, King Crimson, Traffic, the 'Peter Green' era Fleetwood Mac, Cream, The Rolling Stones.

While working I continued my education at WSU/Monteith College. The curriculum emphasis was on humanities, social, and natural sciences, with an opportunity for students to create their own classes. To create a class you needed to be a junior and have a minimum three students working with one faculty member to oversee the process with a presented outcome from the course of study. These were called Cooperative Self Education Courses.

In 1971, a course I co-created with two other students was called Progressive Music. The course was about, "...the growth of the influences of progressivism in pop music and the resultant

hybrid." The other two students were Kent and my roommate Rick, also a Monteith student. Kent knew Rick through Monteith and so we formed the requisite three person class together.

We went to concerts and listened to music. Chicago; Mahvishnu Orchestra: Miles Davis; Renaissance; Gentle Giant; Colosseum; Weather Report; Edgar Winter and Frank Zappa, were some of the groups and artists we listened to and whose concerts we attended. For our final, we went to the home of our professor who had agreed to monitor our class. We met Professor Aaronson in his home and brought a bottle of red wine. We played some of the music on his phonograph I mentioned and talked to him about it.

Rick was the music theory expert and Kent and I talked about cultural and historical aspects of the music, we got an A. Music had been a very important part of my life. I created the soundtrack of my life with the music I listened to and went to see in performance. Once I discovered the joys of music, and the difference it made in my life, I pursued listening to everything I could get my hands on. Styles of music I currently enjoy include electronic, country, jazz, Indian, classical, music that is now labeled either new age or world music. After having written this passage about music and its importance in my life I learned yesterday of music's potential in our everyday lives. A CNN report highlighted the fact that, (there is) *"...Growing evidence that music has neurological, physical, and psychological benefits..."*

My cinematic discoveries provided me opportunities to learn about people and cultures that I would not normally have opportunity to experience. **Kurosawa** (2000), color & b/w, 215 min., written & directed by Adam Low. Narrated by Sam Shepard, readings from Akira Kurosawas' *Something Like an Autobiography* by Paul Scofield. The film is in Japanese with

English subtitles. This excellent documentary features interviews with **Akira Kurosawa** (1910-1998), his family; film scholars & critics; actors and technicians who worked on his films. I came away with a greater appreciation and more insights on someone who is not only considered one of Japans greatest filmmakers, but he is considered one of the world's greatest filmmakers.

He chose cinema as his avocation because he said because it combines literature, theater, painting, and music. In 1936, he got his first film job as an assistant director for Toho Studios Film Company the salary was very low. In order to make more money and survive financially he wrote scripts for which he was paid an additional salary. In 1943 he directed his first film **Sanshiro Sugata** aka **Judo Saga**.

The film that is one of his most well-known and is considered one of the worlds' greatest films is **Rashomon** (1950), b/w, 90 min. This film gives you four different accounts of a murder. The film opens with a torrential downpour of rain. The opening sequence has characters coming in out of the rain to a shelter and they then describe this feudal setting that has included war, earthquakes, famine, bandits, the plague, and fire. The four versions of this story come first from a farmer who goes to the forest for wood and stumbles upon a dead body. Later the story introduces us to a samurai, who encounters a man and wife in the forest. The film is about lies, cheating, rape, theft, and betrayal. A character in the film says, "...in the end you cannot understand the things that men do..." I've often felt that way.

Kurosawa has said, "Human beings all share the same problems, a film can only be understood if it depicts these properly." At the end of production for this film there was a scene shot in a Japanese temple. An Abbott for the temple when Kurosawa came to say goodbye and thank them for allowing production there gave him an inscribed fan.

The inscription said, "Benefit all mankind." Kurosawa's films still provide us with that benefit. **Rashomon** was nominated for and won many international awards. The film was voted by the Board of Governors for the Academy Awards as the most Outstanding Foreign Language Film released in the United States during 1951.

Other important Asian cinema includes the work of **Satyajit Ray** (1921-1992) who is India's most world renowned director. He was born in Calcutta to a Bengali family prominent in arts and letters. Ray's early interest included Indian and Western classical music and cinema. In 1941, Ray attended a school founded by Rabindranath Tagore a Nobel Prize winner in literature in 1913. The school Tagore founded in 1901 combined Eastern and Western knowledge into a "school of wisdom". In 1921, it became a university in Santiniketan. Tagore's influence on India and Ray was profound and lasting because of Tagore's intellect and talent expressed in his music, literature, and philosophy. Tagore's contemporary influence is seen in the fact that both the Indian and Bangladesh national anthems were written by him.

In 1947 the year of India's independence from British rule Ray and a friend Chidananda Das Gupta founded the first film society in Calcutta. Rays' background includes having written many novels including works of science fiction. Ray made a living and a name for himself as a leading graphic artist. One of the books he illustrated was Pather Pachali (Song of the Little Road) by Bibhuti Bhusan Banerjee.

The Song of the Little Road (2008), documentary, color & b/w, 60 min. Produced and directed by Priyanka Kumar. This excellent documentary chronicles the production of Ray's cinema, his influence and renowned throughout the world. A variety of cinema luminaries discuss and access Ray's impact and lasting influence on cinema. This group included filmmakers

Martin Scorsese; Ismail Merchant; film scholar and preservationist Pratha Mitter, Sussex University, U.K.; Peter Rainer, president of the National Society of Film Critics; David Sheppard, film preservationist; Michael Pogorzelski, Academy of Motion Picture Archive; and the Indian musician Ravi Shankar who composed and performed the music for the "The Apu Trilogy".

There are many insights the interviewees express about Rays' films. Ray presented the Indian culture with an Indian perspective very different from the colonial perspective of India. Ray's style albeit a very straight forward and seeming simple style gives us resonance on the affairs of humans that is spiritual, introspective, meditative, captures the rhythms of life, exemplifies the utmost truth, and presents a complexity only great artists can give you.

There are three films from Ray's early career that introduced me and the rest of the world to Indian cinema. These films as a whole are considered a masterpiece and some of the most important films in the world. The Apu Trilogy (1955-1959).

Pather panchali (1955), aka **Song of The Little Road**, 122 min., b/w. This is the first of three films following a rural Indian family in Nischindapur a village on the banks of the Ichamati River. Ray has said that the one film that moved him most before he began this film was Italian neo-realist director Vittorio De Sicas' **Bicycle Thief** (1948) which he is said to have watched more than fifty times. This film is like De Sicas' classic film, real human drama. His shots of nature even in b/w are very expressive. His characters are emotionally engaging. We see the cycles of life and people deal with universal issues.

The film follows the Roy Family, which includes, mother, father, son, daughter, and an aging aunt. Ray's cinema in its essence is like film folklore akin to the documentary work of Robert Flaherty's **Nanook of the North** (1922)*. Ray's film was

nominated for nine international awards and won three Cannes Festival Awards in 1956 including an award as the Best Human Document.

Aparajito (1956) aka **The Unvanquished**, b/w, 110 min. This is the second of three films on The Roy family. We see more of the mores and customs of this Indian family. They have moved from the countryside to the city of Banaras over six hundred miles from their ancestral home. This city is on the Ganges River and it is a holy place for Hindus, their Mecca, or Jerusalem. We see the struggles of everyday life and the opportunities that big cities provide.

Apu the son is finally given an opportunity to go to school and eventually wins a scholarship to university in Calcutta many miles away. The poetic composition of shots and the ease with which we come to embed ourselves in this family's life is all exquisitely done. Awarded the Golden Lion from the Venice Film Festival, 1957

The World of Apu (1959) aka **Apur Sansar**, b/w 105 min. This is the final film on the Roy family of India. The triumphs and tragedies that is the fate of human existence are passionately and sincerely etched into each one of these three films. As a trilogy of films, no finer work in cinema exists. Ray is a titan of humanist cinema. This film was honored by the National Board of Reviews as the Best Foreign Film, 1960.

Ray has a son Sandip Ray who is also a filmmaker as well. He has written, produced, directed, and composed music for nearly a dozen films since 1983 when he made his first feature film.

I met Brenda Lee Wriggles she was born in Australia. She had blonde hair and green eyes. She lived in the Iroquois House. Over time, we were mutually attracted to each other and developed a serious relationship. We began to work together first as neophyte members of the Detroit Film Collective. An opportunity for us to work and be paid came after we had moved into a studio apartment together on Detroit's Eastside near Jefferson Avenue. Brenda and I received an opportunity to work together at a Montesorri approach nursery school, co-teaching a kindergarten class. We got the job because a mutual friend Mary Anne who also worked in the film group with us and provided her recommendations to the owners, which helped in our getting hired. In the mornings, Mary Anne who had been teaching in this combined nursery and pre-school for some time and I taught with her leading, and I assisting her. After nap time for the students and lunch for staff, Brenda and I taught the class together with me taking the lead. Mary Anne had a second hand clothing store called Fabulous Second Hands she had opened and now ran part-time in addition to teaching.

Brenda and I grew close because of our mutual intellectual and emotional connection. We both liked the same music. Music was one of the many things that drew us closer together. Every interpersonal and personal relationship I'd had to that point had been tempered by the level of understanding, openness and respect people have for music.

I think it says a lot to me about that person and their ability to understand things that they are not familiar with. In all the women, I wooed their interest in music and willingness to explore new musical horizons with me as guide was important.

While in Monteith College I was enrolled in a Humanities class & senior colloquium titled *Anarchy.* It was a survey of theories and ideas from early 18th Century theorist to 20th Century anarchists. We had a textbook, which consisted of an assortment of essays on anarchy that included its history and included theory position papers. Over the course of the semester, we met in the evenings at the professors' home.

Eventually with the teacher's agreement, the class meetings turned into a pot-luck I remember wine poured profusely. By mid-semester we abandoned the book, we told the professor he was going to give us all A's. Anarchy!

"Anarchism believes in man, in the individual, and in human love." (5)

Many of us continued to meet for another two semesters in Cooperative Self Education classes. We had an assortment of professors to assist us as we taught and learned Revolutionary Anarchy that was eliminating rigorous judgment norms of school as outlined. We practiced interpersonal anarchy. Students and teachers equal members of a rational thought provoking group. We developed a group consciousness in terms of goals. We continued over six months a core group of six from an original group of twelve. We explored ideas and supportive activities for the group as a Group. We reached new levels of understanding of each other as people and not just students and numbers.

At the end of one semester our class project was a cookbook called the Anarchy Cookbook, not like the real book from the sixties that included information on making home-made bombs, our cook book only had recipes from our many potlucks. My recipe was called Ice Cream Surprise. ½ cup of blueberry preserves, ½ cup of raspberry preserves, ½ gallon of vanilla ice cream. Let ice-cream soften. Mix in preserves. Refreeze. Serve Cold.

While co-teaching kindergarten with Brenda I tried an experiment with the class during the afternoon period when Brenda and I co-taught together. I had a litany of activities-blocks, musical chairs, a water table, books, games, and puzzles in which the children could engage. I called it programmed anarchy the caveat was you could engage in any activity as long as you did not disturb anyone else. So after naptime I asked the

students what they wanted and over the course of a week of learning what good anarchy was, to a child their response when I asked *"What do you want to do to this afternoon?*, their reply was, "Anarchy, Anarchy, Anarchy!"

Our class was in the front of the building so when parents came in they saw us first. With Brenda and I as teachers and our students a very multicultural group that included black, white, Asian, and mixed heritage children, in a very active but controlled environment. This was a positive image and our supervisor Ms. Brown always liked what Brenda and I did with our afternoon class. The owner who had several schools liked our work as well.

A group of filmmakers, technicians, and neophytes working together formed the **Detroit Film Collective**. The group produced a film that allowed me my first screen credit. The half hour documentary was titled **Readin' & Writin' Ain't Everything** and dealt with individuals and families who had challenges related to mental health issues in Michigan at that time which was 1971. A few years later the film won Cine – *Golden Eagle*. In 2010 Rosa's Law, sponsored by Maryland Senator Barbara Milkowski strikes the term mental retardation from the Federal lexicon of all health, education, and labor laws, replacing them with "intellectual disability".

My experience during the production consisted of assisting people who could light, run sound and camera equipment. I was learning from people who raised the money and made the appropriate contacts to shoot in hospitals and homes near Grand Rapids, Michigan. We spent one ten day period during the summer shooting and camped in a nearby campground close to our locations and saved money for production that way. We had a very difficult time meshing experience with energy for those without experience like me. I saw later that, that experience was probably as good an introduction to full on film production as I could have had without being in a union or having school training or experience. I had no serious production experience prior to this production.

Within the second year of the relationship, Brenda and I agreed we both wanted to move from Detroit to California. Several of my friends from the Hancock House were in California and they kept insisting I should move when I would talk to them or receive a letter with pictures. That insisted they had not fallen in the ocean from earthquakes and the weather was better. Brenda and I knew that we needed to make a plan to do this. So we decided to work save money, buy a vehicle to travel in and move to California when we were ready.

I saw an ad in the newspaper, went for the interview passed the written test and was hired on the spot. It was for a fresh flower wholesaler. I was a stock clerk. After Brenda graduated from WSU with her degree in psychology with a minor in physics, Brenda found full time work. She worked as a counselor for an outpatient program run by a group of nuns who wore regular clothes.

It was during those years I began to keep a Journal and have done so on and off since that time. Brenda and I were focused and excited about our future together.

Our lives start as peoples acts of love it's up to us to make the means justify the end or beginning of love – us.

Anger makes you think you're right, peace makes you glow from within to show your love light.

8:30AM, channel 7, movie, drama, **In search of America** (1971), 1hr. 45min., directed by Paul Bogart. Carl Betz, Vera Miles, Jeff Bridges, Ruth McDevitt, Renne Jarrett, Sal Mineo, Howard Duff, Michael Anderson Jr. An affluent family comes to grips with

contemporary values at an outdoor rock festival. A tacky attempt at conveying some of the new ideas and values of the so-called "counter culture". Noteworthy for its temerity to broach these ideas in a made for TV movie at a crucial point in time.

Billie Holidays music has that quiet ever changing blue serenity of the setting sunset.

The cinema tide in the seventies included the emergence of a contemporary American black cinema. The films in this oeuvre are sometimes referred to as "Blaxploitation" films. The word came from the NAACP and CORE who saw these films as exploitive and negative in their impact on the African American community. The press contracted black and exploitation to create the word "Blaxploitation". Blaxploitation begs the question who is being exploited and for what purpose? Images of Black people no matter which/what country produces the films/images of them and what era we look at do not come without some degree of exploitation, for good or ill.

The filmmaker who kicked down the door of profitability in independent filmmaking in America completely outside the Hollywood idiom is **Melvin Van Peebles**. Van Peebles had made and recorded music that presaged "rap" music with his album *Brer' Soul* and made his debut film while living and working in Europe. An original story Van Peebles wrote *La Permission* that was published in France was made into a film in France and entered in the 1967 San Francisco International Film Festival as the French entry to the festival.

The film **Story of a Three Day Pass** was a hit and opened doors of opportunity for Van Peebles. He directed the film **Watermelon Man** (1970) under the Hollywood studio system. The film because of its militancy was not a financial success. Van Peebles saw the paucity of images controlled, produced, and

distributed by Black people in the 20th century. He determined he was personally going to change that. He did so in a way that carries weight into the 21st century and is a beacon for those looking for ways to make independent films and be successful. Van Peebles is now seen as the "Godfather of Independent Black Cinema".

Sweet Sweetback's Baadasssss Song (1971), written, produced, directed, scored, and starring Melvin Van Peebles. The film was produced for less than five hundred thousand dollars and shot in nineteen (19) days. The production crew was mostly people of color and women who did not have union cards or lots of production experience in some instances. There were two white crew members who were in the union but worked on the film for less than union wages because of their belief in Melvin and his vision. Van Peebles opened his film in two cities Detroit and Atlanta. The success in these two cities playing too sold out houses brought wider distribution and recognition.

The film has grossed over fifteen million dollars according to Van Peebles. This film is the first "Black power" film. The Black Panther Party made viewing this film a prerequisite for membership in their then forty-eight chapters. A whole issue of their newspaper *The Black Panther: Inter-communal News Service* with analysis by Huey P. Newton was devoted to this film. In 1969, *Newsweek* did a survey and 92% of Black people supported the Black Panther Party as the legitimate political arm of Black people in America at that time.

The soundtrack for the film featured a then unknown band **Earth, Wind and Fire**. A song from the film featuring the group was used to advertise the film on radio. This has become a film marketing norm and is now common practice to get people to see a new film.

The hero of the film Sweetback is an anti-hero, he did things Black men did not do on screen until that time. He does not die in the end. He never loses his dignity. Van Peebles is a cinematic provocateur like Jean Luc-Godard. Van Peebles deconstructs the Black experience. This film inspired a wave of bad Hollywood copies that left the politics out and made caricatures of black people in trying to copy this singular black film.

Gordon Parks (1912-2006) was the youngest child of fifteen. His family ran a farm. With the death of his mother by age fifteen Parks was relocated to family in Minneapolis. When Parks became a family man himself he worked as a pianist, busboy, railroad dining car waiter, and professional basketball player. He later moved to Chicago took up photography was awarded the first Julius Rosenwald Fellowship in photography.

Richard Wright is the author of <u>Native Son</u> a ground breaking and important novel on the Black experience in America and it is still widely read. Wright met Gordon Parks in 1943. Parks photographed him during Parks' tenure with the Rosenwald Fellowship.

Parks came to New York on that August afternoon, while there; a riot erupted in New York on Harlem's Lenox Avenue. Parks took his camera and recorded the incidents, his pictures showed many black people bloodied by the police. When he met Wright the next day and recounted his experience, Wright admonished the younger Parks, "You could have been killed." Wright inscribed in Parks copy of <u>Twelve Million Voices</u>, one of Wrights' many books, "To one who moves with the new tide."

Parks spent twenty years as a *Life* magazine photographer. Parks also developed his skills as a writer publishing several volumes of poetry, memoirs, and novels. Parks was also an accomplished musician. He composed music for concert halls

and films. Parks was a renaissance man. His first novel <u>The Learning Tree</u> a semi-autobiographical work was turned into the film that marked his emergence as an important voice in American filmmaking also titled **The Learning Tree** (1969)*.

Parks was one of the first black directors to emerge from this important body of black cinematic expression. His contributions to it are cornerstones of it. The film that is said to have helped in perpetuating this wave of contemporary black cinema within the context of the Hollywood idiom is a Parks' directed film **Shaft** (1971)*.

Hollywood was in transition from the studio dominated era of film production and distribution. The shift was to television production in the Hollywood studios and the mid-seventies emergence of videocassettes on which you could reproduce and sell movies. Both black film production and videotape generated major new revenue streams for Hollywood in the seventies. Because of the success of **Sweet Sweetback,**... a white detective story that was in pre-production at MGM was changed to a black detective.

Shaft (1971)*, 98 min., color, written by John D.F. Black and Ernest Tidyman based on his novel. Directed by Gordon Parks, music composed and performed by Isaac Hayes and J.J. Johnson, cinematography by Urs Furrer, edited by Hugh A. Robertson who was nominated for an Academy Award for his editing on **Midnight Cowboy** (1969)*. He lost the Oscar but won the British Academy Award in the editing category for his work a first for an African American. The film stars Richard Roundtree and Moses Gunn. A black private eye who takes nuthin' from the white man, whether business man or cop. John Shaft was a private detective for the times. He was black, proud, and stood his ground in all situations.

Shaft never let himself be treated as less than a man. He was a stud with women and had respect in the streets of New York City. *"A bad mutha..."* - so said the lyrics to the popular soundtrack and theme to the film. Ticket sales and soundtrack album sales made this a film that took the MGM Studios production company and saved it from closing because of its profitability. The soundtrack emerged on the Billboard charts as the #1 jazz and rhythm-and-blues album selling more than a million records. The film won an Academy Award, a Golden Globe Award, and a Grammy Award for Best Original Song for the song *Theme from Shaft* by Isaac Hayes, a first for an African American. With a budget of just over a million dollars estimated, the film grossed in excess of $17 million. A remake of this film in 2000 starring Samuel L. Jackson as **Shaft** was directed by John Singleton a contemporary Black filmmaker who has followed the path of Parks in Hollywood. His film made more than $107 million dollars.

Two more films that came on the wave of Black films were **The Spook Who Sat by The Door** (1973), 102 min., color, script by Sam Greenlee based on his novel of the same name, Co-script Melvin Clay, music by Herbie Hancock, directed by Ivan Dixon (1931-2008). Dixon was an actor with a successful career first in theater, then television and later films. In films besides acting he became a stunt and body double for Sidney Poitier. In his role as Sgt. James "Kinch" Kincloe on the television program **Hogan's Heroes** (1965-1971) a situation comedy about a World War II POW camp and Nazis, Dixon got the opportunity he needed. Because of the success of this program, he appeared in over a hundred episodes he took the steady work and his own time and seriously studied filmmaking. In his off hours from work, he got veteran technicians to teach him what he needed to know. Eventually given an opportunity he directed a lot of episodic television and was quite successful at that.

This film is his second directed feature film was a project he initiated, developed, and helped raise the seven-hundred and fifty thousand dollars needed to make the film. The film stars Lawrence Cook, Paula Kelly, Janet League, and J.A. Preston. The story follows the first black C.I.A. agent from recruitment to training as he become the last man standing and is hired into this covert organization. He works for a number of years and leaves of his own volition. He goes back to the city of Chicago his home town. In a short while, he recruits people he knows first then later enough people to create a small army.

The mission of this black guerilla army is to tear down the military-industrial complex teaching his recruits martial arts, weaponry, guerilla and covert tactics our Spook learned while a CIA agent. These are powerful ideas. The film states in very certain terms that the choice for Black people in America is not assimilation or integration but militancy like that used by oppressed people all over the world.

The next film from this black cinema wave of the seventies that I find one of the most interesting and inspiring of any film from this period is **Brother John** (1971), 95 min., color, script by Ernest Kinoy, music by Quincy Jones, directed by James Goldstone. Starring Sidney Poitier, Paul Winfield, Beverly Todd, Bradford Dillman, & Will Geer.

Sidney Poitier has risen from humble beginnings in the Bahamas to actor of stage and screen to successful film director and is now Ambassador of the Bahamas to Japan. Along the way he earned his first Academy Award for his performance in **Lilies of the Field** (1963) and a second Honorary Academy Award (2002), "...in recognition of his remarkable accomplishments as an artist and as a human being." In 2009, he was awarded the Presidential Medal of Freedom, the highest American civilian award from President Barack H. Obama.

The film **Brother John** was a critical and box-office failure upon its release. At the time of its release, it was part of a two-picture deal that Sidney Poitier had signed with Columbia Pictures. **Buck and The Preacher** (1972) was the second film. It was a financial and critical success. The damage had been done with the first film and so after the release of the second film Poitier concluded his relationship with Columbia Pictures.

Poitier in his autobiography titled *This Life*, says this about **Brother John**: "The idea for "Brother John" came thundering into my mind one quiet evening.... The strange fascinating tale of "Brother John" haunted me until I committed myself to seeing it come alive on film."

To further put this film experiment into perspective here is what was said of the film from the book, The Cinema of Sidney Poitier: The Black Man's Changing Role on the American Screen, "Now that he was a star, however, and other blacks were appearing on screen, Poitier could take chances, explore new properties, and broaden the range of his roles." This film is one of my favorite Sidney Poitier films. It stretched the roles of black men on screen. The film allows you the screen viewer to consider many possibilities for one John Kane, Poitiers character. We owe Mr. Poitier a debt of gratitude for having the courage of his conviction despite its impact on his personal finances and career.

John Kane is a black man not like any black man we've seen before on screen. He has a family and friends from his childhood past whom he visits in the South. His family and friends are dealing with too much small-town and Southern white supremacy. John Kane has several passports stamped with visits to all the major nations and capitols of the world. He has diaries that when viewed by others reveal nothing. Kane is well-traveled, mysterious, enigmatic, unfathomable, confident, self-assured, and articulate.

This is a non-usual image of the black man of the seventies. Those who seek answers don't look here, those who see the value of questions asked but not necessarily answered this film is worth your time. This is a very good film. When they do the Sidney Poitier film tribute this is the film they will surely show first. Many people have not seen it and it is a very compelling part for Poitier.

My own self image as a black man now in a serious relationship with a woman who was not black was one that made me reconsider what I knew about people, relations and interracial mixing, social and romantic. Those black cinema images reinforced what I sincerely knew and believed - the black experience was not a monolithic one.

Brenda and I worked and saved money when we could. We set about finding a vehicle to make the trip to California. We scoured the ads and Brenda saw an ad for an old "airport limousine" for sale for $500 dollars. We went to the address and knocked on the door, the black man who came to the door said come to the side of the house. In his drive way was a pale blue eight-door 1960 **Checker Aerobus**.

He said it had been used by Central Michigan University for their golf team and he bought it from them but now wanted to sell it. It was so long and outrageous we both fell in love with it. Within a week, we came by and paid him. With the assistance of friends, they drove us to pick up the car. Our friends' mouths hung open when they saw the car. When they could speak, they expressed great excitement. Our friends, like Brenda and I, had never seen another vehicle like it on the automobile crammed roads of Detroit, the Motor City.

When we got in the car, I drove. The car had power steering and was an automatic. I had to get accustomed to its length

when turning corners. We always, always got more than one stare when people saw it no matter the day, time, location, or weather. It was our dream travel vehicle. We loved our Checker Aerobus. Our friends when we got it and they saw it all had to have rides in it.

One day we filled every seat and there were four bench seats and a compartment in the back like any station wagon with eight doors would have. Our friends loved it, we loved it, and we always made new acquaintances at gas stations and in parking lots, yes we amazed parking lot attendants. I usually had to park the car. They wouldn't get in it because of its extreme length.

Our plan to save money was working, so we decided to save even more money if possible our friends knew our plan to move to California and saw how serious we were, they helped us in very special ways. We moved from a large house on Seyburn Street on the east side of Detroit with about five other people into a smaller apartment complex to save money.

One of our new friends from the neighborhood of Indian Village told us about it. So we continued to save money and share a small one-bedroom apartment with two cats, Dizzy who was an all-white cat and his sister Bessie, who was a tabby gray color. Meanwhile Brenda and I decided we needed to road test the vehicle after about a year. We both got some time off and decided to visit some friends who had moved back to the land, in Arkansas. All along the road and throughout the trip to Arkansas the Aerobus hummed along beautifully. We got stares galore for sure.

The community that our friends with whom we had lived in the Seyburn Street house Joe and Linda and Marissa their daughter had moved into was amongst a group of young hippies who also wanted to live an agrarian lifestyle. This group

connected with the local old time fifties something ex-moon shiners. The two groups often after a hard-days' work whether in the fields as farmers or jobs in the instance of some of the young hippies and after a days' work sat around together the two different generations swapping adventures and beer. We and the Aerobus were an immediate hit. At one point, we took on a local mountainous area with the Aero-bus and it took the hill with no problem.

One day Joe and family and Brenda and I set off to an area and picked up sassafras roots and took them to the local fresh food market and Joe and Linda exchanged the sassafras roots for groceries. I really felt part of the land in ways I have not experienced since that time. After a few days of going back to the land, Brenda and I left with fond memories and new friends.

Aerobussing it through America it's been such a treat no tricks even, seeing the land walking, planting, smelling, feeling and being really of the land for a change not just on the earth but among its very earth cells. Our next mission with the car was to get it painted a nice new color. With the help of friends, we found a guy in an East side Detroit paint and body shop who fell in love with the idea of painting the car in his shop just for the challenge and the opportunity. The color we settled on was bright yellow.

East side, west side all around this mutha' scratchin' town I'm bent I tell you bent from paying the rent my card has been punched so many times in the name of the landlord I feel like telling that no doing where is the money son of a house with roaches and junk and people son of a beehive motorcycle get your ass on down to my job you buzzard and punch my boss for me.

Eventually Brenda developed an entrepreneurial venture with a girlfriend. It was an old clothes store named Fabulous Second Hands-East. The original Fabulous Second Hands was opened by Mary Anne, co- teacher of the kindergarten class with Brenda and I, it was on the west side of Detroit.

The humor of Charlie Parker his playing of many moods and tempos...

I go to sleep tonight not knowing where I shall live soon whether here or there or somewhere else entirely but does it really matter if it is to life and for love you care.

Creatures of habit traditionally inhabit those places, which are habitable so that they can have it to cohabit and continue with their habits.

Mourn for Bud, mourn for Louis, and mourn for Bessie and do not forget Duke too as long as you are at it mourn, for we will never hear see, feel, experience their likes, impossible, again ever again....

We huddled in the Strata waiting for McCoy and his fellow music makers, we huddled in Ford waiting patiently for the end of the JoJo Gunne scene hoping the Mahavishnu would come and charge us up again for another time another place, those who really knew huddled at the Ibo waiting for Alice, dear Alice loving and sharing us all at once huddling together waiting for the music.

There are two memories of being in an interracial relationship in Detroit that remain. The first memory was of one early morning after being awake all night and in love. It started to rain this warm summer morning so we left my place on Commonwealth Street and began to walk in the rain in the neighborhood. On the way back on a main thoroughfare through my neighborhood, we hear a horn. We turned and it was an 18-

wheeler truck, the driver who was white as he drove by gave us the middle finger salute.

The second memory was a hot summer day. We were living in the Seyburn Street house near Belle Isle Park on Detroit's' east side. My friend Sylvia had come to visit. We had lived together when she was in relationship with a musician, in both the Hancock and Commonwealth House together. This hot summer day Sylvia, her new roommate a woman named Marilyn and Brenda and I went for a walk to Belle Isle Park. There is a multi-lane bridge that spans the Detroit River that also has sidewalks for crossing over onto this island park.

On the way over, we were constantly accosted by men in cars who saw a black man with three white women in shorts. The men showed nothing but disrespect to me and the women. I was a little concerned until we got off the bridge. We spent time enjoying ourselves as much as we could. If we walked as a group, the horns and cat-calls grew more pronounced. We finally picked a spot and sat. I dreaded the journey home. It was more of same on the way home. These women were my friends and my lady. I had to grin and bear it. Those two incidents helped me see what the image of black and white people together can do to people who do not understand what they are seeing. It also reinforced the power of images, understood or not.

A spirit came to me I think; and it said, "Be not afraid, you are well", over and over again. I could feel in a sense its cold essence all about me as I sat unafraid and crying in the dark. It said in part that it was the spirit of my mother's mother and that it was there to protect me. Further, I must awake and be grateful and thankful for I was to be blessed with the gift of life and health and a soul mate to protect and caress me. I was to keep on keeping on and find myself in the drums, to 'just do it' and I would be enlightened. I must love and respect my mate and find life and happiness. I was blessed so I was not to fear. I was overcome emotionally and spiritually. Who or what was I to the life flowing forces in the ethers. Now you understand why I sit here in wonder and amazement. I feel something or someone touched me and I cannot forget or let go of that feeling. You know just on my left it sits watching and touching me.

Midnight greeting the new day early still up and about from previous days' situations, a lot of communications and feelings. I'm wondering how to write something that just is not the same old rehashed version of me from the day before. Other people write in prosaic terms and ideas I can barely even begin to write that way. It's seems to me it's like someone telling you to go outside and look at the color of the air or smell the clouds.

To look anew and see the shadows and the life revealed, to be known by someone and yet be a sweet mystery, to lead someone down a carefully chosen path and both be lost in wonder at the expanse of newly discovered territory to be with and without two can and will be, just be.

The other interracial couple in our circle of friends was Spencer and Wilma. He was a white doctor from Missouri. About a third of all our white friends knew each other from years earlier in Missouri. She was a Black nurse divorced with two young children a boy and a girl. Spencer was also divorced and had two children, two boys about the same age as Wilma's kids. At one point, I baby sat Spencer's kids. It was always fun to meet Spencer and Wilma because when he saw me he would say, "Hey Spencer, how you doing?" and I'd reply, *"Good Spencer, how*

about you?" He and I got a giggle out of that every time and it and our mutual understanding of black/white social-sexual mores helped to make the four of us fast friends.

Nelita was one of the roomers in a small studio apartment in the apartment building we shared. She was just across the hall from us. Once the three of us met and spent time getting to know each other, we became the "three musketeers" headed to California. Nelita was from Brazil. She lived in Brazil during the time of the dictator General Humberto Branco.

The Generals' regime was short (1961-1967) but brutal. Labor unions were banned; criticism of his regime became unlawful, thousands of people who were "suspected communists", including children, were arrested, tortured, and murdered. Nelita described personally bearing witness to some of these events. She talked about what she saw in Brazil. She said she saw people beaten and murdered during her early youth in Brazil in the sixties before she left.

Eventually Wilma and Spencer bought a house a few miles from my parents' home on the west side of Detroit near Seven Mile Road; my parents lived near Eight Mile Road. Spencer and Wilma and her kids offered to have the three of us, Brenda, Nelita and I room in their attic for free. This would help us save even more money for a few months before we left for California. So with the offer from Spencer and Wilma we moved into their attic. Brenda and I shared a small room; Nelita had another room across the hall, in their over-sized third floor attic. We continued to work until two weeks before we were to leave. Our last Christmas in Detroit was 1975. We were going to leave Detroit in January of 1976.

I feel the tension of my decision to quit work, those who care, and those who could care less, those who hope I have a wreck, feelings of resentment, restraint, repression, rejection, rejuvenation, and exaltation. Now the path lies ahead must use my head so as not to be misled. Visions of 'Frisco in my head, planted there long, long ago now reappear as to say "come on out". So I don't doubt that I will get there it's just the adventure from here to there the great Bi-Centennial cruise.

By this time, we had a day bed put in the Aerobus for sleeping which left two bench seats, one up front and one all the way in the back in front of our storage area for the Aerobus. A friend helped us rig up my large and heavy cassette recorder with a wire run to the back so we could hear the sounds from the deck and a bookshelf sized speaker placed in the back of the Aerobus.

The journey from Detroit to California was like the experience of Billy and Wyatt in **Easy Rider** (1969)*. The three of us were determined to leave the city of our lives and life times to that point. I felt the urge to be released from the bonds of having lived in one place all my life. Detroit, Michigan was a good place to escape from. The long cold winters, the gray over cast days that represented sixty percent of the weather patterns. Our friends provided the thread that kept us satisfied with life and unhappy with life all at the same time. We loved our friends but the three of us wanted out of Detroit. So we cast our lot together to move to California. I had friends who had escaped from Detroit, had not fallen in the ocean, and said when we talked by phone, "The weather is better in California."

The three of us left Detroit on a cold snowy January day in rush hour traffic, we were on our way to the adventure of our lives. I drove and felt joy and trepidation when I realized as we were caught in Ohio rush traffic after a few hours that we were on our way to a new life. At twenty-eight, I never imagined that I would be in a serious long term relationship with a woman who

was not black. The three of us were driving South in the dead of winter 1976. Our license tag read Michigan, Water, Winter, Wonderland, the tag was red, white, and blue for the Bi-Centennial year.

CHAPTER THREE

THE BICENTENNIAL CRUISE

1976 was a year when the winter season hung on in parts of the South as fiercely as it did the North. We arrived in Florida having stopped only for gas and bathroom breaks. We stopped in northern Florida, to regroup and while fixing food and walking around to stretch our legs, we decided, this is still too cold. The Florida Keys became our destination for warm weather and a beach that was our goal. I let Brenda take over driving and went and lay down on the day bed in the car and Nelita rode shotgun. Within a few hours we were in the Keys and I awoke to heat and sunshine. Now the question was where we could park this long yellow Checker Aerobus, inconspicuous we were not. Besides the color of the vehicle we had luggage strapped to the roof of the car. We looked like something out of a circus train.

We did manage to find some people who were friendly and loved our car. The car opened more conversations with people who it seemed never realizing who or what we were. They were generally so blown away by the car and its length and color, that we were sometimes invisible because the car shone so brightly in people's minds and eyes. These locals told us the best place for a rig our size that would be free was along the beach near the local Navy Air station. They said the Shore Patrol never hassled folks as long as they were law abiding and peaceful. With some time and one more stop for directions we found it. The sun was shining, we all immediately got into bathing suits and got wet on

the beach came back to our blankets and lay there till the sun was going down when we made a fire and started to prepare our first serious meal since leaving Detroit.

We were now home on the road. **Easy Riders'**(1969)* Billy and Wyatt were like us when they landed after selling the coke, then buying some killer motor bikes and putting their money in Wyatts' gas tank. We were here because we worked hard for three years and saved money to make the move to California. When we started, there were the three of us, when they started there was just the two of them. As time went on our trip became a reflection of the **Easy Rider** trip. For the better part of two weeks we swam, ate, and slept along one of the nicest beaches in the Florida Keys. Our paradise was interrupted occasionally by locals who knew the area. They stayed usually overnight never more than two nights. Our cross to bear for all this sun and fun was, once a week the jets near us did night maneuvers which brought them directly over our heads. So that night for a good four hours it was like being inside a loud machine that you could not turn off.

The low point of our sunny vacation was being accosted by a local white policeman who did not like the image of our interracial ménage-á-trois. He threatened us with incarceration and so we spent the time that he and his family in their camper were there being very subdued. They spent two days there and left. As time wore on Nelita became restless more than either Brenda or I. She grew more restless every day. One day she took off and we did not see her for two days and we got worried. When she did show up she said she was going to stay with a black soldier she met in the area and we should go on to California without her.

We thought this was sufficiently weird so we decided that day to move on to New Orleans and Mardi Gras our next

planned destination. We wound up in a State Park near the Florida/Georgia line. We meet up with some people we had met in the Keys who had recommended this Park to us. We also had work done on the car, oil and lube so we spent one night in our sleeping bag under the stars. Our company that night included armadillos who were beggars and thieves.

We got the car back and drove on into Louisiana. We never did figure out why Nelita suddenly changed her mind about the trip we had all planned to take together. We had gone from three to two. Billy and Wyatt went from two people to three. We did not know anyone in New Orleans. All we knew and heard was that you could sleep in your car on the streets. Well once we arrived we decided to park on the campus of one of the local universities, Tulane.

By the time campus had cleared out near dark we were accosted by the school security who said we could not sleep in our car on their campus. We were also informed that just this year the city of New Orleans had outlawed the sleeping in cars period. So we were stuck. We left the campus area and parked on a street and within a few hours we were accosted again by the New Orleans police. We said we knew and would move.

Before the night was over, after having moved again we were accosted by the New Orleans police again, by this time it was nearing dawn. So we said we would move as soon as it was daybreak, they left and left us alone. We did not get much sleep that first night in New Orleans. We found a parking lot and parked the car and got out and walked around New Orleans. After we found someplace for breakfast we walked to an area that had tourists walking around. We hung out for a while and met some Hare Krishna's, who when we explained what had happened, they offered us a free meal and a driveway for us to park our car.

We found their house, parked in their driveway, and had their food, which was very different from anything I had eaten. After lunch we decided to walk around some more. We were walking north on a street adjacent to a main thoroughfare in the downtown area. Up ahead of us I saw two policemen who saw us and kept walking out of our line of sight as they walked perpendicular on the cross street ahead of us.

When we got to the corner they were there waiting for us. They asked for I.D. Here is what one of the pigs said, "Nigger if you don't get yor' black ass out of the city by sundown I'm going to lock yo' black ass up!!" We were totally bummed out. We went back to the Krishna's house. We got our car, drove downtown to the Western Union office, wired Detroit for more money, which we had arranged to do along our trip. We went to a bookstore nearby, bought some books and parked in the Krishna's driveway for the night.

We went to Western Union the next day, picked up our money and got the hell out of New Orleans. We landed in another State Park and found the showers and came back to the Aerobus, chastened and happy we had survived that ordeal. We watched some ducks that were in the swamp area near our site feeding on bread crumbs and saw that even in the world of ducks there was a clear pecking order.

We spent two days decompressing from New Orleans. We met some other campers our age and later one night before we left we shared some wine and conversations. Our next stop was Dallas, Texas where we had friends. We left on the morning of the third day and called our friends in Dallas and said we were on our way. We arrived in Dallas parked and found our friend Vicky who greeted us warmly and like everyone else when she saw our ride commented, "Man that car is really long and it is beautiful." We went up to her place and rested and chatted

about our experiences in the Keys in Florida and New Orleans. Vicky comment on New Orleans was, "Man what a bummer."

We slept in our car that night. The next day Vicky had to go to work. Her first roommate in Detroit was one of my former girlfriends. Later when Vicky and Brenda became roommates and we continued to marvel at our running into each other in different social sets. Vicky left Detroit and moved back to Texas to pursue her ambition to run camera on movies. She moved to Dallas to do that and had worked her way to camera assistant on movies, commercials and television shows. After work the second day we were in Dallas, Vicky had arranged for us to meet her new friends in Dallas that evening. We went to one of her girlfriend's homes in a part of Dallas that had the "old money" with an influx of young "new money". Her friends were very warm and gracious. He ran an upscale women's wear boutique that clearly was doing well as he described the stress and joy of running his own store. She was owner of a school for ballet and modern dance instruction. She had also spent a decade in San Francisco where she received her education and training as a dancer. So as a result of her San Francisco experience she became a cheerleader and font of information on California and San Francisco.

We found time to explain that the car despite its looks was giving us problems, so they gave us the name of a good mechanic. We left them and thanked them for a wonderful evening. Vicky followed us and our car to the mechanic the next day. She had to work so she took us back to her house where that night we slept on her floor in our sleeping bag. The second day we picked up our car and got the bad news. To replace the part that was causing the problem, a gasket, required that the engine be removed and put back in the car. The option since it ran well and just leaked oil was to keep putting about two quarts

of oil per hundred miles which was the rate at which it was leaking until we got to California and get it fixed there.

So we decided to move on but Vicky had good news for us. Her sister who lived in Albuquerque, New Mexico was making her apartment available to us for a week while she was out of town. She worked as a geologist for the Federal government and often spent time away from home. Needless to say we were thrilled. The caveat was we had to be there within the week before the weekend to get her key. We told Vicky to tell your sister we would leave and get there in time to get her key.

After two days on the road we arrived at Carla's apartment which was on the second floor of a duplex. She greeted us warmly. We walked up the stairs into her apartment which was very tastefully decorated it had wooden floors and beautiful hand-made Navajo rugs. We sat and she told us about the area and about her work and her trip out of town. She said she was very happy to have us stay there and take care of her apartment.

She was pleasant and she said she had some work to do to prep for her trip and we should relax. We put on some quiet music from her collection, on her record player which she suggested we use and relax. We read the books we bought in New Orleans.

We were so quiet beside the music playing that Carla came out of her room to check on us and remarked how quiet we were, which she liked and said we would be headed out to a local restaurant for lunch very soon. The part of Albuquerque that Carla lived in we found out was considered the "old Town" section of the city. This section of the city was an assortment of apartments, multi-unit dwellings, shops, restaurants and it seemed dozens of jewelry stores selling what was Native American made jewelry. We commented on this and Carla said

she was fascinated by this as well and had lived here long enough to know what was and wasn't hand crafted. Most tourists she said couldn't tell the difference, so the stores did well with the tourists. After the meal we went back to the apartment and made our selves secure in her apartment. We said goodnight to her and she said she was leaving early the next day and would not see us as we would be sleep, so we said our goodbyes and Thanks You's, then. She wished us a bon voyage to California. When we did awake the next day she was gone and had left us a very nice hand written note.

Billy and Wyatt in **Easy Rider** went to New Orleans found some whores, dropped acid, and did Mardi Gras. George Hanson is murdered in **Easy Rider**. We were run out of town and were fortunate not to be arrested. We left New Orleans and Louisiana with our tails between our legs, wiser for the experience I hoped. Now here in New Mexico, Brenda and I were in a safe, sane and secure environment after having been away from Detroit almost two months. We left town before Carla returned, left her key and a note and some fresh flowers. We made our way through the desert southwest. It was wide, desolate, foreboding and inviting. As a city boy this journey provided me with more travel than I had ever had. The adventure to date had been very eye-opening as well.

We spent a few days getting to California. We found Highway 1 which runs the length of the state and drove until we found a park that was right on the coast. We stopped there because we saw hang-gliders sailing like big colorful birds from the surrounding hills. We had a wonderful camp spot. It overlooked the ocean. The Pacific Ocean was walking distance and the peaks where the hang-gliders jumped were well within our view. The sound and smell of the Pacific Ocean seemed to open me and all my city saturated pores.

We decided to spend our last few weeks taking our time driving up Highway 1 to San Francisco our destination. That time Brenda and I had together before we reached San Francisco along the California coast was the apex of our relationship. Eventually we made our way into San Francisco. We parked our car along the area in San Francisco that was strewn with odd looking vehicles, that people lived and traveled in. Our vehicle fit right in. This was the Panhandle section of the Golden Gate Park. We found the address of one of my old Detroit friends. This was in April. We had been on the road three months.

I felt relieved that we had arrived at our destination. I knew that no matter what the future held I had reached a major milestone in my life. I did not know what to expect but having made the journey of my life I was prepared to take California and make it my home.

SAN FRANCISCO

Maketa a sista', was shocked and pleasantly surprised when we rang the doorbell to her apartment and announced our arrival. She was effusive and jubilant to see us and we proceeded once inside her apartment to explain some of our adventure in getting to San Francisco. Over the next two weeks besides sleeping in our car we met and stayed with my other Detroit friends George Socha and Jerry Silhanek who each had their own apartments. As time went on I knew Brenda and I were on the last legs of our relationship. We both got what we needed from the relationship a loving and caring partner who helped each other get out of Detroit.

Within a month, we convinced George from my Hancock House and Studio Theater days to move from his closet sized apartment into a flat with Brenda and me. The apartment was on Oak Street which bordered the Panhandle, to which we had become so familiar. George worked as a bike messenger. Brenda and I were going through our financial resources. During this difficult time we met a man who he said he fell in love with the car and wanted to use it to advertise an event he was planning. Little did I know the event he really was planning was very different! His name was Julio he was Hispanic, after a week of riding him around in the car, I saw that he was indeed working with a local group that was planning a public event. The group was involved in opening a restaurant which would be staffed partially by ex-cons. He was an ex-con and now counselor for the program working as media liaison and ombudsman for a group that was called Reality House-West.

One of the people we met who was to be a part of the event was "Papa Joe" Taylor. "Papa Joe" had spent most of his sixty odd years in San Quentin. It was there that the muse found "Papa Joe". While in San Quentin he had developed a knack for sculpture, completely self-taught. His work resembled African inspired sculpture. His worked in various shades and textures of wood was amazing when you examined it very carefully.

The muse found him and it had sustained him in his time in prison. It was clear because his work resembled that of a master carver. Julio got the local press to come to the restaurant pre-opening to see "Papa Joe" and his work. Julio got both papers the Chronicle and Examiner to do stories. The Examiner sent a photographer and thus had the better story. By the time the restaurant had opened Julio and Brenda were living together and I sold the Aerobus to them for five hundred dollars. I got some work as a busboy it was my first job in San Francisco. I worked

long enough to collect unemployment based on this job and my last job in Detroit and quit. Within a month of that I was beginning the process of making my life in my new home San Francisco.

Now in San Francisco a month or so since last made entry being in a very human condition both happy and sad for my life these last few months, years, days, hours, seconds. I'm still traveling inside my head off into some far off space. Living in San Francisco is like a dream, people often times stranger than fiction. I had done what my family and friends did not believe or suspect I would do. This was my opportunity to find my place and make my mark in the world.

My decision to move west was one encouraged by thoughts of better weather, the opportunity to reconnect with friends from Detroit and beyond that I was open to whatever changes or opportunities I could find, make or would come my way.

For blacks in the late1800's post-Civil War America, the West was a place that was far away from Reconstruction and Jim Crow that grew in the South. The western frontier post-Civil War was a melting pot of black, white, Hispanic and Native Americans. More than seventy-five thousand slaves escaped before the Civil War. African Americans were builders of the new western frontier in America.

Buck and the Preacher (1972), 102 min., color, story by Drake Walker, Ernest Kinoy, and script by Ernest Kinoy, directed by Sidney Poitier. This film marks Poitier's debut as director. He took over for Joseph Sargent who was fired because the producers, which included the stars, did not like his point of view for the film. The film starred Sidney Poitier, Harry Belafonte, Ruby Dee and Cameron Mitchell. Belafonte is one of the un-credited co-producers of the film. His Belafonte Enterprises and Poitier's

production company E & R Productions are listed as co-producing companies along with Columbia Pictures, the distributor of the film. The music was composed by jazz great Benny Carter.

This story chronicles some former slaves who have managed to earn money, bought wagons and acquired resources necessary to move west. They are pursued by agents of slave owners who through force by violence want to compel them to return south. Buck (Poitier) the wagon master for the group and the Preacher (Belafonte) meet by accident and become the leaders and guardians of this group of settlers looking to find a better life in the West. The challenges, struggles, obstacles and perils of this adventure make for a very positive statement about black striving that resonated with me.

The facts are many blacks have a Native American branch of their family. **James P. Beckwourth** (1798-1866) whose father was of English nobility and a mother who was a biracial (black/white) slave is one of the most famous trailblazers of his time. Most American history books forgot his accomplishments. In April 1850 he found a path through the Sierra Nevada mountain range leading a wagon train personally through what is now called Beckwourth Pass, a first for anyone. He built with partners the first trading post in what is now Pueblo, Colorado. His ranch, trading post and hotel in the Sierra Valley of California became the city of Beckwourth, California. Because of his frontier skills he was familiar with and opened trading with many native tribes and became a chief with the Crow tribe.

Over time his image in drawings and even in cinema has been whitened. In the film **Tomahawk** (1951) Jack Oakey a white actor plays one "Sol" Beckworth a mountain man and trapper. The struggle of black and Native American farmers continues in the 21st Century. On November 26th, 2010 the U.S. Senate

agreed to settle and pay $4.5 billion over claims of discrimination in lending practices, government mismanagement and access to U.S. subsidy programs for these American farmers.

My friend Maketa Groves having recently graduated from Antioch College/West, San Francisco with a degree in political science was now working in their administration and helped to get me enrolled there. Antioch College is in Yellow Springs, Ohio. The school was among the first to open their doors in the late 1800's to Blacks and women before many institutions. In the late nineteen-seventies and eighties they had programs for people like me who had in the words of Timothy Leary, *"...turned on, tuned in and dropped out."*

The program involved letting you document what you had done with your life to that point, take a year of classes (three semesters) use prior college course transcripts with passing grades if applicable, and get an under graduate degree. They had nearly a dozen centers in the seventies and eighties around the country for people like me. At twenty-eight years old, I was their ideal candidate.

In the fall of 1976 I got a Pell Grant student loan and I was enrolled doing undergraduate study in film making. My work/study job which the school found for me was as the first intern for Newsreel in San Francisco. Newsreel was a group of activists some of whom had formerly worked for the Students for a Democratic Society as an extension of their anti-war efforts. Newsreel distributed Cuban films, Asian films, and a variety of relevant anti-war and other international social issue documentaries including many American made. At one time in the late sixties there were more than a dozen cities with a Newsreel. In 1976 there were three offices: San Francisco, New York City and Boston. Today there is California Newsreel in San

Francisco and Third World Newsreel in New York City. (See Resources)

As their intern I cleaned films, I shipped films, I called teachers all over the country trying to get them to rent films, I watched the films in their library whenever I wished. Eventually I got a key and could come and go after business hours. I used their Steenbeck editing system to edit my undergraduate thesis film. All of their films and my film were 16 mm gauge films. By the time I graduated I had found additional part-time work as an usher at a local movie theater chain that featured international cinema and I worked part-time at KPIX-TV, as a casual part-time film editor. This was all within the first fifteen months in the city by the Bay.

During my tenure with Antioch as a result of a school assignment eventually I continued to teach myself about Black cinema. This history included discovering George & Noble Johnson, Oscar Micheaux, Spencer Williams Jr., and other forgotten pioneers of Black cinema. My course work was titled, *Third World Cinema in Perspective*, it was part of my independent study.

The work included a series of conferences with Ed Guerrero, PhD., then a professor, at the San Francisco Art Institute. Another filmmaker who was on my degree committee, Tony Williams, introduced us. In the course, I was "...seeking to understand cinema as art and communication tool, perspective on the Third World influence as part of this process."

Here is what Ed wrote for my portfolio, "During the twenty-five hours that Spencer and I spent together he more than met my expectations as far as the quality and level of his output in film work. I was particularly impressed with his thorough knowledge of Third World and foreign films. The thing that is

important in terms of his development is that he has been able to integrate the best elements of these films into his own aesthetic. Over-all I am quite satisfied with his skills and his development."

Ed is currently part of the faculty of New York University and has written *Framing Blackness: The African American Image in Film*, Temple University Press, 1993.

During my undergraduate film study an **Independent Black Cinema Film Festival** was held at the San Francisco Museum of Modern Art. Here are some films from the festival:

Bush Mama (1976), produced, directed and edited by Haile Gerima. This film portrays the inner life of a black woman struggling to survive in contemporary Los Angeles. We see her anguish as a result of society's denigrations and the confrontations of which she seems to have more than her fair-share. She struggles for survival every day, sometimes she wins, and sometimes she does not. Barbara O. Jones delivers a gripping sensitive portrait .The story draws you into the life of this sista' as she deals with the affects/effects and pressures of the black experience. This story does not wallow in misery it is black social realism.

The festival featured three films by Oscar Devereaux Micheaux (1884-1951), **The Girl From Chicago** (1932), **God's Stepchildren** (1936), and **Lying Lips** (1939), b/w, feature films. Micheauxs' films show the black middle-class in a positive perspective. He successfully showcases the black experience including sights and sounds of black owned and operated businesses. Scenes in nightclubs with men and women performers serve as segues and interludes in his films that show people in the South what life was like 'up North'.

Prior to the festival I had heard of Micheaux but had not seen his films. Micheaux was the first great black filmmaker in America. He made films from the silent era until 1950, when he made his last film. There were other independent black filmmakers prior to Micheaux but none achieved the level of productivity that he did. Micheaux was an entirely self-taught filmmaker.

Micheaux began his entrepreneurship as the salesman for his parents, who had been slaves. They were farmers whose products Micheaux sold in the city of Metropolis, Illinois. From there Micheaux left home at seventeen worked as a Pullman Porter saved his money and moved to South Dakota in 1905 and became a homesteader. From farming he turned next to writing novels and selling his self-published novels door to door to mostly white people in the Dakotas.

Next he began the Micheaux Film and Book Company with offices in Sioux City, Iowa, then moved to Chicago and later Harlem. He even sold stock in his company to white farmers around Sioux City. Between 1918 and 1950 Micheaux wrote, produced, directed and occasionally had small acting parts in his films and personally distributed more than two dozen silent films and another dozen and a half sound films. Micheaux was so astute a filmmaker that his distribution entirely financed his film production.

In 1992 a Micheaux film was discovered in a Spanish cinemateque, with Spanish inter-titles. With its discovery it is the earliest surviving feature film by an African American. That film **Within Our Gates** * (1919) was re-edited with new English inter-titles.

Tuskegee Subject #626, (1976), 30 min., color, written and directed by Leroy McDonald. This is a fictional account of one

man's reactions to a brutal and insensitive real government experiment that actually ran for forty years named the, "Tuskegee Experiment". In this U.S. government run experiment black men were given a venereal disease injection, then left untreated and were never told about it. This film personalizes that awful misuse of government power.

This film chronicles how one man reacts once he knows the awful truth. It is a case of too little too late. The cast is uniformly excellent with a very strong performance by Robert Earl Jones (James Earl Jones, dad). You wonder at the temerity of the government and at the lows to which it will stoop in the name of the state.

Allensworth (1976) written, produced and directed by Thurman White. This film is a social history documentary. This film is the story of an early Black California pioneer and his efforts for change for his people. Lt. Colonel Allen Allensworth (1842-1914) established the first black settlement in California in 1908. The settlement became a municipal district in 1914 and finally a state historical park in 1969. This documentary uses a montage of interviews and other documents to trace the development of the town.

Five on The Black Hand Side (1974), color, feature film, 96 mins., written by Charles L. Russell, based on his play, directed by Oscar Williams. The film stars Clarice Taylor, Leonard Jackson, Glenn Turman, Virginia Capers and D'Urville Martin. This is a forthright and righteous film on Black family life. It is a very funny film. A family fights to grow and not be stifled collectively and individually. The mother realizes after twenty years her potential to be more than a housewife. A son strives for his own identity. The father can't quite march in step with today after a twenty year Army career. The daughter is in love and about to be married. Add some funny neighbors, a fast talking, jive walking

neighborhood, a local barbershop filled with an array of characters and mix well with some African social mores. Serve it funny side up. This is a lesson in the humor of life.

I made a concerted effort while still in undergraduate film study to see the work of many American filmmakers. My interest was in filmmakers considered mavericks in the Hollywood film idiom.

John Cassavetes (1929-1989) while well known as an actor was also considered by many the Godfather of American independent feature film making. In his directorial work he used improvisation as a technique with the film script as a beacon for sailing into the creative unknown. He worked with actors who were his real life friends and his wife Gena Rowlands. She is terrific in **Faces** (1968) **Husbands** (1970), **Minnie and Moskowitz** (1971), **A Woman Under the Influence** (1974)* and **Gloria** (1980), but she is monumental with Cassavetes as her co-star in the film **Love Streams**, (1984), color, 141 min. Original play and script by Ted Allen, Executive Producer and cinematography by Al Rubin. Cassavetes and Rowlands play a brother and sister who both challenge conventions.

He is a womanizing alcoholic writer she is a collector of pets, husbands and the troubles of life. The film is visceral without being too cerebral, when they are on screen together in this one it is truly electric, a million volts. This film little seen and poorly received critically is Cassavetes' last film as director. I would argue it is one of his best. *"...many recognize that Cassavetes' techniques have become central to the vocabulary of contemporary cinema."* (5)

Samuel Fuller (1911-1997) began his filmmaking career as a journalist while still a teen working for the New York Journal. Later he had novels published. Fuller got work as a screenwriter

in Hollywood in 1936. After military service in World War II, his directorial debut was for a western he wrote based on an article; it was the film **I Shot Jesse James** (1948). Fuller says of his work, *"Film is a battleground. Love, hate, violence, action, death...In a word, emotion."* (7)

Shock Corridor (1963)*, b/w, with color, 101 min. produced, directed and script by Sam Fuller, starring Peter Breck, Constance Towers, Gene Evans, James Best and Hari Rhodes. This is a love story about two reporters who work undercover. Cathy (Towers) works undercover as a prostitute. Her fellow reporter and love interest Johnny Barrett (Breck) is determined to win a Pulitzer Prize, at all costs. Barrett (Breck) is a journalist with 140 IQ is in a psychiatrist's office rehearsing for playing a neurotic to get admitted to an asylum to solve a murder there.

This is a line from the film. Euripedes, 425 BC, *"...whom God wishes to destroy he first makes mad...".* He is warned against doing this by his boss, his girl and others who care about him. He sees himself in the mold of Charles Dickens and Mark Twain writing icons he admires. He conditions himself for a year to play this role of a neurotic. *"Hamlet was made for Freud, not you..."* says his girlfriend Cathy to him before he embarks on what he believes is a golden opportunity. He has to create a Jekyll/Hyde character. The Editor of the newspaper is involved in his scheme. His girlfriend helps by playing his sister who, brings charges against him to get the process started by signing a complaint about his instability.

In this murder mystery psychiatric expose we meet several people in the asylum that are potential witnesses to the murder who are all unique anachronisms. Stuart (Best) who believes he is a confederate soldier. He is really a shell shocked Korean War vet. The most vivid character from a very personal perspective for me in the film is a black man, Trent Bowden (Rhodes), who

imagines himself a "white supremacist". He was the only black student in a southern school who has a mental breakdown from the extreme prejudice he experienced at school. He carries a blatantly racist sign. At another point in the film he steals a pillow case and makes a KKK hood. He continues his madness with lines like *"...get that black boy before he marries my daughter..."* as he attacks the only other black person in the asylum.

Comedian Dave Chappelle used such a character in his television comedy series **Chappelle's Show** (2003-2006). Clayton Bixby, Chappelle's character was a black man who is blind as he imagined he was a "white supremacist", Chappelle made his social/political point with comedy.

Fuller made his social commentary about the insane nature of racism at a time when civil rights issues were on the front pages of American newspapers and on television. The third potential witness to the murder is Dr. John Bowden (Evans), a Nobel Prize winning scientist who went insane working on nuclear projects. The hot button issues of the time are addressed by the characters and psychosis of these three witnesses - war, race and nuclear power. Fuller also takes a major swipe at mental health care of the time in this film. The color sequences which are used as very effective moments representing psychotic episodes of some of the patients. The color sequences were shot by Fuller and are his home movies.

In the eighties Fuller made another film that looked at the sickness of racism. It is appropriately titled **White Dog** (1982). In this film a "white dog" is trained by its white owner to attack black people. A black man is hired to deprogram the animal which has killed. The controversy surrounding this film and its ideas prevented it from seeing a wider audience at the time of its release.

Orson Welles (1915-1985) in his lifetime was awarded the French Legion of Honor from the "Academy des Beaux Arts"; Cannes Film festival Co-Grand Prize for **Othello** (1952); an American Film Institute, Life Achievement Award and an Honorary Academy Award. This in no way reflects the artistic achievement level of Welles. He received many other living and posthumous awards. It is his very personal vision and dedication to his art that is revered and often revisited.

In 1938 he produced, directed and starred in the radio performance/event of that decade. That was "The War of the Worlds", a radio drama made of H. G. Welles science-fiction thriller. The radiocast produced real wide spread panic in the state of New Jersey where the story is set, among many people who were listening to the radio-cast. It made him an overnight sensation nationally.

By age twenty he had co-produced and directed an all-black cast voodoo production of Macbeth, funded by the Federal Theater Project that ran in the Lafayette and Adelphi Theaters of New York City. At twenty-five he co-wrote, produced, directed and starred in an acknowledged cinema landmark, **Citizen Kane** (1941)*, 120 min., b/w.

Welles was a social activist from his early days in radio. By 1946 with assistance from the NAACP, Welles recreated the plight of a black war veteran from the war in the Pacific who had received a battle star. Isaac Woodward, Jr. was the victim to an unprovoked police beating in South Carolina that left him blind. Welles recreated the case for radio highlighting the injustices of racial tensions in America. "I was born a white man and until a colored man is a full citizen like me I haven't the leisure to enjoy the freedom that a colored man risked his life to maintain for me." (8)

One day I saw a local repertory film house was doing an all-day Orson Welles marathon. I had to go. On the bill that day was **Lady From Shanghai** (1948); **Touch of Evil** (1958)*; **The Trial** (1962); **F is for Fake** (1973), color. Welles' personal story is of one who was labeled a "genius" by family, friends and the press. It was Welles dedication to an independent vision that made him a maverick in and out of the Hollywood idiom of film-making. Welles stands apart from his many American contemporaries. He is bold, talented and egotistical enough to try and fail in a more interesting fashion than many more popular American directors.

In this marathon the early films **Lady From Shangai** & **Touch of Evil** are economical and action propelled, these two films twist and turn with suspense, murder, melodrama and fluidity. The cinematography in **Lady...**, by Charles Lawton and in **Touch...** by Russell Metty in both films is excellent in their use of black and white for subtle and nuanced images. The latter films **The Trial** and **F is for Fake** both these films left me puzzled by the story construction and execution of ideas. The body of Welles work consists of a strong sense of confidence in concept. This is so lacking in many more prolific American directors as to be a deficit.

Touch of Evil has been reissued. The DVD package contains a veritable Welles-copia consisting first and foremost of the restored version of this film noir gem. The film was restored based on the original Welles notes to the studio after he saw their studio edited and released version. Bonus material includes commentaries from star Charleston Heston, Welles and other film luminaries. The film takes us on a journey of murder, kidnapping, corruption and obsessions. Welles was never better as the oversized, overly ambitious police detective. He is someone willing to bend the laws towards his version of justice.

You're never at a loss for interest in this one. This is one of Welles' best films as actor and director.

My degree from Antioch was in film making I graduated in June, 1977. A full time job at **KPIX-TV**, a CBS affiliate, opened which required a degree I got the job and began working full time in fall, 1978. I worked with two other editors in a room shaped like an L. As you opened the door Charles Jackson who was black, was at bench one, I was at bench two and John Kerns who was white, was around the corner, at bench three. Our department was called 'Film Make-up Department'; we made the 16mm films ready for air. We put breaks in the films, making segments for running with commercials. We timed, put run times on the film, cleaned the films and also had the power of a censor.

My American cinema education was further expanded with this job at **KPIX-TV** as editor for the **"Red Eye Theater"** of this local San Francisco, CBS affiliate. They ran American films from midnight to four or five AM. They were one of the first stations in the area to be on more than twelve hours a day and eventually all Bay area stations were broadcasting twenty fours a day, seven days a week. During this period I edited for television sometimes in a busy week of work as many as fifteen to twenty American films that were produced between the nineteen-thirties and the nineteen-seventies.

B movies originally played the bottom portion of a double-bill of feature films in movie theaters. The B movie was not considered as well made or the film that put butts in seats, the A movie of the double bill did that. Television because it was not how good is it? But how long is the film and how many can we get? B movies filled the airwaves and hours of television programming. **KPIX-TV** at that time was part of the Westinghouse Group of half a dozen stations and so the films

were rotated from one station to another. The films were well worn and the copies we aired had clearly seen better days. But at the time of night they were shown sponsors were happy to have someplace to put their commercials. So the station made more money with their all night movies.

As someone who appreciated the work required even for the B movies my goal was to make the segments as long as possible. I had to contend with the Traffic Department which decided how many commercials were run during the midnight to dawn time period. Eventually I established a rapport with the supervisor in traffic. I was able to get her to drop one sometimes two and occasionally more commercial breaks. Some nights the commercials were fewer so my segment run times for the films could be longer. Thus the viewers would get longer segments of films between commercials. This was for me one of my minor triumphs in the fight to see the films air and the viewers' not be run away by too many commercials and too many short segments for the films. Despite our station at that time being the only one broadcasting at that hour.

The filmmakers whose work I came to admire in the B movie genre included the films of Budd Boetticher; Todd Browning; Roger Corman; Andre DeToth; Edward Dmytryk; Val Lewton; Don Seigel; Douglas Sirk; Jacques Tourneur; Raoul Walsh and James Whale. Their films made mostly through the major and minor studios that dominated film production exhibited moments of craft, did more than just tell a story with pictures and sound, bore the stamp of the director even in the studio/factory regime. Their films, when uninterrupted by commercials, provide more than just a pleasant viewing experience.

Within a year John retired from our film department. Alex Wong who was Asian, was hired to work with us. His prior editing experience had been as an editor with BBC, Hong Kong,

on documentaries. After a year, Alex grew bored and moved to news film editing. I helped get my roommate and long-time friend George Socha hired first as a casual film editor. He was doing vacation and sick day relief with us. When Alex moved to News Editing, George was hired to a full time position.

Because of changes in the technology the Film make-up Department was not threatened with complete extinction as all the films were being transferred to video. This resulted in their being only one full time job in what had been a three person department. So we were fortunately given the option of moving to other technical areas at the television station. My roommate George chose to become a video editor for the News Department. I chose to work with people in the Production Department to be re-trained as a stage manager/floor director.

George and I moved to 47th Avenue, two blocks from the ocean into a nice two story, three-bedroom house with a garage. George had a back yard now for his dog Ursa, a dark Shepherd. One of our roommates Cliff played classical guitar.

Another moment moving on to a new place in this San Francisco space what better way to end this portion of the story than right here on Oak Street now on to 47th Avenue and the end of the American world as I know it right next to the vast open space of the ever widening Pacific Ocean drift away on a sea of me and my shadows of dreams.

AFRICAN FILM FESTIVAL

In 1978 there was an African Film Festival at a local repertory film house, the Four Star Theater. It was on the other side of the Golden Gate Park from where we lived. We lived in the forties on Forty-Seventh Avenue it was in the Sunset Section of the city.

The theater was in the Richmond section of the city in the thirties. The Festival ran for six nights. The festival featured the films of, **Ousmane Sembene** (1923-2007) who was born in Zinguinchor-Casamance, a village along the southern part of Senegal. I had read and heard about him so I made sure to be on-line early. My instincts proved correct because every screening I attended was sold out. Sembene and his films are part of what W.E.B. Du Bois described almost ninety years ago. Du Bois saw that the study of Africa and the African Diaspora as a seamless whole.

Sembene spoke Wolof, his native language and fluent French, the language of the Senegalese colonizers. His love of movie going began while still a teenager. His life included work as a mason, carpenter, mechanic, dock worker and union organizer. Sembene was a sharpshooter in the French colonial army during World War II.

His artistic endeavors began with writing poetry, short stories and later novels. Of his ten published literary works seven have been translated into English. His formal education did not go past middle school. Sembene in his various jobs worked from an activist perspective. He was keenly aware of the need for political and social change in Africa. He was interested in helping the disenfranchised and marginalized. His activism influenced his artistic temperament. After migrating to Paris at age forty he

decided to complete his formal education. This was something to which I could relate.

His continuing education led to him spending a year learning cinematography in the Soviet from director, Marc Donskoi. Sembene saw cinema, as offering the opportunity to reach large audiences with ideas that spoke to the average African of his time, reflect the social and cultural mores of Africa and reach other international groups with his cinema. He began making films of his novels.

It has been said of Sembene... "African filmmakers are like griots, they carry the living memory and conscience of their people, in their films; he has a definite social function to fill." (9)

The production of his first film based on a short story in 1963 has been described as having ushered in the dawning of an authentic African cinema. That film is titled, **Borom Saret**. All of Sembenes' films have been subtitled and translated into English, French, German, Japanese and Chinese.

The films I saw at the Festival were **Black Girl** (1966), b/w, 65 min.; **Xala** (A curse) (1975), 123 min. color; **Ceddo** (The people) (1977), 120 min., color; **Mandabi** (The Money Order) (1968), 90 min. color. Sembene has a gift of a keen insight into the plight of his African brothers and sisters on the street level and their daily grind and routine of the life for those in the cities. He is a careful observer of the tribal customs and religious mores and their influence in the lives of Africans. His camera is as fluid as any I've seen. He is a poet and a bit of a philosopher in his dialogue that evokes the spirit of African life and rings with words and phrases that sound as if they were right out of ancient texts with their universal wisdom and truth.

Sembene is powerful at weaving the necessary elements to speak for his African family with his cinema that examines the

components that have shaped African minds. Sembene illuminates the issue of African materialism brought about by capitalism juxtaposed with religious and social practices that are laden with the weight of centuries. The yoke of colonialism is very visible and these elements all go to form films of such depth that you are drawn inexorably into them.

Issues of alienation, subjugation (mental and physical), detribalization, frustration and the process of differences in cultural and social mores are poignantly illuminated with his films. Sembenes' skills in his sensitivity to structure and composition are part of his work that is clear in its social and political commentary on the 20th Century African.

In many countries in Africa, schools libraries and amphitheaters bear Ousmane Sembenes' name. Sembene has been recognized as the "father of African cinema". Sembene has received awards for his oeuvre from Film Festivals in Berlin, Cannes, Carthage, Karlovy, Los Angeles, Marrakech, Moscow, San Francisco and Venice.

August 1979

Involved in a new job assignment at KPIX-TV, I am now floor director/stage manager. Better pay and more interesting than film editor. As I look back. This requires a certain degree of mental and physical agility not required for film editing. Now I work with real people (talent, producers, directors, engineers, writers and production assistants) contrasted with the thousands of celluloid people I dealt with in preparing film for air. Now I actually help studio floor direct our on air product specifically the six and eleven o'clock news shows.

After the first few days of nerves and mistakes, I am now becoming more confident. Also due to some praise and

encouragement of a very beautiful and talented lady newscaster. Wendy Tokuda an Asian reporter was just starting her work as the weekend anchor. She was very supportive and encouraging of me my work as the lead floor director for the weekend news. It's amazing what the ego does with a bit of flattery and encouragement.

If we could all just give a little more along the lines of praise and encouragement to one another on an individual and day-to-day basis on all levels of work no matter what the job or experience of the person, I am sure it would go a long way towards improving and bolstering the conditions we all work under. I must remember these very simple but prosaic words.

Now approaching my thirty second year of life and I still am in need of making myself conceive, believe and realize the many dreams, ideas and concepts that I find important. This mass media education I'm getting is something people would gladly give money and sweat to get and here it's not so much I'm given it, I earn my money I'm sure, but the experience and exposure will and is standing me in good stead for future and present use. As a conscious soul in search of self and a communication artist embarked on a quest for a better world, made better by a closer understanding of all people intentionally and universally through the power that is communications from basic to the most sophisticated electronic.

August 1979

Wednesday evening, the first day of second full week as floor director/stage manager I was waiting for production of a local public affairs program production to begin. My only required work was to put up and call out information on the

program slate. The rest is all done in the mix and on the boards for Studio B.

I still feel queasy about ten minutes before I begin the actual work of a live show. I had dinner tonight and even though it was very good I ate only a third of it. My body is making some sort of dietary change, I can feel it. The most invigorating thing I ate today was a very sweet and juicy nectarine. It tasted better to me than my dinner somehow, which cost eight dollars, to find out.

Slated local public affairs programs that are about Third World people. One of the co-producers is Francee Covington who is Black. She and her producer have taken this seven-year-old show that was on the ratings skid, turned it around, made it a dynamic, topical, fresh, and lively, and increased its ratings two hundred percent. It shows that minority oriented programming can be dynamic and informative and interesting. It makes me proud to be here at Channel Five to see it happen. The program was called **All Together Now.**

As stage manager and floor director, my job was to direct cameras usually three and talent sometimes four or five people. My directions were based on a script and direction from the director and producer in the booth. I got my instructions over headphones. For every one person whose face you see on-air at that time at least ten people were responsible for making them look and sound good.

REALIZE YOUR ENERGY

My friend from Detroit and mentor at Antioch - Maketa and another sista' Evelyn who was a music major at Antioch the three of us had become close friends and formed a non-profit organization which we called **...realize your energy...** (**R.Y.E.**) – A non-profit tax exempt organization was founded in 1977 for the promotion of innovative, cultural, educational and career advancement for " people of color" and "working class individuals". Evelyn Hatcher had transferred from the main Ohio campus to the San Francisco campus. Evelyn and I made my thesis film together. She was my big unrequited crush and star of the film.

The Premier party for our organization featured my thesis/self-produced film **Strivin' and Survivin'** (1977), was in December 1979. The title song was written and performed on film by Evelyn. The film is in color and seven minutes. The film was my visual love poem to Evelyn. She talked about her life and family and sang two songs, including the original title song.

In addition we screened a film I rented from a distributor, **Jammin' the Blues** (1944)*, 10 minutes, b/w. This film was directed by a Swedish filmmaker Gjon Mili who had worked as a photographer for **Life** magazine. With music impresario Norman Granz as Technical Director, Mili assembled and presented Black jazz artists in a very stylized production of Black music, song and dance. The film featured Lester Young, tenor; Jo Jones, drums; Harry "Sweets" Edison, trumpet; George "Red" Calender, bass; Marlowe Morris, piano; Sid Catlett, drums; Barney Kessel, guitar; John Simmons, bass; Illinois Jacquet, tenor; Marie Bryant, vocals and dance; Archie Savage, dance. It is narrated by Knox Manning.

Jammin' the Blues was nominated for an Academy Award in 1945, in the Best Short Film Category. That evening after we screened both films, Evelyn performed a few songs acappella including *'Strivin' and Survivin'*. We served soda and desserts we bought at a local bakery and took donations. The event was in Ft. Mason a giant office complex that formerly housed U.S. Army offices but now was filled with art and art related organizations and had large open spaces for events.

The Elephant Man haunts me still not like the solid impact of **Ordinary People** (1980), which was immediate and visceral as **Jimmie Blacksmith....** haunted/ haunts me so too does the **Elephant Man** both dealt with cruelty and the effect of positive and sympathetic vibrations on two distinctly unique men, John Merrick, aka "The Elephant Man" because he was so grotesque, **Jimmie Blacksmith** half white/half aborigine because he was part Black alright they never let him forget and he never let them forget either!

The Elephant Man, U.S., 1980, b/w, poignant, difference as a detriment to progress in their society, very good lead character performances, cultural fascination/repulsion for the different/the unusual.

The Chant of Jimmie Blacksmith, Australia, 1980, color, cultural   socio-psycho-economic   portrait,   superlative photography, exemplary music, strong cast, solid script.

Maketa invited me to a Thanksgiving party that some ex-Detroiters were having. Later some of those people came to The Premier of my film and debut for our non-profit ...r.y.e... One day I was taking the trolley to work at **KPIX-TV** and saw a woman from those events and I remembered her. Bonnie was sitting there, we recognized each other and I sat down. We chatted and she was effusive that day, she proceeded to tell me it was her

birthday. She said she was going to her studio to work on some new paintings. We exchanged phone numbers. Bonnie Boren is five feet, ten inches, with curly red hair. She bears a striking resemblance to Vanessa Redgrave. Bonnie's background includes having a Bachelors of Science in design from the University of Michigan, School of Architecture and Design & an MA in printmaking/painting from Columbia University

So when we began to spend more time together her background in the arts and her serious part-time avocation painting and drawing meshed with my film aspirations. Within the first six months of our relationship, we got an opportunity to work together on a project and be paid. Bonnie worked with the **San Francisco School Volunteers** a multicultural group of women who coordinated guest speakers from, the arts, business, education, technology, to visit the San Francisco public schools as supplemental curriculum. They also helped parents, students and teachers with resources that schools always seem to need. The **SFSV** decided they wanted to produce a slide show on school busing, using the first day of school as the point of interest for the script.

Bonnie convinced them that we could produce it. We were paid half up front to get photographers, sound recording technicians and equipment. Bonnie and I split up into two crews as producers with a sound person and a photographer.

On the first day of school in the Fall of 1980, we recorded interviews with some parents and students. Within the week, we recorded interviews with a few teachers. We produced an eight-minute slide show. The **SFSV** loved it. Eventually Bonnie and I using resources available to us brought our slide show, which consisted of two slide decks synchronized with music and narration, and videotaped it from a screen set up in a studio. The

videotape became the first program we produced together. It is titled, **Hand in Hand** (1981), 8 min., color, video.

I recall hearing the love of my life being called a fighter, a heavyweight, does that make her a knockout, I know I'm knocked out by her tenacity, voracity, capacity to be such a strong powerful and tender and warm moving force in many people's lives not just my own as if true love wants to be held but more likely just seen for what it is and forever shall be....

Bonnie and I had dated for more than a year and by now, George and I had moved into separate single apartments so I was living alone in a small one bedroom, Bonnie had a small one bedroom and eventually Bonnie and I decided to move in together. This is what we went through to find a place as an interracial couple in San Francisco in 1981. First, we used the agency that had helped my former roommate George and I find the place near the ocean. The representative who Bonnie and I met was not the same lady George and I met. This woman was an older white lady. We met her at the potential apartment where she began showing us the apartment and the building. Then she said, *"We don't like a lot of parties in the building."* Bonnie immediately got upset and expressed it to the agent and that viewing and our use of that agency came to an end.

I was disappointed in the person we met. The original agent also a white female from this agency when George and I met with her to rent a house from her, asked us to bring Georges' dog along to the agency. We met the agent, the dog was well behaved and it went very well because we got that place, dog and all. Next Bonnie and I began to use the newspaper to find ads of places for rent.

We found one ad that Bonnie called and when we got there, a white woman opened the door and made it clear from body

language and demeanor that she was not thrilled to see the two of us together. We looked at more places, and we were beginning to get frustrated in our efforts. Bonnie finally saw an ad for a place a block from where I was living on Fulton Street. We called and the man told us to come to the back of the house, which had another, entrance on a small street called Ivy. Ivy Street was big enough for one car at a time, with a line of cars parked along its street. Some homes had front doors on Ivy.

We got to the address we saw a door and a garage door and rang the bell near the door. A Hispanic man answered from the second story balcony that he would be right down. Fernando Exposito we found out was from Cuba, he is a designer by profession. He took what would normally be a storage area in the basement floor of a two story Victorian building and made a boxcar length apartment.

From the Ivy Street entrance, it had a cement driveway for one car; it had a back porch, a room that on one side had a pantry-sized kitchen that also hid two boilers for the building hidden in a shuttered closet.

Surrounding the shuttered closet, this pantry had a gas stove, cabinets, small kitchen sink and a refrigerator. The next room had a fireplace, the front room was big. The whole place was carpeted. He added doors to make the front room closed to the rest of the apartment, the front door to the apartment was under the stairs to the main building and led to the primary entrance on Hayes Street.

Our address was 766½ Hayes Street. Bonnie fell in love when we entered, I tried to tell her to be cool, but she was gushing the whole time we were there. We settled on a price filled out applications with references, wrote him a check and moved in

shortly thereafter. This was in fall of 1981. We lived along one of the steepest hills in the city.

New address after thirteen odd-very odd months in 859A Fulton, 94117; new place large and expansive in our new home together Bonnie and I, now one roof, one address, one car, one life together and apart but always together.

To Bonnie,

Late October evening, early wee hours, as I sit here I am enamored, inescapably, enraptured, enthralled and completely overcome with this feeling, this feeling in my heart that just has me and I do believe us and it is very OK with me right now, I love you.

I could not believe Pat Greer and old time friend from Detroit and the Hancock House alumni circa '68, who came to these shores with Ma and Pa Greer on their America 81 cruise in the wagon with Volvo mats all over the rear interior stick shift Chrysler. She simply radiated like those people, the Greer's, do when they really feel good. We spoke at length about the past, the present and the future, hers, mine and ours. The last night we spoke after a party then drove to Santa Cruz, whatta' cruz to return Maketa and her son Michael home. On the way back to the dock of the bay we spoke at length on people, George, Jerry, Bonnie, Michael, Maketa, Detroit, friends and relatives and really opened up to hearing and talking we had a two hour trip it was late 1am and there was so much to say. She really radiated, god I can see her form in silhouette against the night highway, she glowed positively!

Because of a renegotiated I.B.E.W. contract for the production department stagehands, floor directors, stage managers I am going from full time to part-time permanent

work. After having lived together for nine months, Bonnie and I had begun producing a documentary series on racial mixed marriages and biracial people. This began in earnest with meetings with racially mixed couples and friends with biracial children in July of 1981.

Now end of dusty KPIX trail setting self in motion for a new episode in the odyssey of San Francisco, mission: impossible. Have definite plans and taken steps to secure good work at other stations in the area. Meanwhile **Interracialism: The National Denial** takes form with a proposal off to the Film Fund, god speed... Taping continues Monday with a very beautiful couple, he is Moroccan and she is Japanese.

Now second week without daily KPIX 3:30 to midnight, Wednesday to Sunday grind. I don't miss it. I've been very busy everyday producing **Interracialism: The National Denial** and working two days for a total ten hours at **KQED-TV**, Public Television in San Francisco. A start of what I hope to be more freelance work. A two-day workweek suits me fine plus a few casual days here and there. There is talk of a part-time gig if the news expands to two hours.

Working in broadcasting and on news, I got to see stories start from what is called a 'thirty second reader'. The talent reads copy there is no visual other than say a graphic super-imposed in a box next to the talent on the screen. Over time, I saw stories go to a minute length of copy with a voice over of talent reading copy to a full two-minute story done by a field reporter. The talent introduces it and we roll the videotaped story. The Jim Jones story was such a story. In November, 1978 more than nine-hundred people are said to have "committed suicide" and Congressman Leo Ryan and four other people including a news photographer were killed in Jonestown, Guyana, South America. I

watched this story grow until it ended in horror. People who survived called Jonestown *"... a slave-camp run by a madman... "*

Jim Jones specter haunts Amerika a spirit in search of a peaceful resting space but in Amerika, there is no resting space for the specter of Jonestown it goes unburied a huge abyss of unresolved karma and ideas. Go away specter go haunt the souls that refused to believe evil existed, exists, and insists on a human sacrifice.

Howard Finley (March 18, 1921- September 17, 1981)

September 1981, Detroit

I am home again ever so briefly till Friday, arrived Monday AM, buried Howard today, step-father of twenty years now gone, cancer got him. Day filled with burial, funeral, people, places, memories, joy and pain. People of Howard's' church gave him a royal send off with a fire and brimstone sermon by minister who raised much san' about Brother Howard and his contributions to their church and community. Death is ever present, ever there, everywhere.

September 1981, Detroit

Spent day with mom and Luke, mother's appointed helpmate, appointed by Howard before his death, very thoughtful.

Afternoon spent with Judy Adams another long time Detroit friend and saw her do her radio show on **WDET-FM** called "Morphogenesis" which is her daily radio music expression /impressions/confession/lesson. It was a rare and tuneful treat.

Then later we talked at length about life, people, relationships, etc. The world, the cosmos we still communicate an enormous amount to each other.

Came home had a fine dinner called friends to come to Thursday evening Detroit Premier of **Interracialism: The National Denial**, a work-in-progress. Later talked to Jerry and Jeff went to their house and spent time vibing on the past the present and the future.

By November using our own funds and lots of donated resources we had produced, shot and edited enough material to schedule a benefit fund raiser using our finished half hour "pilot' program as part of the event. The fundraiser included not only the screening of our "pilot" but a live performance of jazz by artists in racially mixed marriages with biracial children. By December after the event, we had raised money to continue production.

December 1981

Now at end of two weeks at **KQED**, wrap of **Up and Comings'**, second season and at **KPIX** two weeks of vacation relief. It seemed like a long two weeks in which I felt I got stronger at both stations in terms of establishing my ability to work as an effective stage manager/floor director/stage hand.

Up and Coming (1980-1982) was a 30 minute twenty-five episode **PBS** series. It was created and produced by Avon Kirkland an African American. The series focused on a middle class Black family the Wilson Family. The father owned a construction company the mother was an executive in a bank. The three children two boys and a girl were precocious and talented. The series was an exemplary dramedy. My work on the series production was two nights a week as a stagehand. I was

responsible with a crew of technicians for changing, constructing and painting if necessary the sets for production.

1982 will be challenging and exciting year as the year closes in triumph for some defeat for others. I look forward to being kinder, patient, tender, stronger, tougher, smarter, wiser, more money wise, unafraid, helpful and always true to myself, my love mate, my mother, friends, people, the planet and the eternal plan.......

Day six of my mother's seven and a half day stay, she leaves Monday morning. Her stay has been pleasant and uneventful. She has had good weather and a chance to see the city superficially at best but she has at least seen some of the city. Last night a few friends came over and met mom. I'm a different person though.

Mother has come and gone. She was glad she came and happy to leave content in the knowledge that her one and only son is alive and reasonably well in San Francisco.

Ironic beauty that is what it feels like. For two years, Bonnie, I, and friends knocked ourselves out trying to independently produce a serious program on the subject of racial mixing. People who were critical to our work were first, John Pagan. John is biracial Puerto Rican and African American. He wrote his master's thesis in social work on *Interracialism: The National Denial.* He was co-producer and our on camera host & narrator of our program. The second person was Herb Ferrette who was our chief technician/editor/co-producer. Filmmaking is collaborative even more so for independent filmmakers. People donate their time and energy because they believe what you are doing is important.

Together we had produced a half hour "pilot", titled *Interracialism: The National Denial.* During some idle time

while working at KQED-TV, PBS, I showed this program to another brotha' a fellow stage manager named A. Hole (not his real name). I found out he later took my ideas to the NBC affiliate **KRON-TV** and in December produced a ten-minute segment for a magazine format program. The segment he produced dealt with racially mixed marriages and biracial people. In March of 1983, we sent our "work-in-progress" to **WGBH-TV, PBS** in Boston. They viewed the tape, and lost it and did not want to help us.

CHAPTER FOUR

In the spring of 1982, I met Una Van Duvall who was co-chair of the **Los Angeles Black Media Coalition**. The **Bay Area Black Media Coalition** part of the **National Black Media Coalition** was producing our Third Annual Media Conference of the Western Region. Rudy Marshall was chair of our local group and Pluria Marshall was chair of our National group. Una and one of the **LABMC** co-founders Ella came to our event to see how we did a conference so they could replicate our conference in Los Angeles. **The NBMC, BABMC** & **LABMC** were advocacy groups for Black people in all phases of media regulated by the Federal Communications Commission, which included radio, television cable, fiber optics, and satellite. At one point, there were nearly a dozen cities with **Black Media Coalitions** in the eighties. The fruits of those efforts can be seen in black images in front of the camera, as well as all the black technicians you don't see behind the camera. Our work laid the foundation for that. Newspapers were also important to our mission but not regulated by the FCC. The **NBMC** was founded by, black people concerned about our lack of adequate representation in the key areas of media namely, ownership, management, and technical jobs. I had been a key volunteer with the BABMC almost since its inception in the San Francisco Bay area, in 1980.

Bonnie and I were still trying to develop interest in our documentary. We continued to write proposals and send our two films, **Hand in Hand** and **Interracialism: The National Denial** to foundations that were willing to view our proposal and

programs. In March, 1983 we sent our package of programs and proposal to the Creators Equity Foundation.

My film education continued. Jean Luc-Godard's film **Everyman for Himself** (1980), color, 87 min. is one of his most autobiographical films. Godard whose work always seems to me to be a deconstruction of the cinematic process and language. He continued delving into his own personal issues never more so than in this film. Godard labels each section of the film with titles that are apropos to his métier - Commerce, Sex, Cinema and Communications. The affection and despair that are conveyed by this film speaks to the decade of the seventies. After the sixties was such a disappointment for many people of my generation. The war mongers still seemed to control the profile and fate of our country. The election of Jimmy Carter brought hope. The election of Ronald Reagan brought us to a social, political, economic posture that today we are still trying to recover from. Despite people today telling the lie that Reagan was somehow a savior for this country. The seventies seemed to me as the decade in which I had personally come of age as a man and a working filmmaker. Cinema offered solace and inspiration from my own personal business and artistic failures. In this film Godard uses a variety of cinematic techniques quite effectively, slow motion photography, stop motion and the editing is quite affecting.

The music Godard chose to enhance his story and techniques is an eclectic mix and includes progressive rock, electronic and classical music. The story focuses on three people in a large metropolitan city, looking at the human and universal qualities of contemporary urban life in France. Godard has in his significant body of work moved from what would be considered the fringe of French cinema because of his style back to

mainstream and then back to the fringes. Godard is an unparalleled director.

In 1984 as a freelance stage manager I got the opportunity to work on a video production with Fred Friendly. He was the first president of **CBS News** during the Ed Murrow years and later worked with other CBS icons, newsman Walter Cronkite and **60 Minutes** producer and creator Don Hewitt. He was retired from CBS and was working now as an independent producer with public television financial support and distribution for his productions. This program was one of many he produced using an eight person panel discussion with a law professor as the moderator.

The topic we shot was on media and business. The panel included representatives from **Mobil Oil**, **Coors**, **Seagram's**, a Superior court judge, **N.Y. Times**, **CBS**, **L.A. Times** and **NBC**. We rehearsed one day with the moderator and shot the event live to tape the next day. I assisted another stage manager Frank Zamacona who had gotten me the gig, I knew him from our time together at the public television station. He had left the station and was now working successfully as a freelance stage manager and director. Cinema/media is political it is about survival of the fittest, those who can do.

In 1984 I began to work part time as the Project Director for the **Bay Area Black Media Coalition**, a non-profit group that advocated for African-Americans in all phases of media. The project I was given was to survey San Francisco Bay area radio, television and cable companies. My focus was employment statistics. I gathered this data over many months using the Public Files at each radio or television station or cable company.

Any US citizen can access this information as is their right since the Federal Communications Commission licenses these companies. So you can visit any cable company, television or radio station and ask to see their Public File, during normal business hours, Monday through Friday.

The facts were in 1984, less than 8% of the full time employees at twenty two stations and companies surveyed were African Americans. African Americans statistically in the nine counties considered the Bay area, represented roughly 15% percent of the statistical population in those counties in 1984. My position as Project Director for the **BABMC** served to improve access for me in other areas as an independent filmmaker and now social/political activist.

So are things better now for African Americans in media today? Consider this. Of the 85 films released in 2009 by the six largest film companies- Paramount Pictures, Sony Pictures Entertainment, 20th Century Fox, Universal Pictures Walt Disney Studios and Warner Brothers, 93% of the directors are white and are an average of 45 years old, 93% are male, there are two black directors with releases amongst this group. In 1999 the **Directors Guild of America** report on diversity whose statistics include non-studio films found African Americans worked on 5.4% of the total days that are covered by a guild film contract. Women worked 7.4%, Asian Americans 1.5% and Latinos 1.1%. (10)

I had learned the importance of advocacy and organizing with the **Bay Area Black Media Coalition**. When given the opportunity I did not hesitate when asked to work on behalf of first the **National Association of Broadcast Engineers and Technicians (NABET)** as a Shop Steward. While a film editor I

worked on negotiating with management our perspective in a union contract.

Work conditions, hours and pay are issues that all workers blue or white collar must deal with. Unions provide the leverage that an individual just does not have in negotiating with management regarding working conditions.

I also knew that I was not currying any favor with management by doing this. My work with the **BABMC** helped me see that a greater good is served by speaking up and not laying down when dealing with companies whose sole interest is money. People who provide the labor are the necessary component for companies to make that money. I learned more about what actually goes on with management and their interactions with labor from a very personal perspective. My experience with unions made me more conscious of the needs and concerns of workers.

How do you get a union job not being in a union? Once I was hired as a film editor I joined the union and paid dues. Once I was promoted to a new position I joined that union and paid dues. When I made the transition to became a stage manager/floor director/stage hand I was a member of the **International Brotherhood of Electrical Workers** (**IBEW**) and again I worked as a Shop Steward and negotiated our perspective on a union contract. Cinema has dealt with labor issues and workers in a variety of films.

John Sayles an independent producer said that while in college he majored in sports and foreign films. Between 1972 and 1979 he acted in theater, wrote and published short stories and novels and was even nominated for a National Book Award for his novel *Union Dues,* published in 1979. Sayles first serious

film work came when director Roger Corman had him write the script for the film **Piranha** (1978). Sayles frustration at not being able to get more of his scripts to screen led to him producing and directing his first independent film, **The Return of The Secacus Seven** (1979). Sayles has said of his body of work, "I'm not making independent films as a stepping stone to something else." (11). Sayles tackles the issues of labor and management with an original story based on real incidents. The film is set in Mingo County, West Virginia in 1920. The story is also loosely based on his first novel. We see the United Mine Workers struggle to organize mine workers. **Matewan** (1987), color, 135 min., written, produced, directed and edited by John Sayles, starring Chris Cooper, James Earl Jones & Mary McDonald. In telling this story Sayles provides ample opportunity for us to be both sympathetic and informed about the conditions which miners must endure to survive and provide for their families. We see how management in their efforts once workers are organized to break the strike by pitting poor whites against blacks and later Italian immigrants. The film was nominated for an Academy Award for Best Cinematography by Haskell Wexler and won the PFS award from the Political Film Society.

In April of 2010 in West Virginia in the Upper Big Branch coal mine twenty-nine (29) people died. This is the worst mining disaster in four decades. Massey Energy owners of the mine have a history of safety violations and have previously paid millions in damages for prior mine disasters.

In October 2010, thirty-three (33) Chilean miners were rescued after being trapped sixty-nine days in a mine 2,300 feet underground. A billion people watched the rescue telecast around the world. The Chilean miners were very lucky because

they survived. Some workers are forced to work in almost inhumane conditions.

Paul Schrader did not see his first film until he was seventeen. His family's Christian Reformed Church beliefs saw cinema as part of the corruption that is of the secular world. Schrader while enrolled in a cinema course at Columbia University was like Alice going through the looking glass. He graduated and enrolled in film study at UCLA. Schrader wrote film reviews for the L.A. Free Press. He made his initial film mark with his thesis, which was published in 1972 titled *Transcendental Style: Ozu, Bresson, Dreyer.*

His first successful film script was **The Yakuza** (1974) a film about gangsters in Japan. His next major script triumph was **Taxi Driver** (1976)*. His first film as director is **Blue Collar** (1978), 114 min., color, script by Paul & Leonard Schrader, music by Jack Nitzsche, starring Richard Pryor, Harvey Keitel & Yaphet Kotto. The music which accompanies the opening credits is a throbbing bass heavy blues. We see shots of workers along an assembly line making autos in the plants of Detroit. We meet three auto workers Zeke (Pryor), Jerry (Keitel) and Smokey (Koto). Zeke and Jerry have families. Smokey is a bachelor and an ex-con. The trio is looking to make ends meet and a little extra money so they decide to rob their local union. They find something more valuable than money a way to rise above the labor floor. The cost is one that they will regret having to pay.

After the robbery along the way they find that their union and the company share similar goals. They come to realize the plant is short for plantation. The company pits the young against the old, the lifers against the newbie's, blacks against whites. The

three union workers are out flanked by strategies all designed to keep everyone in their place.

I can say from personal experiences workers need to hold their union representatives and management accountable for their actions. The history of unions is one that includes a variety of influences both good and bad. Unions are no better or stronger than the lowest paid most recently hired union member.

The film when released and screened was endorsed by the auto workers who saw it. Since the major auto companies would not let the filmmakers shoot in their plants they shot all the plant scenes in the Checker Motor Corporation, in Kalamazoo Michigan. Checker made the Aerobus I drove from Michigan to California. The trio of Pryor, Keitel and Kotto give some of their best performances on film.

Michael Schultz after graduating from Marquette University moved to New York and got work as an assistant stage manager and later as an actor. In 1966 he got his first directing work at Princeton. He later was staff director for the **Negro Ensemble Company** for two seasons. His Broadway debut as director was for the acclaimed *'Does a Tiger Wear a Necktie?'* for which he received a Tony nomination and the production was the Broadway debut for Al Pacino.

Schultz moved to Los Angeles opened an office and cold called the studios for work as director. He successfully navigated that process and directed a lot of episodic television. He has directed some classic films **Cooley High** (1975), **Car Wash** (1976), **Greased Lightning** (1977), the TV movie **For Us the Living: The Medger Evers Story** (1983).

The Schultz directed film that deals with labor and workers in their quest for fair pay and better working conditions is **Which Way is Up?** (1977), 94 min., color. Script by Carl Gottlieb and Cecil Brown, produced by Steve Krantz.

This film is a remake of the Italian film **The Seduction of Mimi** (1972) directed by Lina Wertmuller. Schultz and Pryor had also worked together on two other films from this period **Car Wash** (1976), **Greased Lightning** (1977).

Richard Pryor has delivered some very entertaining comic turns in feature films. In this film he is given the opportunity to play three different characters Leroy Jones, his father Rufus Jones and the Reverend Lenox Thomas. We see Pryor as a farm worker in the fields of California. Ramon Juarez the leader of the Affiliated Farm Workers comes to his farm and Pryor becomes a hero accidentally and is seen as an inspiration to farm workers. The farm workers are in a struggle to organize the farms owned and run by the Agrico Fruit Company. Pryor's' rise to labor leader as Leroy Jones is ultimately co-opted when Agrico makes him a supervisor of the workers. Pryor imbues all three characters roles with his usual comedic panache and genius. The point of labor versus management is only slightly subverted by this comic twist on workers organizing for better pay and working conditions. The other important issue besides solidarity among workers that is addressed in the film is the importance of the family.

The film has a good cast of supporting actors that includes Lonette McKee, Margaret Avery, Morgan Woodward and Marilyn Coleman. A well-known California theatrical troop El Theatro Campesino supplies many of the other supporting cast and their founder and director Luis Valdez is acknowledged as the founder of modern Chicano theatre and film and plays the labor leader

Ramon Juarez in this film. Valdez has directed two notable films dealing with the Hispanic experience **Zoot Suit** (1981) and **La Bamba** (1987).

Bernardo Bertollucci was born and raised in a village near Parma, Italy. His first major artistic influences included his father who was a poet and later a film critic. His father took him to films in the city and the young Bertollucci saw cinema and the city as mythic experiences. After the publication of Bertollucci's first book of poetry his experience working with fellow poet, countryman and filmmaker Pier Paolo Pasolini on Pasolini's **Accatone** in 1961 convinced Bertolluci that cinema was where he would best serve his muse.

Bertollucci's film directing career began with his first feature **La commare secca** aka **The Grim Reaper** (1962). The film from his body of cinema that made him an internationally known artist was **Il conormista** aka **The Conformist** in 1970. The film received an Academy Award nomination for Best Writing, Screenplay Based on Material from Another Medium and won the National Films Critics' Awards for Best Cinematography by Vittorio Storaro and Best Director for Bertollucci.

The film that made him part of the group of filmmakers whose name and films you knew and wanted to see was **Ultimo tango a Parigi** aka **Last Tango in Paris** (1972). Because of the frank language and explicitly candid sexual scenes the film was a sensation and a critical and financial success. The film was nominated for two Academy Awards Best Director and Best Actor for Marlon Brando. This success with the films' producer Alberto Grimaldi led Grimaldi to encourage him and consent to produce his next film.

Bertollucci's mother was born in Australia of Irish-Italian heritage because her father was in exile there because of his fervent political beliefs. Bertollucci joined the Communist Party in Italy because of his reaction to the corruption of bourgeois society and that led to a period of psychoanalysis. For his script to follow-up the success of **Last Tango...** he wanted to express his regard for workers and peasants, the lower classes who are the foundation that make it possible for the upper classes to survive and thrive.

Novecento (New Century) aka **1900** (1976), script by Bertollucci, Franco Arcalli & his brother Guiseppi Bertollucci, cinematography Vitorrio Soraro, music by Ennio Morricone. The director's favorite version of his epic film is five hours in length with two acts. The producer released to theaters a three hour and fifteen minute version. The director later supervised the editing for a four-hour American released version. The DVD is 315 minutes, five-hours fifteen minutes. The film achieved more success in Europe than America.

The story follows the birth of two boys on the same day. One boy is the son of Il Padrone the landlord and land owner and the other the son of peasants. They grow to young boys together always in competition with each other. They become men and go off to fight in World War One. When they return the peasant becomes a leader for workers' rights, the land owner's son is a bourgeois ne'er-do-well. Robert DeNiro who plays the ne'er-do-well becomes a Fascist and Gerard Depardieu as the peasant becomes a Communist. They are both at their best in this film.

The story in two acts ends April 25th, 1945 the end of World War II. During this journey of discovery we are immersed in both families and see the inexorable split in their relationship but they

are tied together by the land which gave them both the gift of life. Burt Lancaster and Sterling Hayden two American stars of another time give some really wonderful performances here as the grandfathers of the two boys. The film also has some fine very visceral performances even in the young children in the supporting cast. Berotollucci has created a visual novel in this film every scene makes you excited to see the next. The cinematography is very crucial to the dynamics and style of this film even when viewed on a small screen. We watch the characters grow and develop during the four seasons and there is much care given to use a lot of natural lighting to great effect. The film was shot over a forty-five week period to achieve this sense of the four seasons more accurately. We grow empathetic to the workers and their struggle for better working conditions and fair pay for back bending labor.

Should the workers of the world unite there would be certainly more emphasis on fairness and equity in all aspects of employment. The communist system is dead except in China and Cuba, the capitalist system is on the ropes and ultimately the workers still provide the labor that keeps systems more engaged in the bottom line than in making things equitable for those who provide the labor. Bertollucci's, *"...films are part of cinema and, in this sense his films have never, not mattered."* (12)

Meanwhile my neighborhood began a ten year spiral downhill. What were once a few drug dealers was now a colony in a partially closed large pink colored tenement. It was a three building complex that took up a block directly across from our flat. As time went on the junkies and dealers took over the building so the neighborhood became more of a challenge. Bonnie and I took to exiting the apartment using Ivy Street our back door and coming in the front door only when absolutely

necessary. Because of the noise at night in the neighborhood we moved our bedroom from the Hayes Street side of the apartment to the back, the Ivy Street side. Double doors that separated the front from the back of the apartment helped to insulate us partially from the night commotion. Our landlord finally put up burglar bars around the building. So did our neighbor next to us on the right of us on Hayes Street. It is quite a sight these two very attractive colorfully painted Victorian buildings surrounded by these hand crafted specially made burglar fences. At the end of the decade attractive low income housing replaced the dilapidated housing and the entire community became one of the places to live in San Francisco.

On the work front at **KQED-TV**, I still had to work with A.Hole on occasion. I was always uptight whenever I worked with him. One program I worked on often and without A.H. was the **McNeil-Lehrer News Hour** when they had a local guest beamed to their program from our station by satellite. One memorable program included a discussion with a local scholar who was in our studio debating Dr. Sam Epstein whose book The Politics of Cancer and the subject of cancer was the focal point. Epstein was in the McNeil-Lehrer studio.

Since World War II the U.S. has grown from producing a billion pounds of chemicals to 350 billion pounds in 1984. Sixty thousand different chemicals are used in the U.S. and another 700 to 1K are added every year. Dr. Epstein cited that one in five will die from cancer. Cancer mortality has increased at 1% per annum over the preceding ten years with incident rates increasing at 2% per annum. The local scholar from the University of California @ Berkeley in our studio flailed at Dr. Epstein who shredded his arguments with facts. I especially

enjoyed this debate despite the ominous nature of the information I had learned about cancer.

The public station seemed to come up with new and creative ways to raise money, for many years their televised auction of goods and services with people bidding by phone was a staple. This year they also did a wine auction. I worked ten hours on this production. They let people bid by phone but this auction included a small audience of bidders in the studio. They netted sixty-thousand dollars in the several hours the show was on the air. The CEO of a local semi-conductor company in Silicon Valley, who sat in the studio audience, bought twenty thousand dollars of wine by himself. The cheapest bottle sold was for one hundred and fifty dollars and the most expensive was sold for two thousand dollars to the CEO of the semi-conductor company.

Besides keeping a regular journal and a film journal, I began in 1982 to keep a TV Journal - Dedicated to hope.

February 11, 1982. I worked at the public station on the *first* digital recording of music for broadcast, yesterday. Several artists from the **Windham Hill Records** performed. The audio was pre-recorded on digital and played back through the studio so that the performers could mime synch to their previously recorded in a sound studio performances. Playback of the finished program was on **KQED-TV** and to be simulcast in stereo over **KQED-FM**, **PBS**, both firsts. The studio recording on videotape used three cameras, one mini-cam and two studio cameras. One song performed by George Winston on piano titled "Moon" used two fog machines, one of which I ran, to create some nice effects with the studio lighting. I feel like I've finally begun to do things that are fun and advance the state of the art. This is no mean feat

these days with television being so advanced from a technical perspective, these days. This **Windham Hill** experience was interesting and edifying, more now than in the moment. The sound engineer Helen Silvani won an EMMY for her work.

Also more work @ **KQED-TV**. February, 18th, 1982. I worked on a television rendering of a play by a local author. The play chronicles the cowboy era. It is called **Cowboy**. The play includes excerpts from other sources including books, films, speeches, etc. The emphasis is on retelling the saga of the American cowboy. The cast and author are associated with Chebault College which is in Contra Costa County, which is east of San Francisco by about sixty miles. We rehearsed last night, we videotape tonight. This same Contra Costa County was recently in the headlines for its racially motivated attacks against black people in their community. Cowboys and Contra Costa County go hand in hand.

February 19th, 1982, 3:30pm

Finished shooting **Cowboy**. We started production yesterday at 4:30pm we rolled tape around six pm. We had our first meal break at nine p.m., we had our second meal break at midnight we wrapped production at four a.m. a full twelve hours. Quote from script, "...most cowboys were young with an average age of twenty four and one out of three was either Mexican, black, Native American or had some Native American blood." Not one person of color was in the cast for television, so much for history. The producer of this program who also directed won an EMMY for his work as director.

A free-lance stage manager job that came to me was working for the **Marcus Foster Education Fund** an organization that honored the memory of the late Marcus Foster. Foster had

been the city of Oakland, California Schools' first Black superintendent for over 35 years in the Alameda County School district. He was murdered while doing his job. After his death an elementary school in Oakland was named in his honor. The **MFEF** did an annual formal dinner/fundraiser honoring local outstanding black Oakland school graduates. This year they honored Aleta Carpenter who was Station Manager at a local Oakland radio station and the Hall of Fame baseball player Joe Morgan who was still playing at that time for the Oakland A's baseball team. The event was a success. I was of course pleased that I had helped.

Before I came to California people in Michigan warned me about the earthquakes. Living in San Francisco and California in general you get adjusted to feeling tremors on occasion. This year we had a 5.9 - 6.2 tremor, which was the biggest shock I had felt.

I submitted material for an article to a local magazine called *Cinezine.* The editor called me and complained about my writing style and the manner in which I had put the material together. He said that with a heavy rewrite and additional information he had put together an article. I knew I would not get another opportunity with that magazine.

The article was about film archives and film distributors in the San Francisco Bay area. I chronicled, or so I thought, **California Newsreel, One Way Films**, the **San Francisco Public Library** and the **Pacific Film Archive**. The article was published and despite the editors chagrin at my writing I had my first freelance byline.

Repertory Art cinema houses in San Francisco was my source for continuing cinema education. Repertory Art cinemas

operating in 1984 included **The Parkside** Theater on 19th Avenue, **The Strand** on Market Street, **The Cedar** on Cedar Alley, **The York** on 24th Street and the **Surf Theaters** chain that included four cinema houses around San Francisco. Films changed usually daily or at most a film might run a week if it was being premiered. Through repertory cinema houses I was introduced to many international filmmakers from all over the world; historic; contemporary; silent film.

Kings of The Road aka **Im lauf der zeit** (In **the course of time**) (1976), 175 min, b/w, produced, written and directed by **Wim Wenders**, Germany. Cinematography, by Robbie Mueller & Martin Schaefer; music, by Axel Linstadt; starring Ruediger Vogler and Hanns Zischler. In German with English sub-titles. Grand Prize Winner at the Cannes and Chicago Film Festivals. Edifying escapade through German consciousness. Two men bonding as friends after meeting literally by accident, on the road of life genre film. I am reminded of the American made films **Midnight Cowboy**, **Easy Rider** and **Scarecrow**. Wenders makes an outstanding contribution to the buddy/road genre. Wenders is part of the German New Wave that includes directors, Werner Herzog, R.W. Fassbinder, and Volker Spengler.

Wenders' plunge into serious study of film-making began in Paris where he spent more than a year watching over a thousand films at the world renowned Cinémathèque. He returned to Germany and enrolled in a German film school and from there worked for United Artists, German studios in Dusseldorf. Wenders made short films and eventually graduated from film school with the completion of his first feature film in 1970, **Summer in the City**, the films' title and the film are inspired by the American pop group the *Lovin' Spoonfuls'* song of the same name.

Traveling film projector repairman Bruno (Ruediger Vogler) meets Robert (Hanns Zischler) after he pulls him from a river where he has attempted suicide by driving into the river with his car. Bruno is kind and gentle with Robert and takes him along on his journeys to repair film projectors. They travel along the border of the then still divided East and West Germany to small towns with movie houses that need film projector repairs.

They slowly form a bond, in the course of time. Bruno talks always about film and projectors and decry's the many local movies houses closing entirely in small communities or to showing a more programmed bill of fare or becoming X-rated movie houses. They talk about the Americanization of German life and Americas values seeping into German consciousness. The dialogue is intense, emotional and deals with issues of change. The mood of the film is maintained by the script, the performances and the cinematography. The cinematography reveals a keen sensitivity to composition and light. This is readily apparent in scenes shot at night entirely by moonlight without the aid of additional lighting. The fresh freedom of a road adventure is adroitly crystallized in the music score. Wenders' can certainly be said to be influenced by American pop culture. Cinematically there is the influence of Japanese director Yasahiro Ozu, whose work dealt with human emotions and ordinary people in conflict, much as this extraordinary film does.

In July of 1984 I got an opportunity to videotape events in and around the **Democratic National Convention**. This was the year of Jesse Jackson's first serious effort to run for President. I managed to line up three camera people who wanted to work on shooting an independent film just to have access to the convention. Sue, who is white was one of the people I met during the racial mixing project, she has a biracial son. Sue

introduced me to Jim who is black. Jim had lined up some free videotape, the DNC passes necessary for access to the event and some students and one camera.

We agreed verbally to co-produce the production with our focus being the Jackson campaign. Sue was also interested in working with us on the video production and also wanted to record audio for **KPFA-FM** the public radio station in Berkeley, CA, for which she had produced programs. The students were from the **University of California at Santa Cruz**, their participation was in exchange for them being able to use their audio equipment to record material to be aired on their school radio station, for that we got forty hours of videotape from the school for production. The passes necessary to get into the event required that I be on-line every morning at **DNC** press headquarters no later than 6:30AM to get the passes we were allotted six, per day. Once the allotted number of passes for independent media was gone, that was it.

Over the course of five days in July we shot events of the **DNC** and a post-mortem of the convention in Berkeley, California, sponsored by the *Black Scholar* magazine, it was called *The Making of a Black President, 1984*. We used the forty hours of videotape and shot interviews, convention floor activities, rallies around the convention site, various caucuses and the Black Scholar event. Scholars and activists spoke about the Jackson campaign. Their lectures provided the social, political and historic focus we needed to tell the story of Jackson's historic campaign. As independent filmmakers we saw there was a double standard by the mainstream media in their coverage of Jackson as a political candidate. "Jackson's biggest problem is that he's never been identified with any issue except civil rights and civil rights is not an issue today." (13)

We videotaped interviews with black people, Asians, Hispanics, social activists, politicians and scholars about the Jackson campaign. They voiced their need to have representation that reflects their concerns and articulate the imperatives behind those concerns.

They voiced their need to make a change in, "...patriarchal attitudes, egocentricity, scientific single vision, the bureaucratic mentality, nationalism and the big city outlook..." (14) because of the detrimental effect these attitudes are having on our society. Civil rights *is* still an issue today. We worked three years on producing and finishing the material we shot.

In late July of 1984 I participate in a first time Black film-makers workshop, sponsored by the **Black Filmmakers Hall of Fame, Inc**. of Oakland, CA. The **BFHOF** is a group established to honor blacks in literature, theater, music, film and recordings. In 1984 they organized and sponsored a film workshop and invited, two dozen filmmakers from the San Francisco Bay area, Chicago, Washington, D.C., New York City, New Jersey, Houston, Philadelphia and other cities from across America to spend three days learning from and interacting with Hollywood and veteran independent black filmmakers and screenwriters. I was a participant filmmaker again in 1985. By 1986, I moved from participant to the role of paid Coordinator for this event.

Film instructors over the course of the three separate yearly workshops included among others Gordon Parks; Topper Carew; Lonnie Elder III; Avon Kirkland; William Greaves; Michael Schultz; Stan Lathan; Louis Peterson; Booker Bradshaw; Carroll Ballard and Hugh Robertson. Half the attending participant filmmakers were women. I met and made friendships with many of the participants.

March of 1986 I began one of my most daring cinema ideas to date. The previous year I had attended the 28th **San Francisco International Film Festival**. I found it wanting. Of the many films shown only three could be considered representative of the Black or Diaspora perspective. I decided to do something about that. I contacted the **Bay Area Black Media Coalition**; **Los Angeles Black Media Coalition**; **National Black Media Coalition**; **National Black Programming Consortium**; **Bay Area Video Coalition**; **Film Arts Foundation**; **Association of Independent Film and Video** & **Women that Make Movies**.

I explained the paucity of black representation in the prior film festival I told them I was an independent black filmmaker who wanted more black representation at the **SFIFF**. I asked each group for their support, if only in name for a **Black Cinema Series** as part of the 29th **SFIFF**. They all agreed that I could use their support to lobby the **SFIFF**. When I called the Artistic Director of the festival explained who I was and the support I had, he agreed to meet with me. The **Black Cinema Series** was co-organized with two other members of the Bay Area independent black cinema community, Elena Featherston and Jacques Taliaferro. The dozen films we selected for exhibition included an animated film from Cuba, documentaries, films by San Francisco Bay Area and Los Angeles independent black filmmakers, short dramatic films and the film that was the highlight of our series and really the festival, was Spike Lee's, **She's Gotta Have It** (1987), 84 min, color.

Despite a sudden local power failure during the screening that lasted about twenty minutes, no one left the auditorium. The film was started again from the beginning and when it was over Lee and Tommy Hicks an actor in the film who was present for the screening received a prolonged standing ovation.

The distributor for **Island Pictures** came from Los Angeles to the event to see the film and they eventually distributed the film. The film was made for around two hundred thousand dollars grossed over nine million dollars in first run release.

In early fall of 1986 I began to use my social, political and media contacts to work with a group of likeminded black journeyman filmmakers and technicians, including novice media makers. We called ourselves **Picture This**. We formed to promote the distribution of international cinema and the production of cinema that speaks to an international audience. We were also interested in finding outlets for our own work as black filmmakers. There were usually between ten and fifteen people who showed up at our initial meetings. The first event we produced together was a film exhibition fund-raiser. Members of our group had experience four-walling theaters. So we decided to rent a local repertory cinema movie house for a night, hoping to exceed expenses and make a profit.

In November of 1986, we had the West Coast Premiere of **Lien de Parente (Next of Kin)**, 1986, color, 90 min., the film was written and directed by Willy Rameau, a black French filmmaker born in Martinique. One of the members of our group Floyd Webb had been instrumental in screening this film as part of the Chicago **Blacklight Film Festival**. The original novel on which the film was based was by an American author. This was also Rameaus' first feature film as director.

The film starred legendary French cinema icon Jean Marais and newcomer Serge Ubrette in his film debut. The story follows Marais who discovers, at the funeral of his now long estranged and recently deceased son, that he has a grandson. The grandson played by Ubrette is black. With the son's death he

now becomes the guardian and parent for the teen. Thus begins a mix of racial and generational conflicts that spoke to an international audience. With promoting, marketing, and the assistance of the **Black Filmmakers Hall of Fame, Inc.** in Oakland, CA, together we arranged for Rameau to be flown to San Francisco from Paris, for the screening. We made a profit.

In March of 1987 we had an article about our fledgling efforts chronicled in **The Independent: a Film and Video Monthly** magazine based in NYC. Mia Amato a free-lance writer and an acquaintance of one of Bonnie's friends wrote a glowing article on our efforts. In the fall of 1987 our group did a tribute to **Hugh Robertson** (1932-1988) a veteran black filmmaker whose work as editor on **Shaft** and **Midnight Cowboy** earned him accolades. He was Awarded the **British Academy of Film and Television Arts Awards** for his editing on **Midnight Cowboy** (1969), making him the first black American to win this award. As a director his work in television earned him an Emmy Award and later he earned recognition for his prowess as a feature film director. At the Tribute to Robertson we produced, we presented two of his feature films, **Bim** (1976) and **Obeah** (1987) and again we are able to make inroads in exhibition of films by black directors about the black experience.

In early spring of 1986, because of my media activism, I got a call from Julie Mackaman of the **Film Arts Foundation**, an organization for independent film and video makers, I was also a member. Julie called and said a woman had called their offices looking for someone to teach video to inmates of the San Francisco County jail system.

The program as I learned from calling and talking to Ruth Morgan was a **California Arts Council** funded program. Ruth

was the local Coordinator for the **Artists in Residence** program. The program allowed artists from different artistic disciplines, to teach these disciplines as visiting Artists in Residence, to people in the local county jail. Ruth Morgan explained that the previous instructor of the video class, a white female, had been unsuccessful in really having an impact or imparting much information to the inmates. We talked at length and I convinced her that it really required two people not one to do the subject and the students any good. I also told her I was interested in teaching the class. So she said OK, send my resume along with my associates and some samples of our work as filmmakers and she would be in touch. I really did not want to hazard this alone not knowing what to expect.

Al Marshall, the other instructor of the class, and I had known each other for more several years. Al was the processor technician for the film lab at **KPIX-TV** for their film unit. When film was replaced by video he was retrained as an engineer in many phases of television production. Al and I began to work on independent film projects together. He was one of our co-producers on the documentary on the Jackson presidential campaign. When I broached him with this new job possibility he was definitely interested.

After reviewing our resumes and tapes, within two weeks Ruth Morgan assured us of the job and asked that we help her write a proposal to raise money to videotape a drama class that was being done for the first time with inmates in the 'work furlough' program. Work furlough allowed people still under jail system supervision the opportunity to live in a group residence and to go to work full or part-time and return to the residence after work to complete their sentences.

The drama class had only been done at the San Bruno jail which was the city south of San Francisco that had the larger of the two jail facilities for the City and County of San Francisco. Ruth thought that because this was a new dimension to the Artist-in-Residence program she believed that a video of this would help with future funding.

Another component of the 'work furlough' drama class was to be six performances at two different community centers with a live audience for the students and their production. Ruth wanted both rehearsals and performances recorded. The instructor for the drama class was a well-known actor in the area who had been a member of the San Francisco Mime Troupe, Shabaka aka Barry Henley. Shabaka had been teaching drama to the inmates at the San Bruno jail facility for two years prior to the 'work furlough' program. We videotaped several class rehearsals, one public performance at a community center and also recorded follow-up interviews with the instructor and some of the drama students after release from jail. This all happened between May and September of 1986.

The music class taught by local musician Rudy Mwongozi, would for the first time allow him to teach people released from jail after completing their sentences, who had been in his music class at San Bruno. Continued music lessons for those who wanted to pursue further instruction once released from jail.

So we also videotaped his San Bruno music classes as part of our on-going documentation of the Artist-in-Residence program. We were originally slated to start teaching video in the fall of 1986. Because of space issues, more classes being taught and not enough rooms, we did not begin teaching video until February of 1987.

Once we started teaching the response of the students after two - four hour classes which included about a dozen men and women was positive. One student dropped the class immediately after it was clear we were going to be doing real study and work in the class. The first week curriculum consisted of extensive lectures that we gave with an overview of media. We talked about radio, television, film, new technologies, gave a media quiz and had a homework assignment. The highlight of our second day on the job was while we were having lunch in the smallish employees break room a *Code 3'* went out over the radios all the guards carried. In a flash the Guards dashed for the exit and one guard went across a table that was empty. The previous day Al and I had been sitting at that same table. If anyone had been sitting there they would have been trampled.

I realized then this was not your everyday school. When one of the Guards returned I asked sheepishly, "Did you guys put the fire out?" his reply was "The fire was out when we got there, they're usually out when we get there." 'Code 3' means trouble on the tiers or an officer is in trouble and needs immediate assistance.

Week two was spent viewing two documentaries. The first documentary was on Africa. The documentary made the case for the historic roots of racism as being economics. The students saw the informative aspects of the class and liked the perspective presented to them because it was an aspect of African history that they had not considered. The second documentary was a live jazz concert. The interest in the two subjects proved to be an inspired juxtaposition this was evident in our post viewing conversation. We then watched the programs a second time with the sound turned off. Al and I described and analyzed the images and ideas and the way in which the programs were produced.

The first film was a historical documentary, the second film a live music concert with audience. We described the techniques, the different production styles and analyzed the visual content of each program. We discussed the use of narration to embellish and enhance the visual content. We also described the documentary using a single camera technique versus the performance being recorded by a multiple camera technique. We deconstructed the material.

Because there were two of us teaching this allowed us the opportunity to give special attention to people who showed more aptitude than other students. The original curriculum outline we had for the first five weeks was revised. The group absorbed material at a faster rate than we had anticipated. Our team teaching technique proved itself and the Principal of the jail school confided to us there was a waiting list of people who wanted to take our class. The school curriculum included adult basic education; math; reading; tutoring; English; typing; GED; offset printing; horticulture/landscaping; culinary arts and automotive technology.

The **Artists-in-Residence** were teaching – music; theater/performance; painting & drawing; ceramics; creative writing; sewing/handicrafts; quilt-making and dance/exercise. There were also counseling services that included financial aid; referrals; application assistance and post release planning. Al described the environment after a month as being "Just like high school only with bars."

Al and I have also had some refreshing exchanges and interchanges with other artists, specifically the music and creative writing teachers, which led to several collaborations of our classes working together. During one of our lunch breaks Al

and I are approached by one of the inmate food service staff. He was a former student who dropped the class. He said our lowered class enrollment because of people dropping the class was because we made the class too difficult. In questioning the afternoon class session I got positive reinforcement. Students said that they enjoyed our approach and technique and wished they had a chance to attend the class more than two days a week. They wanted to learn and not just go through the motions they were content to work as we had been. A math teacher who had worked for **NASA** and that we saw in passing said that he had also heard good things from his students who were in our class about our work.

In our tenure working in the criminal justice system as artists we became aware that there were elements within the system that reinforced the negative behavior of the people there in jail. In a magazine titled '*The Incident Report*' published by the San Francisco Sheriff's Department in the February/March, 1987 issue, a member of the Correctional Counselors staff wrote:

"...videos and books presented in the county jail glamorizing crime and violence project the wrong kinds of images to prisoners. Sensationalizing the criminal life styles originally responsible for their incarceration negates the rehabilitative goals we are trying to achieve in the Sheriff's Department. Crime and violence are not exactly the best themes to present to prisoners during recreational time in jail."

I wrote a letter to the magazine in reply to those comments, "Media can and does shape our perceptions. Vance Packard, Marshall McLuhan, Wilson Bryan-Key these authors have shown clearly we can become what we see and hear, prolonged passive viewing of particular types of material can be harmful. Muzak,

the canned music we hear in malls and stores has been subliminally programmed to discourage shoplifting and employee theft. This has saved companies millions of dollars. Censorship is not the issue but rather the fact that a wider variety of program material is available now than at any time in American media history.

Our video class after watching an excellent series of programs on civil rights produced lively and animated discussion and interaction among our students. For the black inmates their sense of their own recent history expanded, it was clear and evident in their comments. A white female inmate responded to the scenes of whites attacking Blacks by commenting, "... what's wrong with those white people they must be programmed in some way...", indeed they were, but even she recognized this after we made clear what 'programming' means in the context of the video production class curriculum. Our curriculum emphasizes and reinforces the need for our students to be more active in their television viewing and less passive. It is clear they have learned the lesson."

We taught until the end of 1990. Over the next year we took material we had recorded including student shot material and produced a 53 minute documentary on the entire San Francisco County Jail, California Arts Council, Artists-in-Residence program. That program is entitled, **Art From Jail: Artists and Inmates Creating Art**, 1990, 53 min, color, video.

This documentary shows artists working with the inmates, we see the artists who talk about their process working with inmates, and we see samples of students' work in a variety of disciplines. The disciplines were video, painting and drawing, quilt-making, creative writing, dance, music, ceramics. The

Sheriff, jail staff, the program coordinator and former inmates who were in the art program talk about the value and use of arts in the criminal justice system. The finished program was funded by the **San Francisco County Sheriffs' Inmates Services Department**, **California Arts Council** and the **National Endowment for the Arts**.

In the fall of 1986 I got another byline with the newsletter of the **Film Arts Foundation**, the Bay Area organization of independent film and video makers. September, Vol. IX, # 7, p.3, "African filmmaker visits Bay Area". Ben Diagoye Beye from Senegal was on a U.S. tour to meet Black American filmmakers and he came to the FAF to show his work and see the work of local Black filmmakers. His film **Black Prince of St. Germaine**, is a short film satirizing one African's experiences adapting to life in Paris.

Beye cited influences on his work such as Frantz Fanon, who wrote extensively on the Black colonial experience in <u>Black Skins White Masks</u> and <u>Wretched of the Earth</u>. **Seyseyeti** is in the tribal language of Senegal, Wolof. This film is a docudrama on polygamy. A black girl in the film who rejects polygamy says, "The real fight is between the exploited and exploiters." His films are very evocative.

America in 1987 was sowing the seeds of economic peril because of the two terms of Ronald Reagan as our President. Reagan started his first term as President by destroying one of the most powerful unions in the country, the Air Traffic controllers union. He then went on to create laws that totally deregulated Wall Street and its practices. In 1987 Oliver Stone chronicles the financial practices of the time in his film **Wall Street** starring Michael Douglas who won an Academy Award as

Best Actor as a character who is a well-known Wall Street mogul. Gordon Gekko, Douglas' character lived by the expression, "Greed, for lack of a better word, is good. Greed is right. Greed works."

Bernard L. Madoff is the sociopath responsible for the biggest financial fraud in U.S. History. He is the most notorious thief of Wall Street with his "Ponzi scheme". He and it are emblematic of the deregulation aftermath of the Reagan years gone horribly wrong. Madoff bilked hundreds of people out of 65 billion dollars. Madoff successfully laundered money and committed securities fraud because no one was watching the financial store from the government side. A private citizen analyzed the Madoff finances and as early as 2000 and again in 2002, 2005 and 2008 notified the Securities and Exchange Commission, our government agency overseeing Wall Street, of his suspicions. The SEC did nothing with this information and let the money madness virtually tear down the capitalist empire not just in this country but the world capitalist system, with the worst Recession since the nineteen-twenties of the last century. In December 2008 Madoff, admitted that his company and his financial house of cards was all a lie. It is clear the SEC was asleep on the job. Madoff received a 150 year sentence at his trial and later prosecution.

We sit now huddled in our homes wondering if tomorrow we will have a home or will we become destined to join the masses of people being turned out of their homes because of the greed of several generations of business executives gone array, sanctioned by the Federal government.

We had a public premier of our finished program **5 Days in July**, (1987), 28 min. color, video in August of 1987. Prior to that

premier as we were still putting our program together Bonnie and I went to a film screening across the Bay in Oakland. We had heard that another independent filmmaker was producing a program on the same subject as ours, the Jackson campaign. We watched the white female producers program in a public screening she had arranged. After the screening we introduced ourselves and told her who we were and what we were doing and she said she had heard about us and our program in progress. Her program when finished had many of the same people we interviewed for our program. Her program was about forty five minutes. She had done I thought a better job than we had. I personally was crestfallen and I know Bonnie was again a little disappointed that here again we had spent several years of our life producing something and someone we did not know had taken our thunder.

Here is the up side of our finished program. The premier of the program was part of an exhibition of **Bay Area Film and Video** at the **Oakland Museum**. Other exhibitions included the **5th Conference of the National Alliance of Third World Journalists/Film and Video Festival** in Atlanta, GA; **Peralta College Cable TV**, Alameda County, CA; **Viacom Cable Access,** San Francisco; **Cast Iron TV**, NYC; **New American Makers Series**, San Francisco. The program was purchased by the **San Francisco Public Library**-Main Branch, Video & Deaf Services and the local **Rainbow Coalition** bought four copies.

In my undergraduate thesis part of my course work was an independent study course called *Hollywood: American cinema*. I took many hand written notes on an assortment of films and filmmakers and collected that information for a film journal in 1977. My professor **Fred Sweet**, PhD, wrote in his evaluation of my journal, "In this course the student was expected to attain a

critical understanding of the American Film Industry. Spencer demonstrated sophisticated understanding of the industry. I grew to rely on his ability to generate ideas and initiate exciting discussion about film. Spencer kept a film journal that demonstrates a deep commitment to whatever he undertakes to study."

I continued my film journal over the next decade and had enough material in 1988, to retype my journal notes into a computer and print a sixty page book outline; the outline titled, *'Beyond Hollywood: a resource guide to independent film making, 1920-present'.* I am refashioning that material into my cine biography. That film journal turned book draft in its original construction had seven chapters. American independent filmmakers; Black cinema; international cinema; San Francisco Bay area filmmakers; Hollywood, mavericks and masters; cinema masters; assorted filmmakers. This cine biography will fold many of those films into this cinemoir.

My journey to get my undergraduate degree took ten years. I started Wayne State University/Monteith College in 1967 and eventually got my undergraduate college degree in 1977 at Antioch University/West in San Francisco. Between starting school in Detroit and finishing school in San Francisco there was a lot of living and growing up. So ten years later I wanted to get a graduate degree. In between again was living life while pursuing a career in broadcasting and independent film making. I found a program that worked for me. The one I chose was **Columbia Pacific University**, in San Rafael, CA. The program offered me the opportunity to do as I had done with the under graduate program. My mentor for the program and process was **Norma Armon**, Ph.D. I submitted documentation for the graduate level film classes I had taken with the **Black**

Filmmakers Hall of Fame, Inc., in 1984 and 1985. Documentation of my work in broadcasting, my written thesis, and two documentary productions and a written thesis that included the script of both films and in fall 1989 I received my master of arts in film and television production.

From my written thesis, "This process has been valuable because of the manner in which I have begun to analyze, describe and improve my ability as a film maker. I see the value of written documentation of the production process as a way of improving my ability as a producer and communicator of ideas to my film making associates was well as with people who know little if anything about me or my work. This process represents a major milestone in my development as a serious filmmaker."

There were many films and filmmakers that were cited in my thesis as influences. A filmmaker whose work I grew to respect and love was **Luis Bunuel** (1900-1983). Bunuel was born in Calanda, Spain. From age six to fifteen he studied at a Jesuit school, whose curriculum was one that dated to the 18th century. His views on religion exhibited in many of his films can certainly be dated from that experience. Later in school he studied, entomology, zoology, agricultural engineering, natural sciences, and history.

While attending the University of Madrid he met artists Salvador Dali, Federico Garcia Lorca & Rafeal Albertini. He left Madrid for Paris in 1925. He eventually studied cinema at the Académie du Cinéma, Paris. A filmmaker who he acknowledges as an early influence was Fritz Lang of Germany. In time Bunuel worked with French filmmaker Jean Epstein whose mentor Abel Gances' films Bunuel said he disliked. Bunuel worked on Josephine Baker's **La sirene des tropiques**, 1927, Ms. Bakers'

first film, as an assistant director. With money from his mother to make his first film Bunuel created a sensation with his first short film **Un chien andalou** (1928) 17 min., b/w, silent. He co-wrote this film with fellow Spanish countryman, surrealist painter, Salvador Dali. His use of surrealist montage in this film was the talk of European art and cinema circles.

Bunuel's films are capable of creating transcendence for the viewer. We transcend the mundane aspects of day to day life that Bunuel depicts so passionately in all his films. Bunuel creates a transcendent experience with his film mastery. He clearly and adroitly delineates the sacred and profane aspects of life. His films can be seen and enjoyed more than once. He has a significant body of work from silent films to his last film for which he was nominated for an Academy Award for Best Writing, Screenplay Based on Material from Another Medium, **That Obscure Object of Desire** (1978).

A Bunel film that struck me when I first saw it and still resonates with its brilliance today is **The Young One** (1960), b/w 95 min. **The Young One** was also released in the U.S. as **White Trash**. **The Young One** won a Special Mention Award at the Cannes Film Festival and was nominated for the Golden Palm Award.

Bunuel made films in Spain, France and Mexico, many of his films are in Spanish or French. **The Young One** is only his second English language film, Bunuel's other English language film was **Robinson Crusoe** (1954). **TYO** stars, Bernie Hamilton, Zachary Scott, Kay Meersman, Claudio Denton & Graham Denton. Hamilton is best remembered by American television audiences as Lt Harold Dobey on the seventies cop show **Starsky and Hutch**. Hamilton also had a twenty year-long parallel career as a

music producer of gospel and r & b music. The original story for this film is inspired by a Peter Matheissen story titled *The Travelin' Man*. The cinematography by Gabriel Figueroa is one of the highlights of this film. Figueroa was cinematographer on many of Bunuel's films during his time working in Mexico.

The film deals with the issues of race, sex and the finite world view of man. Bunuel has an infinite world perspective, he takes in everything in his cinema; he excludes nothing. Hamilton portrays Travers, who is a black musician falsely accused of rape and is now on the run, yearning for freedom he makes his way to an island off the Carolina coast. The island seems deserted because, it is a game preserve. The preserve has a manager, called Miller (Scott) and one other inhabitant a young woman, called Evvie (Meersman). They are both white. She is a teen age girl whose grandfather has died leaving the game warden as her guardian. The game warden sees himself as a potential love interest for the young girl, until Travers arrives. The young woman has not been taught racism and is open to and entertained by Travers playing his clarinet for her. Their friendship threatens the relationship of the game warden and this young girl. The film is on some level a comedy of manners about poor people. As only Bunuel can, he has us following our noses to places that we would never suspect that we would go, with this very simple story. His story and characters reveal as insightful a perspective as you're likely to see in cinema on race issues.

I miss Bunuel as much as any filmmaker whose work I have come to know, respect and admire. Bunuel's body of work stands the test of time. Bunuel in all his films displays a very certain and solid sense of humor. Many times you discover in his films there are moments of great humor where you might not expect it. My

journey in cinema discovery was aided and encouraged by a filmmaker like Bunuel. I am pleased that I was alive during his lifetime and got to know about him and his work in my explorations of cinema. In his lifetime Bunuel was nominated for nearly three dozen awards and won more than a dozen awards for his films that were exhibited in festivals in Italy, France, U.S., Mexico, U.K., Berlin, Denmark, Spain and Moscow.

Because I was working part-time still for **KPIX-TV** and only on weekends, the social life for Bonnie and I was always a problem. If we visited friends over the weekend I always had to leave midday to get to work for my 3:30 to midnight shift at work. The exception to this was when I took my vacation days which was paid time off. The reason I was allowed vacation time was because I was part-time permanent staff. So over the course of the year I had about ten paid vacation days which allowed me to take those weekend days off.

On October 17,1989 while watching the start of the first Bay Bridge World Series, Oakland vs. San Francisco on television a magnitude earthquake 6.5-7.1 happened. The biggest since 1906, which was an 8.0. The center was Loma-Prieta, which felt the initial impact of thirty Hiroshima bombs. There was a mushroom sized cloud of fire smoke in the Marina which was made on land fill. Phones were down, roads blocked. The Cypress Freeway collapsed. The Bay Bridge had a section collapse. San Francisco/Oakland was 100 miles from the center of the quake. It happened around 5pm, rush hour. The house wiggled and the earth rumbled like never before I was scared out of my wits. I bolted to my back door and the back yard and the rumble stopped. After I collected myself I called spoke to Bonnie at work and found out she was OK. We survived several days of an uneasy feeling as the aftershocks got to 4.7. Not funny! The

World Series resumed after 10 days the A's swept San Francisco, 4-0. The Bay Bridge was down for a month. (15)

My life has been a potpourri of images, people and ideas. **Langston Hughes'** (1902-1967) life was not like mine. He understood that he wanted to make the arts specifically writing his métier at an early age. I realize that words and images in its many forms whether books, films or music aided in producing someone who sees the great value that an artistic temperament has for people with the courage to pursue their dreams and ambitions with the arts. Hughes was and is a great beacon for people no matter your ideas or ideals.

Langston Hughes: The Dream Keeper (1986) 58 min., color, documentary. Produced and directed by St. Claire Bourne (1943-2007). This program was part of a **PBS** Series called **Voices and Visions** on American Poets. Arnold Rampersand the biographer of Hughes describes Hughes family background as distinguished. His family included ancestors who had died at Harpers Ferry with John Brown. One of his grandfather's was a distinguished Kansas politician during Reconstruction. Hughes had his first work published in his high school newspaper.

By the time he had arrived in Harlem in 1921 to attend Columbia University he was determined to make writing his full time avocation. In the program Hughes is recognized as the greatest poet of the Harlem/Negro Renaissance. James Baldwin describes Hughes as both "...gallant and weary..." Hughes first published work is homage and a gateway. It represents the marriage of the rural folk traditions that produced gospel and blues and the new literary traditions of black poetry - *The Weary Blues* (1926).

The poet and African American arts progenitor Amiri Baraka describes the original reaction from the black community to Hughes work as producing embarrassment. The black bourgeois did not understand that Hughes because his life included time working as busboy and other labor intense jobs represented the working class in his words and ideas. Over the course of his life Hughes was challenged by the struggle of most artists, financial solvency. His patrons over the years helped to make that struggle easier but some patrons had neither little affection nor any understanding of his work and its import. Hughes in his life wrote essays, reviews, poetry, plays and even attempted an aborted film production in the USSR with twenty other young black artists in 1938. Because of Hughes support for liberal and left causes Hughes was made to testify before the House Un-American Activities Committee in 1953. His testimony was given in a private session. Hughes in order to continue undeterred by the forces of narrow minded "Red baiting" had to repudiate his earlier work for those causes and institutions that he supported. He did not have to name names, small consolation.

By 1953 Hughes was the Dean of Negro writers. His influence was international and had reached the shores of Africa where Leopold Senghor the former president of Senegal said that, "...Hughes was the greatest Black poet and a major influence in African negritude..." The program mixes Hughes words read by him and are also illustrated by dance and performance to great effect. The program is a loving tribute to a great artist.

St. Claire Bourne (1943-2007) the producer of this film was someone I had an opportunity to meet and interview. His life was one that blossomed from his families influence. His father St. Claire Bourne Sr. was a well-known journalist. Bourne the younger got his opportunity to learn about filmmaking while

working on the **PBS** series **Black Journal** the first national black public affairs program under the tutelage of that programs creator/producer **William Greaves**. Bourne in his lifetime produced a significant body of documentary films that he himself described, "...define black people as they themselves would define themselves and stretched the documentary style..." (16)

William Greaves St. Clair Bournes' film mentor began his artistic career with the visual arts, later dance then acting. His frustrations as an actor led to his career making films. He apprenticed in film in Canada. He made documentary film his primary métier but was executive producer on the Richard Pryor feature film **Bustin' Loose** (1981). Because of his significant body of documentary film work and longevity, Greaves in the words of film scholar Don Bogle is "...considered the Dean of independent African American documentary filmmakers."

This is one of Greaves finest productions. **Ida B. Wells: Passion for Justice** (1989) 60 min. A documentary that chronicles the life and works of an early champion of human rights, black civil rights, women's rights and as important a journalist as America has produced. Wells is credited with beginning a campaign to stop lynching of black men. She chaired the Anti-Lynching Bureau of the National Afro-American Council. The documentary features interviews with people who put her pioneering work for justice in perspective. Toni Morrison narrates and also read the words of Ms. Barnetts' chronicle of American history a unique very important, passionate and singular voice for justice. In Greaves own words the film "...details a modus operandi for people who want to get into political activism." (17)

Over the years that I worked weekends at **KPIX-TV** as my primary source of income I developed a knack for finding a variety of media related jobs with the other five days that were available to me. The city of **San Francisco Hotel Tax Grants for the Arts**, **San Francisco Arts Commission** along with several dozen other foundations and charitable contributors created a Festival to honor the New Millennium, the year 2000 in 1990. The Festival was to be a showcase for newly commissioned art in all the disciplines – music, visual arts, theater, dance, film/video. I became involved originally as a judge for the film/video section of the Festival. So I helped to select the filmmakers who were to be given money to create new original work for the Festival.

Ashley James a well-known Bay area filmmaker was the Curator for the film and video section of the program. Ashley called me and asked me to take his place because he was too busy with other projects to work on this as well. I happily agreed and made arrangement to meet the Festival directors. After meeting we agreed on a salary and I talked about my responsibilities and saw an opportunity and became the Fiscal Sponsor using my non-profit organization **...*realize your energy...*** for the film and video section of the festival, in addition to being Curator.

Originally there were to be six commissioned new works made for the Festival. Over time one artist dropped out and only presented an already completed work as part of the Festival. The remaining five artists including a multicultural group went on to complete and premier their work as part of the Festival. The Festival was set to run for most of the month of October, 1990. The film/video Commissioned work was slated for screening by mid-month. The program grew to include the renowned Renaissance man Gordon Parks as part of a three day film/video

showcase in the Festival. We brought Parks in to be present for a screening of one his many films.

I was fortunate to work with Gordon Parks while he visited the San Francisco bay area. I was his chauffeur for a day of lecture and reception honoring his achievements. During his "Novel to Film" lecture demonstration at San Francisco State University he asked me to read the passage from his autobiographical novel where Newt, the central character of his novel losses his virginity during this passage. He told me later he liked my reading of his novel, my chest swelled.

The film of Mr. Parks Sr. that I selected to be part of the **Festival 2000** was **Leadbelly** (1976), color, 126 min. The opening and closing motif, a shot of the blazing sun saturating the screen across which comes a lone figure on horseback, serves as an appropriate framing for this musical biography. Huddie Leadbetter was born in Louisiana in the late 1880's, several different years are listed depending on your source, to a share cropper family. But by age thirteen he was a touring musician playing with his uncle. Huddie played accordion, guitar, harmonica and piano. By 1915 he was collaborating musically with the legendary "Blind Lemon" Jefferson. This was his apprenticeship to playing for money on the streets of Dallas, Texas.

Over the course of his life "Leadbelly" as he came to be known, killed two men, served time in prison, was twice pardoned yet continued to ply his musical abilities to become completely original in the American musical annals. His repertoire grew to include children's' melodies, ancient folk ballads, blues, work songs and field hollers. He was a progenitor of the folk music idiom.

With the musician nonpareil Josh White they proceeded to make Hootenannies very successful at the well-known, Village Vanguard in New York City. In 1940 "Leadbelly" hosted a regular radio show. His influence on other contemporary musical idioms is without question. His music on CD is a lasting tribute to the fire and passion which served as the blast furnace for his talent and his moments of near madness. Roger Moseby is very good in his role as "Leadbelly". The voice of "Leadbelly" is supplied by Hi-Tide Harris, a wonderful blues artist in his own right. Between Moseby and Harris the director has captured the quintessence that was the legend of "Leadbelly". This film is a wonderful tribute to "Leadbelly" and his music.

There is an excellent autobiographical film on Gordon Parks based on his book, *Half Past Autumn: A Retrospective,* 1997. The film, titled **Half Past Autumn: The Life and Works of Gordon Parks** (2000), is an hour long and directed by **St. Claire Bourne**.

As Curator and now Fiscal Sponsor for **Festival 2000** I met with all four individual artists and the artist group that were the commission winners. Now I was involved in making sure that their works were being produced. In addition as fiscal sponsor when money for their Commissions was made available I had to write them checks so they could continue and complete their work. The film/video section was mostly a success. The Festival ran into financial difficulty and many other commissioned artists and their works that were scheduled to be part of the Festival did not happen.

As an example there was no money to pay Mr. Parks. He however covered himself by accepting a guest lecture separate from the Festival. He appeared and Lectured at the S.F. Art Institute which covered his expenses. He was not happy when

the Festival Director told him as he took the stage before we screened his film the Festival could not pay him. All the Commissioned film/video artists received all of their money, five thousand dollars each.

We successfully presented their work on October 17th, 1990 at 7pm in the AMC/Kabuki Theater in their main auditorium to a two/thirds full auditorium of appreciative film goers. Through my contacts I made arrangement for the productions to be shown later on **PBS**, **KQED-TV** over two nights. The filmmakers were paid for this one time airing of their films. The audience over the two nights was over 100K homes in the Bay area.

I learned a lot about success and failure from this experience. Lack of money and planning are the reason for the failure of the Festival. Not enough funds being raised as the Festival grew and not enough ticket sales before and during the Festival to make the whole event successful. Artistically it left a bad taste in the mouth of many artists, arts organizations and the City of San Francisco. A lot of blame for the failure of the event was laid on the Director of the Festival. But from an insider's perspective, it was a great idea that needed more time and money than was given to it. My non-profit ***...realize your energy...*** profit did not get a standard fee as pass through agency for the artist's money. I was only paid for my time as Curator.

Francee Covington, a former producer at **KPIX-TV**, now doing independent production and long-time friend told me about a project that came under the aegis of **City Hall** and the then mayor, Art Agnos. The project was called the **Video Van**. The city of **San Francisco's Parks and Recreation Department** oversaw and ran a **Gang Prevention Program**.

Young men and women were recruited to become street counselors in more than half a dozen communities that had recreation centers from which these counselors would then talk to young people and hopefully prevent them and assist them in their efforts to stay out of street gangs. Money for this program came from the city and the Federal government. They wrote another grant and got money to create a **Video Van**. The van was supplied with video cameras and support equipment and was to be sent to more than half a dozen Parks and Recreation sites with video equipment to interest the young people ages twelve to seventeen in using the equipment. The program needed four people to work part-time. I applied for and got the position of supervisor of the Video Van. I then interviewed and hired three more video trained individuals.

One of the video makers I hired was one of the artists I had met through Festival 2000, Ulysses Jenkins. The schedule for the four of us was three days a week each working about twenty hours a week in two teams going to the centers to teach video production and document various recreation center events. Our success was tempered by the social and political mores of San Francisco. The city is one of the most diverse in America. The recreation centers were placed so that only occasionally would we encounter a center that had a diverse group of young people. Often what we found was in the Mission district a mostly Hispanic community our young people were Hispanic. In the Western Addition center, which was in the African American section of the city our clients were African American. In the Chinatown Center our clients were mostly Asian.

The Video Van crew consisted of four African American men. In America the racial divide is tempered by an inherent lack of knowledge of other ethnic groups based on limited contact

between the groups. Language, proximity, social mores all contributed to the distance between the various ethnicities of San Francisco.

This is best illustrated in the work of a ground breaking filmmaker from this period. The director **Spike Lee** graduated from Morehouse College in mass communications. He earned a teaching assistant position at New York University. He garnered notoriety with his film **Joe's Bed-Stuy Barbershp: We Cut Heads** (1982) which received a student Academy Award Nomination. His third feature film addresses the issues of race relations head on.

Do The Right Thing (1989)*, 119 min., color. Lee takes a warm summer day in Brooklyn a neighborhood he knew as a native New Yorker. In this film Lee takes the issues of race and ethnic identity and tears the notions apart during the course of the film. We see African Americans and Italians go at each other over a clear lack of understanding of who and what the other group is about in the un-melted pot that we call America. Lee's abilities as director were never more challenged than this very personal and powerful film. Twenty odd years later this film is a primer for looking at the issues of race and ethnic identity. Lee is the most important African American filmmaker in the latter part of the twentieth century.

The issues of this film have not gone away because I believe we have become more entrenched and divided along ethnic and racial lines. Lee's films chronicle the African American experience in many different settings and bring insights with the subjects he chooses to illuminate.

Macolm X (1992), 201 min., color. This film is a biography of one of the people most responsible for the expansion of Black consciousness in the latter half of the last century. Malcolm X was a visionary social political theorist whose ideas rivaled Dr. Martin Luther King's for the allegiance of African Americans striving for social and political freedom. The fact that this film was made and Lee's commitment to get it done and into the mass market is a testament to Lee's abilities as filmmaker and as cinematic social activist.

Clockers (1995) A film that deals with the ravages of drugs on the African American community.

Get on the bus (1996) A film that chronicles a dozen men going to the Million Man March and their individual and group issues as contemporary black men in America.

Bamboozled (2000) The rise and fall of black people in television.

A Huey P. Newton Story (2001) A documentary / performance tribute to an important American political theorist.

Jim Brown - All American (2002) Documentary on one of America's most important athletes.

Miracle At St. Anna (2008) African American soldiers of World War Two, little honored even less recognized for their contributions to the Allied victory.

Lee's body of work represents some high points in the black experience on screen in Hollywood produced and distributed films.

Where is America today regarding race and Black/white interactions now with the first black President? In the summer of 2009 Henry Louis Gates Jr. a nationally known African American scholar was arrested in his home after a white police officer came

to his home because of a reported burglary in progress. Dr. Gates established his identity and that he was in his own home. Because Dr. Gates became incensed and said he was being racially profiled in a way that caused the white police officer to take personal umbrage towards Dr. Gates and arrested him for "disorderly conduct". In the fall of 2009, former President Jimmy Carter told NBC in an interview, "I think the overwhelming proportion of the intensely demonstrated animosity toward President Obama is based on the fact that is he is a black-man, an African American."

Within a month of President Carter's remarks which received a lot of criticism, an interracial couple in Louisiana was denied a marriage license by Keith Bardwell a white Justice of the Peace in Tangipahoa Parish. He said, "I'm not a racist. I just don't believe in mixing the races that way. There is a problem with both groups accepting a child from such a marriage." The couple a Black man, Terence McKay and Beth Humphrey a white woman working with the American Civil Liberties Union created enough public pressure around Bardwell's views that he ultimately had to write a resignation letter to the Secretary of State of Louisiana within weeks of his comments.

My experience in the **Video Van** never achieved the level of racial animus I just enumerated. The young people tended to be open to using the technology to create rap music videos, videotaping skits and dance routines. It became an important adjunct to the **Gang Prevention** program and provided me an opportunity to increase my own personal understanding of the value of diversity in a city like San Francisco. The diversity of San Francisco is always what made my life there very rich. We produced a ten minute documentary within the first year of my tenure with the program. The ten minute video program

highlighted the activity of the **Gang Prevention Program** and presented a view of the work of the Van at various centers documenting the social and political activities of many of the ethnic communities we serviced. The **Video Van** crew and I were able to develop our skills in other projects. In June, 1991 we participated in the **Pro Arts Open Studio** event. We had rented a studio space in Oakland with our collective resources. We began to have contact by Vid-Phone with other artists regionally and internationally. We produced events and Vid-phone interactive programs in conjunction with these artists.

At that time video-telephone communications was the medium we used, utilizing a long distance telephone line to transmit audio and video signals over the telephone system. The screen which would accept a camera in-put could then be transmitted. The images from the video camera were transmitted by way of a slow scan still image which could be changed every ten seconds. The audio in order to be continuous and interactive required a second phone line to send audio only.

The **Open Studios** event was our most ambitious project. Over the weekend of June 8th & 9th, 1991 we had live Vid-phone connections with five separate locations KA/OS Network, Los Angeles; Western Front, Vancouver, Canada; Electronic Cafe International, Santa Monica; Van Gogh TV, Germany; Electronic Cafe, Phoenix. We called ourselves **O'RYE Studio**. We ran video programs by local artists; we had live performances of music by groups and individual artists and had poetry readings.

We served coffee and took donations. More than two dozen artists including the **Video Van** crew - Ulysses Jenkins, Jahn Overstreet, Paul Baker and myself put the whole event together. We achieved our goal which was to promote, produce and

present artists of color and other artists in a video cafe environment to locations near and far via video telephone communications technology. It was our most ambitious and successful undertaking as artists working in collaboration. The days before **SKYPE**.

Because of my continued community outreach I met with a group that had successfully obtained the license of a public television station UHF channel license. This group of African American entrepreneurs had succeeded in getting the license to the channel because **KQED-TV** a VHF channel and **PBS** affiliate also had the license for **KQEC-TV** a UHF channel. The management of **KQED-TV** told the Federal Communications Commission that they took the UHF channel off-air because of financial issues. The FCC found out that this was not true. So a group of African American entrepreneurs successfully challenged and won the rights to the channel. Over time a committee of interested individuals began to meet to develop strategies and implement the steps necessary to bring the station on-air as the first African American owned and operated public television station on the west coast.

I got involved because I understood the importance of their having a license to begin to operate and broadcast programs from a different perspective. I volunteered my time initially. When the station was set to begin on-air operations I was hired as a Program Associate. My job included program selection, producing the log of on air activity and many times getting the programs to the facility from which the pre-recorded programs were beamed. That was Sutro Tower, it is a 1000 ft. tall. It is taller than the Transamerica Pyramid. It sat on the highest hill in San Francisco. The corporate offices and transmission site were separate. Initially we also used a separate studio to produce live

and videotaped programs. The station was renamed **KMTP-TV** which stood for minority television programming. http://www.kmtp.tv/

As an independent filmmaker, I was aware of a variety of sources for program acquisition. One of my first contacts was to **Native American Public Telecommunications**. Their Founding Director Frank Blythe after I called and once he understood our need for programs he was very generous to us. He supplied us in short order with probably more than sixty hours of programs by Native Americans and other filmmakers about the Native American experience. We had unlimited run of their programs. http://www.nativetelecom.org/about_us

In San Francisco my contacts in the Asian community with a group now called the **Center for Asian American Media** led to an agreement for limited run and showcase for about thirty hours of programs by Asians and other independent filmmakers on the Asian experience. http://www.asianamericanmedia.org/.

In the mid-eighties I had already established a relationship with the **National Black Programming Consortium,** members of their group had supported and attended the **Black Cinema Series**, I had curated that was part of the **San Francisco International Film Festival** in 1987. So **NBPC** became another source for programming for the station as well. http://www.nbpc.tv/

Because the programs we ran were on ¾ inch video cassettes our offices were not equipped for me to screen programs which were one of my duties. So I made arrangements to take bunches of tapes to the Film Arts Foundation, http://www.filmarts.org/ a street car ride away and view programs, a few hours a day a few days a week just to keep up.

I know that our use of a wider variety of program sources besides the main PBS archive of programs brought us viewers and supporters that were seeing images and ideas that neither **KQED**, **PBS**, San Francisco nor **KTEH** the **PBS** station in San Jose had not seen fit to show or showcase to that point.

We acquired a few local independent productions, but the main body of our programs came from the **PBS** archive of programs on a variety of subjects. We ran programs of a greater variety from their archive that featured people of color. It was clear our programming made an impact in Bay area Public television. Within months of our going on -air the other public stations in the area were showing a wider variety of programs on people of color than they had previously shown.

The idea for this memoir in this form mixing cinema and the actual events of my own media journey was developed by a combination of influences. In California I was exposed to ideas that molded and shaped my consciousness in ways I had not imagined or dreamed. Taoism, Theosophy, Psychosynthesis, esoteric astrology, African religions, metaphysics, Tarot, Kabbalah and meditation were some of the philosophies and teachings that aided me in my own personal quest for knowledge. I wanted to better understand myself and things I could see and things I could not see but existed in realms of understanding unfamiliar to me.

Dr. Alfred Ligon (1906-2002) was the owner of one of the longest continuously operated Black-owned book stores in the nation which he opened in 1941. **The Aquarian Book Shop** was located in south central Los Angeles. In 1955 he founded the **Aquarian Spiritual Center** where ten years later he developed *Black Gnostic Studies,* a curriculum of knowledge where he

taught metaphysics, astrology, Tarot, Psychosynthesis and other occult subjects. Some of his students published a magazine *Uraeus: The Journal of Unconscious Life*, the journal was founded in 1977. The journal was a self-described "Aquarian Age Journal". Its purpose was "...to motivate and to inspire, initiate seekers, increase awareness and expand consciousness, encourage scholarly research into self-religion and history." Dr. Ligon was a member of the magazines Board of Advisors. I found the magazine in San Francisco's oldest Black book store **Marcus Books**, one of the oldest independent Black bookstores in the country founded in 1960.

Through the publishers of the magazine I learned that Dr. Ligon was coming to San Francisco to teach classes over a weekend I immediately registered. He said, "...the things we see going on around us are phenomena of nature; they are copies of the pneumonic world. The latter dwell in the heavenly realm while the former are of the earthly realm." The import, impact and value of his influence on my knowledge of self and ideas older than written records are inestimable.

Cinema has the ability to help us see things beyond the mere images and ideals that they convey. **Chris Marker** was a philosophy student when World War II erupted in his homeland of France. He worked with the French Resistance forces. After the war, his temperament led him to write poetry, short stories and contributed to Frances leading magazine about cinema ***Cahiers du cinema***. Marker who was devoted to travel during the years after the war and worked as a photojournalist and produced a magazine/book as contributor and editor of a series of limited edition books each book was devoted to a particular country. These books combined facts and impressions of the photojournalists used to create material for each book.

Later Marker wrote novels and began to produce films independently and in collaboration with other filmmakers like Alain Resnais working on Resnais film **Night and Fog** (1955) which documented the Nazi death camps. Marker made **La Jetee** aka **The Pier** (1964), 27 min., b/w. it is his only fiction film using the bold stroke of mixing still images, narration and a small amount of film footage. The story is about a man who is in some un-specified time in a post-apocalyptic future devastated by nuclear holocaust. Those left alive live in vast underground caverns below the surface of the Earth.

A prisoner in this subterranean world is volunteered and sent through time travel back to change the past to prevent the war that destroyed and devastated the life of the time in which he lives. We are never sure if the man is psychotic or in a dream. He has the challenge of the decaying world in which he is living, the ideal of the past and his hope for a better future with his efforts to change the past somehow.

In mediation there is an exercise where you sit silently and look deep within yourself to find a moment in your past and see it and be in it; then consider a moment not yet realized in your future, see it and be in it; then see yourself in the present; then consider all three moments simultaneously. This film is like that meditative exercise. **La Jette** is very challenging for me in seeking to understand its story and message much like the process of writing this book. Terry Gilliam the iconic and manic filmmaker has made a feature length inspired homage to Marker's film called **Twelve Monkeys** (1995).

In 1991 independent film-makers and Hollywood combined to produce and distribute nineteen films that were written, produced, directed and starred African Americans. Not since the

seventies had there been that many films nationally distributed featuring the African American experience. The films ran the gamut from comedy to drama. In this group of filmmakers there was a group that had been labeled as the "L.A. Rebellion". Many of its' members graduated from the U.C.L.A. film program. Some bright moments in Black cinema emerged.

Charles Burnett is the son of Mississippi émigrés who moved west to find a better life. The influence of family is central to perspective. In his study at the U.C.L.A. film school, Burnett acknowledged literary influences as the writer, James Agee, cinematic influences include the Dutch filmmaker Joris Ivens, the U.K.'s Basil Wright whose humanistic approach to film making all contributed to creating a very serious attitude in Burnett regarding the entire film making process.

His first feature as director came and went and did not receive the national or international distribution of his latter films. It did receive awards in Europe, that film is **Killer of Sheep** (1977)*, 84 min., b/w. It is Burnett's thesis film. The film also is now part of a box set of Burnett films available for the first time on DVD. The film is a very visceral and engaging film. The central character of the film works in a slaughter house for animals. The Black family and the social mores of the seventies are etched with a very poetic social realistic perspective. Burnett's use of popular and classical music serves as an effective counterpoint to the images and activities of the people in this very memorable film. Henry G. Sanders and Kaycee Moore as the husband and wife are very effective and compelling in their performances. This is a very carefully crafted film. You cannot be just a viewer, Burnett draws us into this family's life and we are changed by that experience. The children and the scenes with the children are very realistic and telling.

In 1990 Burnett made the film **To sleep with anger**, 101 min. color, that received good critical review and modest national distribution. Danny Glover, one of the films co-stars was compelled by the project and Burnett's strengths as director to become a co-producer on the film as well. This film is a look at the Black family social mores of the nineties.

Burnett's social realistic perspective again draws us into a deeper understanding of its family and the stress of living, loving, learning and overcoming the obstacles of family life, internally and externally induced. The patriarch of the family invites an old friend from back home who comes to visit to stay for a few days. The events that transpire over a week in this family's life address the values, ideas, superstitions, strengths and weaknesses of its individuals and the collective family, friends and assorted neighbors. There are moments of great tragedy and comedy. Burnett has made another compelling and timeless film.

I meet George Hill, PhD from Los Angeles. Una Van Duvall an officer with the **Los Angeles Black Media Coalition** and their Media Conference was what brought George and I together. George is a black author and educator. My book-in-progress _Beyond Hollywood_ was my introduction to him. I gave him a copy to read and critique. George and I immediately began a friendship. George was a very resourceful person. When we met he had co-written and in some instances co-published at least a dozen books.

Within six months after the conference we were exchanging phone calls and packets of information by mail on black cinema. We began very shortly to write free-lance articles together that were published in a variety of magazines from Los Angeles, San

Francisco and national magazines and newspapers on black cinema.

George had developed many contacts in the black Hollywood community through his books, articles, lectures and attendance to Hollywood events where Black stars and Black technicians working in the film and television industry attended. By 1989 George and I had developed a book idea, an A-Z encyclopedia of Black filmmakers silent to sound. We put together a draft using material from both of our individual archives on the subject. After not having any traction for many months with that idea, George being his usual resourceful-self came up with another book idea. This one we would co-publish together. That book *Blacks in Hollywood: Five Favorable Years, 1987-1991* was co-authored and co-published by us in 1992 and we printed a thousand copies. Daystar Publishing, Los Angeles, CA, 1992, Library of Congress # 91-73723. The book featured over forty film reviews and over forty television programs including TV movie reviews. Plus information on awards won by black actors and technicians.

Through George's contacts we got a wonderful full two page review of our book in the *Black Scholar*, Vol. 24 No. 1 by W.F. Bell. "These authors have presented such unique and fascinating material on the cultural presence of African Americans in Hollywood these past five years..." My partner Bonnie was extraordinary on this project with us. She took over the layout and design of the cover. The cover was great it featured a photo montage of b/w pictures of a few dozen black actors, television personalities and filmmakers. The photos were acquired through one of George's contacts.

Bonnie found the printer and supervised the choice of typeface and the printing and binding. She is rightfully listed as editor on the book. I owe her love of me and my efforts at writing a great deal. Our best sale of the book was to the New York Public Library which bought about forty copies. Again old resourceful George had a contact. So this was now part of my bag of tricks, not just published writer but published author, albeit as co-author and co-publisher.

Having met other independent black filmmakers through my work and study of film I corresponded periodically with a fellow filmmaker in New Jersey. Linda Gibson and I met through the **Black Filmmaker Hall of Fame Independent Filmmakers Workshops** in the late eighties. Whenever we talked on the phone always we seemed to be complaining about distribution of our films. Finally, one day we said, "Let's do something about that". We put together a proposal and submitted it to the **National Association of Media Arts Centers: Media Arts Development Fund.** We wrote a proposal for presenting a conference on distribution of work by independent Black filmmakers. We got several thousand dollars, which was given to my non-profit **...realize your energy...** which was the fiscal sponsor for this event. Linda and I were both pleasantly shocked and happily surprised. Now we had to put up or shut up!

The conference was organized by members of an Executive Committee composed of the following individuals; Cheryl Chisholm, Director **Atlanta Third World Film Festival**; O. Funmilayo Makarah, Film/Video Maker, Curator/Founder, **In Visible Colors**; Michelle Materre, founding partner, **KJM3 Entertainment Group, Inc. and Marketing Director, Educational Video Center**; Cornelius Moore, **Distributor,**

California Newsreel; Linda Gibson, Video artist & distributor, **California Newsreel** and myself.

We created a plan of action and continued to write proposals to raise the funds to produce the event, a two-day conference. Over the course of another year we raised enough money for the event. We paid people to write four (4) position papers so we had a shared body of knowledge for the conference participants. We hired a facilitator for the event Lillian Jimenez, founder, **National Latino Film/Video Festival**, media consultant, independent producer and funder. Denise Maunder was hired as our Travel Coordinator who helped us with the travel arrangements for the people we were to invite. We found a location about three hours outside the San Francisco area in northern California in Geyserville, called **The Pocket Ranch**. The ranch was designed as a conference and meeting center with facilities for housing and feeding groups.

The purpose of the conference was to develop strategies for the expansion of African American independent media in non-theatrical distribution, both profit and non-profit. Including the participants, the organizing committee, our coordinator and a technician to audio-tape all of our meetings there were thirty-one people involved. We rented several vans and drove to the ranch from San Francisco. So in July 1992 the event went off without a hitch.

djovida a talented technician we knew audio taped all the sessions so we had material for transcription and enough material to produce a report that highlighted much of what happened at the two-day event. We paid someone to transcribe the tapes. We paid one of the event participants to edit the transcript material.

Issues we addressed in the conference included - market fragmentation; market diversification; new delivery systems; production; packaging and promotion; critical discourse; profile of the Black media audiences; grassroots marketing strategies; Black independent media resource centers; audience development; the status of African American film/video distribution; strategies for promotion/distribution; international markets for non-theatrical distribution; home video market; subsidized library collections; Black College Satellite Network; strategies for the future.

Along with the edited transcript of the conference and copies of the position papers and other conference related material we published a seventy page report. The report was titled, **Available Visions: Improving Distribution of African American Independent Film and Video Conference, July 24-26, 1992**, 12/92 was the date of printing and publication. We mailed over three hundred and fifty copies of the report to the conference participants and a list of organizations across the United States including our funders and even sent copies to the United Kingdom.

Our funders were the **National Association of Media Arts Centers; National Video Resources (The Rockefeller Foundation); Ruth Mott Fund; San Francisco Arts Commission; San Francisco Foundation; Time Warner, Inc.; National Black Programming Consortium; Wallace Alexander Gerbode Foundation**.

My life with my partner Bonnie had begun to change. Within the second year of our relationship Bonnie and two business partners opened a store. The location was in her former studio space, on Hayes Street, two blocks from our flat. It was called

Nuts About You. The store specialized in a wide variety of nuts, candies & chocolate confections. Later sale of coffee both cups cappuccino style and coffee beans and ground was added to the products sold. After a few years it was clear the store was occupying more and more of Bonnie's time.

At holidays especially from Halloween through Valentine's Day she was a blur of activity with at one point owning two stores and managing staff. After more than a decade together we got to a crossroads. We sought couples counseling. We did about six weeks of counseling and it made a big difference in the quality of our relationship. Besides our relationship and working on media projects together and running her business Bonnie found time to continue her artistic ambitions. She produced a series of pen and paper sketches whenever we went to jazz concerts. She had been doing this since before we met. She would mostly sketch and listen only occasionally looking at the paper. She had been drawing jazz musicians for years it was her way of listening. She described the material in presenting it for exhibition, "The line tells the story - the mood, the tempo, the sound and the relationship of the musician to the instrument." Some of her finest work from this series was exhibited at the New Orleans Hilton in 1988. One of my favorite drawings in this series was her rendering of 'Dizzy' Gillespie. She captured that elevated bell of his trumpet that was distinctly 'Dizzys' and the portrait vibrant as his music.

One of Bonnie's abstract paintings inspired one of her fellow artist's a weaver. Tricia Goldberg wove a wall size tapestry using Bonnie's original painting as the design. This work once completed was eventually selected to be part of what became the **World Tapestry Today**, touring exhibition and catalogue, 1988-1989. The show traveled to Melbourne Australia; Chicago,

Illinois; Memphis Tennessee; New York City; Heidelberg, Germany & Aubusson, France.

As time went on being a part-time everyman, trying to get enough work to pay my share of the bills produced its own stress. My work was contingent on my availability from one job to the next. Sometimes during the Christmas holidays especially I really felt lonely, especially if I wasn't working despite my understanding on some level that her business demanded her time. As my longest lasting lover/friend/creative partner Bonnie was clearly a significant part of who I became as individual and partner. Other contributing factors to the demise of our relationship include my weight which ballooned from stress and having a completely irregular schedule and strenuous work being my only exercise and still working weekends at **KPIX-TV**. I woke up one morning and told Bonnie I thought our relationship was over. She did not understand in that moment which was a difficult one for us. Bonnie and I separated by the early fall of 1993. As I continue this look into my life then and now I see the distance I've come.

The director **Jane Campion** was born in Wellington New Zealand; her college studies include anthropology and painting. She pursued media studies in the Australian School for Film and Television. Campion produced several films prior to **The Piano**. This film is her most widely known and successful film to date.

The Piano (1992), 121 min., color, written & directed by Jane Campion. Starring Holly Hunter, Harvey Keitel, Sam Neill, Anna Paquin. The film won Academy Awards for Holly Hunter as Best Actress; Anna Paquin for Best Supporting Actress; Campion for Best Original Screenplay. The film was nominated in nearly a dozen countries for almost eighty awards and won more than

fifty international film awards. Campion was the first female director to win the Cannes Festival Palme D'Or Prize.

Ada McGrath (Hunter), a mute with a young ten year old daughter Flora (Paquin), is bound to a marriage made by her father for money. Adas' new husband Alisdair Stewart (Neill) and his neighbor George Baines (Keitel), eventually find themselves in a love triangle. The location for the film is the 1850's on New Zealand's, South Island. The film speaks to the heart of love and loss. What price do we have to pay to get and keep love? This is a question I had to confront. This is the central question of this exquisite film.

I was in a very loving relationship for many years with the same woman. It was the longest interpersonal relationship in my life. In looking deeply into myself I knew that life had changed me and my heart. In **The Piano** Ada plays piano and it is her voice and her heart. Besides her music her daughters love sustains and keeps her. Adas' piano makes the journey with mother and daughter by sea to this tropical island.

All their worldly possessions are taken from their ship which brought them to the island, by small boat to a beach. They spend a night on the beach waiting patiently for the husband and a small band of Maori natives to bring them to their new home. Adas' husband at first is reluctant to bring the piano from the beach to their home. A neighbor makes a trade with the husband for the piano, if he can receive lessons. Thus begins a series of seductions based on the number of black keys representing the number of lessons the neighbor is to receive. An inexorable sexual seduction ensues. George the neighbor has fallen in love with Ada.

When they get to the lesson where they are in bed naked together, George realizes he has won her lust but not her heart. The husband with the help of the daughter discovers the lovers. The husband who has been cold and distant later tries to find his better more gentle nature, to no avail. The tropical rains, the jungle, the island, the interaction of the Europeans with the Maoris are part of the many layers of this oceans deep love story.

I had been in love before and was very in love when Bonnie and I moved in together. The couples counseling really helped me to begin over time to see myself better. I have always followed a non-traditional path as an African American in a European dominated society. To find love and happiness in the arms of a white woman more than once made me a traitor to some parts of my community. I heard and knew that people said, "...he talks black, but sleeps white..." and was told later, "...while you were in California letting white women lick all over you..." When I reached my early twenties I saw all people as human and treated each person I met as such until they proved otherwise to me.

This film is a wonderful metaphor on the incongruous juxtaposition that love can create whether we believe in it, feel it or understand it. True love is a gift. I value love more today, than at any time in my life. I see that love has helped me, hurt me, molded me and made me the person I am today. My mother's love, my families love, the love of my friends, the love of someone special. Sometimes loving acts from strangers can touch us and change us and open our eyes to loves wonder and unfathomable qualities.

In November of 1993 I was volunteering with the Mill Valley Film Festival in Marin County, that effort led to my getting the

opportunity to co-produce a silent film premier revival. **Oscar Micheaux** (1884-1951) was the most important independent African American filmmaker in the first half of the 20th Century.

A copy of one of his early films **Within Our Gates** (1919)*, b/w, silent, 74 min. was to have its West coast premiere revival as part of the M.V.F.F. We raised funds and arranged to have live musical accompaniment for the silent film. Mary Watkins, piano and India Cooke, violin, composed and performed original music for the film screening. We also arranged to have a panel discussion with several local film scholars after the film. The program was sold-out. The event was funded in part by local foundations and non-profit organizations, my non-profit **...realize your energy...** acted as the fiscal agent for the event. The response to the silent film accompanied by live music and a panel of film scholars was tremendous. Tony Williams a filmmaker friend arranged through his contacts to videotape Mary & India talking about their process of composing and performing for a silent film, videotaped the panel and other event related proceedings and produced a ten minute film on this historic event.

In December of 1994 after having worked since 1977 at **KPIX-TV**, I am lain off. My replacement is a white guy who was a casual employee when I started. He was given my two day a week stage managers position. I am devastated. One of my anchors in life was released and I am adrift now not sure what I will do to survive and pay rent and bills. Work was my number one issue, not enough. Now that I was no longer on staff at **KPIX-TV** and had no regular job.

I was trying to get work with three separate unions to which I belonged – **IBEW** (International Brotherhood of Electrical

Workers); **NABET** (National Association of Broadcast Technicians); **IATSE** (International Alliance of Theatrical Stage Employees and Motion Picture Machine Operators).Each union provided a variety of work as a stage manager for broadcast production live or videotape; stage hand and technician doing audio, carpentry, electrics, props. I continued working on a casual basis in broadcast television but my work now included live theater, live music concerts, audio-visual presentations for hotel conferences, feature film production, public events.

Over the years of working on various film, broadcast and theater productions I worked with a litany of people who are recognized household names but in hindsight I see that I was making history with some of the people I worked with. I worked at **KPIX-TV** with the *first* two African Americans ever hired to work as on-air reporters in northern California broadcasting. They were **Ben Williams** a former journalist for the San Francisco Examiner and **Belva Davis** who had worked in radio. They opened doors and made a difference with who they are and their perspective on stories in the San Francisco Bay area. At **KQED-TV** I worked with **Allen Willis** one of the first African American technicians hired to run studio and remote camera. They all had paved the way for me and other black people to work in broadcasting and being there to see others from their community participate in this medium that is regulated by a Federal agency but never seems to live up to its potential as a major agent of change for the good.

The work I performed in theater was for the Nederlander Theaters and the other employment was working at all the large performance and event venues in town like the Cow Palace, Moscone Convention Center, Palace of Fine Arts and all the major hotels. My former partner Bonnie and I shared the car we

bought together despite living separate lives. She needed it for her shop related work sometimes. I needed the car to get to work when there was work. The car had already been parked in a secured lot in our neighborhood for several years. This was to prevent damage or theft because of the changes in the neighborhood. This made sharing easy, when done the car would be in the lot for the next person.

Searching for work and income I made contact with an African American producer and he commissions me to write a script on "race" movies for a proposed CD-ROM, covering the "race" movie period 1900-1950. This creates a rift in my relationship with a fellow black filmmaker. My friend dislikes the producer I am working for and sees it somehow as a personal affront to him, because they had a parting of the ways over this same production. Shortly after that two more close black male friends who I had been in the media trenches with decide that my friendship with them is over as well. I'm cut loose from the moorings of my friends and feel like a dingy set adrift in an ocean.

I had taken a copy of <u>Blacks in Hollywood</u> and mailed it to half a dozen publishers and one responded favorably. In addition to <u>BIH</u> upon request I sent Alicia Merritt of Greenwood Publishing a copy of the draft of the original book concept on black filmmakers George Hill and I had developed. Greenwood liked the concept and said they could only pay one person. George being the gentleman he said, "Spencer write the book, I'll check the material and write the Forward to the book".

Unfortunately I thought I needed an agent so I found an agent using my first book as mailer and introduction with the Greenwood letter of interest in the new book as entrée. I

solicited nine agents and signed with an agent, signed with Greenwood and started writing my second book. Over the next eighteen months I had a routine when I was working in theater, I'd get up early before sunrise, write for several hours, take a nap and work evenings in the theater. If my work hours were different because my work assignment was different I amended my writing schedule. At one point I got carpel tunnel syndrome from writing and had to wear a brace on my left hand.

I loved working in live theater in the Props Department. One of my supervisors Ron Hunkiewicz took me under his tutelage and made sure to request me for his Prop crew in theater. As a result I worked on touring companies of **Fiddler on the Roof** with Theodore Bikel, December '94; **Grease** with Mackenzie Phillips, Rex Smith, Davy Jones & Sally Struthers. **Blood Brothers** a British production with David Cassidy and Petula Clark, February & March '95. I barely had time to think between working and writing my first book under contract. I saw myself certainly as fortunate and productive.

I met a woman while working in theater; she worked in wardrobe, while I worked in props. She was white, divorced with four grown daughters. Louise's daughters were all out, on their own, some were married. She lived in San Jose, which is south of San Francisco. We dated and fell in love. Louise Connors is a very kind, loving, supportive and inspiring person to me in so many different ways. While we were together I was writing my second book. She was very encouraging and supportive while I was writing book #2 and even did some research for me.

In 1994 while still writing book number two I got a teaching opportunity presented to me. Tony Williams a film maker I had just worked with on the Micheaux project contacted me about a class on Black cinema. Tony had been one of the first black filmmakers I was introduced to when I got to San Francisco and said I was interested in film making. Tony said he had been approached by a former class mate who was now head of the African American Studies Department at City College of San Francisco. She wanted him to teach a Black Cinema class. Tony knew of my own media productions, my having taught video production and my recent self-published book and thought I would be more suited, as he was not interested. Within a year after pitching the class, developing the curriculum which included our book <u>Blacks In Hollywood: Five Favorable years, 1987-1991</u> as class text, it was not until a year later because of issues with scheduling at the school that I was able to teach the class on **Black Cinema**. The course I created became a three hour credit course that met once a week for three hours. It could be used as credit to the University of California and California State University systems. So the challenge is how to be available for work and not be available one day a week so I could teach the class.

My first year entailed teaching what I thought the students needed to know about the history of **Black Cinema** from silent films to contemporary films and some international black cinema, in sixteen weeks. This was a lot of information. I was up for the challenge.

After a year I was able to get a second class started called **Contemporary Black Cinema**. So I divided the black experience into two periods roughly 1900-1950 and 1950 to today. I was still teaching one class per semester. I had some of my most satisfying moments in my life, in the classroom. I let the students offer suggestions via the tests on improving the class. Once they understood their critiques would help the class and not affect

their grade the critiques became more helpful to me as a teacher. In the process of teaching the class for five years as Adjunct Professor I tried to create a safe environment for discussion and expression in the class.

My favorite moment in my class was our end of semester talk. This is when the students have taken their exams done their final projects and we just talked about life and what they learned in class. One young woman talked about a very personal experience related to the class work. The Asian female said that one day going home, by BART the mass transit from San Francisco to Berkeley across the Bay, she was mugged. She said her attacker just snatched her purse and ran and that he was African American. She also let us know that because of her experience in the class and what she learned she was not going to let it affect her opinion of African Americans.

At the end of one semester my students gave me a very special memento, a small ceramic tchotcke book whose cover read – A Special Teacher. The book was opened to a small set of bears one a teacher the other a student who gave the teacher a bright red apple. Inscribed on the page opposite the two bears was, *"Teachers shape tomorrow, one inquisitive young mind at a time."*

My mother remarries in September of 1997. James Jackson is now my second step-father. They had lived together for a few years so I was not surprised by this. I was happy for her. My second step father married my mother while I was in San Francisco. I did meet him and one year they came to California and Louise and I spent some special time with them including my Mom's birthday. Louise made a cake and put candles on the cake that would not go out. Finally after a minute or two Louise

told Mom, James and I they were special candles designed not to be blown out. We all laughed for a while about Mom trying to blow out those silly candles.

I finished book number two. In the fall of 1997 my second book <u>Reel Black Talk: A Sourcebook of Fifty American Filmmakers</u> is published then the air is sucked out of the room. It is a hard back book priced at eighty dollars ($80). I am sick. I remained sick for many days and nights over trying to imagine who is going to buy my book. Universities and schools not the general public for which I wrote the book.

I made an encyclopedia with my first solo book as author. Today you can go to Amazon.com and buy my book or an e-book reader version. The publisher Greenwood Press sells an e-version only, now. Mores the pity! Vital information locked up and tucked away from the audience that needs to see it. I'm still sick. On the Amazon website my agent is listed as an author on the book. I don't even care anymore. I received a check recently from sales. It beats a poke in the eye with a sharp stick.

I continued to work in a volunteer capacity with the **Bay Area Black Media Coalition,** advocates for African Americans in all phases of media. We are still holding our annual Conference, part of my yearly volunteer duties. Attending the conference is a young African American woman who introduces herself to me and mentions that we had met before at another conference. I nod in a friendly way. Later she joins our group and becomes an active member. I ask her for a date after a meeting. After several dates we are smitten with each other. I tell Louise Connor. My arrangement over time with Louise was that we were not exclusive. She understood. We are very good friends today.

Lisa Rhenette Grant, was born in 1966, three months after I graduated from high school. So there was an eighteen year difference in our age. Lisa told me near the beginning, "...*age is only a number...*". Like all new relationships in the digital age, electronic mail became a major source of our early communications with each other. Lisa saved our early e-mails some of them are presented here because they tell our story well to a point.

October 10, 1999

Lisa,

I had a wonderful time Friday PM/Sat. AM. It was easy being with you. I appreciate your charm, wit and intelligence. Let's get together again. Let me know what you think.

Warm regards, Spencer

October 20, 1999

Lisa,

Sounds like you've been busy and stretched in terms of time and by the unexpected aspects of life. How are you? Would you like to get together this weekend? Any fun things you've thought about doing but not had an opportunity to do?

So let's stay in touch, Peace, Spencer

October 21, 1999

Hi Spencer,

Life is a trip. I called myself coming to the aid of friends in need by pet sitting while they made the funeral arrangements in Washington since I couldn't go myself, just to lend my support and now, I've found that I'm a lot farther behind in my own personal matters. I feel like I am totally out of control and that I would need at least a week to pull myself together. The funny thing is that I have made some many commitments to other people, there's is no way I can get that time, so I've taken myself into a perpetual black hole in life and I don't know how to get out!

The time I spent in Pleasant Hill was great because it was only me, the dogs and the cat to think about, but I didn't realize until now that my life is on a roller coaster that I can't get off. I've also realized that it's a roller coaster that consists of nothing but positive influences; I just wish I could find a way to control it better. You probably have no idea what I'm talking about. I am rambling on, but I just feel like I'm reacting to situations around me rather than being in control of them. I probably sound like the biggest basket case.

I had to make a job related transition from depending on work on-again and off again with the unions to something a little more permanent. The good news is City College was able to provide additional income by allowing me to work in the schools administration to make financial ends meet. Besides teaching one class a semester.

October 22, 1999

I received your email. Thank you for responding and being so honest. I appreciate that great deal. I'm not sure what your interests are but I think being honest and upfront with each other from the beginning is important. Let us plan to get together the weekend of November 5-7 if our ever-changing schedules permit. The following weekend is the BABMC Roast, Saturday November 13th. Would you still like to go together? Let's continue to chat in cyber space. Stay strong and as special as you are. I mean that. Lisa

November 03, 1999

Subject: Response and hello again

Lisa,

Are you coming to BABMC meeting Saturday? Would you like to spend some time together this weekend? Are we still on for BABMC Roast?

Regards, Spencer

From: Lisa

Yes, Yes, and Yes, I'll call you when I get back from Oakland on Saturday, or call me @ 11:00 and I can tell you where I am. Looking forward to hanging out.

Have a blessed day! Lisa

November 10, 1999

Dear Friends and Colleagues,

My stepfather James Jackson passed away Monday, November 8th. As many of you know he was ill for quite some time. I know he is resting in a better place now. I'm leaving Thursday, November 11th for Detroit. I'm returning Thursday November 18th to SFO. Please send cards only to:

Florence Jackson
Robert Bradby Drive
Detroit, MI

or to

Spencer Moon
San Francisco, CA

If necessary call my mother's home or my cousin Thelma's home, it has voice mail. If you want to do more than a card my mother and I have agreed that a donation to your favorite charity in my stepfather's name is more appropriate.

Regards, Spencer

November 10, 1999

Spencer,

I'm so sorry to hear of your stepfather's passing, but you're right he's in a better place. If you feel the need of a friendly ear, I'm here for you. Also I will let Rudy know. We'll talk when you get back.

Stay strong & sweet Lisa

December 1, 1999

Lisa,

How are you? What is new in your neck of the woods? I'm doing well. My mom is much better now. She will come and spend at least a month here with me at some point later in the New Year. I would like for you to meet her. Are you going to the Coalition meeting? Do you need a ride? We can talk and catch up a bit on the way over. Would you like to spend some time together after the meeting? Spencer

December 05, 1999

Spencer,

I'm writing this at 11:30 because I have slept all day. I don't understand why I woke up now, except that your E-mail was on my mind and I wanted to say thanks again. I really appreciated and enjoyed the ride home today. You are an angel of mercy. It would be great to meet your mother when she comes. I was thinking that maybe you could bring her with you to one of the BABMC meetings. That way she would be able to get a firsthand glimpse at how valuable a contribution you make here.

I was just thinking that I might owe you an apology if I made you feel uncomfortable with my attitude today, with the demanding hours of the new job, and the hellish commute back and forth, I know that I am blessed, but I'm really tired. The sleep I had today was the most I've had in a couple of weeks, and it was starting to take a toll. I'm going to go eat now, so I'll say good night. Hope we'll chat again soon.

Stay Strong, Lisa

December 28, 1999

Spencer,

I hope your holidays are filled with joy and that the days to follow are too. You deserve it...What did you do on Christmas and what are you doing on New Year's? I'm going to spend it at a friend's house. I haven't seen her in ages and we've got a lot of catching up to do. Since I moved out here, I haven't had a chance to see anybody. I hope the teaching is going well...and the other gig. I really appreciate that you sent me that wish list from Karen. I really needed to laugh. It's getting harder and harder to find humor in anything.

I do find some solace in "All My Children". I know it's only a story, but I get comfort in knowing that the characters' lives on the show are a heck of a lot worse than mine. I have a love/hate relationship with this time of year. I love and respect that it's supposed to be the day for the birth of Jesus, but it's also the time when we're caught between a rock and a merchandiser. For example, they sell the Nintendo 64 console to you for $100, because they know that your kid's going to want every video game they see... so they charge you $60.00 a game. And I don't remember the last time Macy's charged me $7.00 to wrap something I bought there.

'Tis the season to be ripped-off. And if I heard another Christmas carol, I was going to scream. You must think that I'm the true to life grinch. I just resent what Christmas has become. And now here comes Kwanzaa, a tradition that I'm beginning to gain a lot of respect for. I love the idea that we as a community get together and promote positive and creative ideas. Are you going or have you gone to any Kwanzaa ceremonies? There's one coming up in your neighborhood. It's on Dec. 30 at the Center on Fulton & MacAllister. It's after work, and I think that my Godson is going to perform. I still have to go to work on Friday, so I'm going to stay at girlfriends in San Francisco. Hope you can come. I'm going to go get ready for work now. Hope to hear from you soon either by phone or e-mail. Stay Strong, Lisa

December 30, 1999

Lisa,

Happy holidays. I spent Christmas with Louise in San Jose. I'm spending New Year's Eve with her again in the South Bay again. Girl you're blessed. No, Kwanzaa events this year. I have plans for the pm of the 30th, sorry. It is nice to communicate with you over this holiday season. We need to plan further in advance, for now anyway, when we get together.

FYI - BABMC, 1/8 & 1/22. Twice a month since we're now officially in conference mode. I'm much more conscious in general especially during these holidays. I try especially hard to maintain an equanimity. I start teaching a second class this month at CCSF/John Adams, with the second class I'm now 40% time. I wrote an article on my trip to Chicago for the National Writers Union/National Diversity Retreat II. It will be published in our Local 3 newsletter, which is called Hear Say. Best for the millennium, Spencer

I joined the Local chapter of the **National Writers Union** as a way to network with other writers and to take myself more seriously as a writer. My volunteer work with them led to my being asked to represent our Local at an NWU- Diversity Retreat in Chicago.

As it turned out my efforts to get that second class to teach were thwarted by the head of our Department of African American Studies. Needless to say I was very disappointed when I realized ego was involved in my not being able to teach the second class, his not mine. The idea of the class at the John Adams campus of City College of San Francisco was initiated by their Dean.

December 30, 1999

Hi Spencer,

Thinking of each other...that's sounds like a plan. You are right I am blessed to have good friends, a loving family, and a job adequate enough to support me. Kudos on your article. I'd love to get a copy when it comes out. I just know it's brilliant. I woke up really late this morning and between running around trying to get ready for work and packing for tomorrow and then

missing the last commute bus, it just got too hard, so I called in sick. I forgot how wonderful playing hooky is. I have the whole day to organize and develop a plan for next year. My boss told me that I'm going to be working in San Francisco on Friday, which works out perfectly with my staying over at my girlfriends. Have a great New Years.

Getting stronger in 2000, Lisa

January 5, 2000

Happy New Year Homie!

Just wanted to say hi and tell you that I just received the BABMC mailing. I think it was put together well, but I'm still disappointed that my job hindered me in helping out with it. I know it was a lot of work for Rudy, Ruth and Val to have done by them. I guess the most important thing is that they got it done. I also think it was a great idea to include the entire year's schedule. I'm really excited about the website. I think it will be a lot of fun and a lot easier to disseminate information to everyone. My New Year's was a eye-opening experience.

I hope your New Year's was more eventful. I know school started for most colleges on Monday. Hope your class schedule is working out. Two classes is a lot of work. Have you heard anything else about the article that's going to be published? If you're going on the 8th, I was wondering if I could get a ride and maybe we could hang after. I am babysitting with my Godson for Sunday, so his mom can get her study on. I know this is short notice, and if it's inconvenient, I'll understand. I'd appreciate it if you could get back with me by tomorrow so I'll know how to pack. Stay Strong, Lisa

January 19, 2000

Lisa,

Thanks for listening to my tale of woe. I appreciate your willingness to be there for me. Any idea what you'd like to do Saturday after the meeting? By the way you did not answer my question? Think - one down, two to go!? So, what are the other two things on the list of three that you thought we'd never do together? If it is too personal or you feel uncomfortable answering, that's OK.I had fun when we were together last.

Regards, Spencer

Spencer,

Thanks for sending me a copy of your article. You should really be proud of yourself. On that other question, did I say there were three things specifically? I didn't really mean three. Hanging out in the first place could be considered one. It's just that you get an impression of someone when they're in a certain kind of place, and then when you actually hang in a different environment, you realize that the impression was totally false.

I'm glad that we're able to get to know each other on another level, because now we get to see who we really are. I'm looking forward to hanging out with you and discovering more stuff about each other. Maybe we can get together again Sunday before I go home. I'll call you Friday and we can discuss it. Stay strong, Lisa

January 26, 2000

Hi Spencer,

How the heck are you doing? I'm O.K. I've been packing everything up in my department, but I interviewed for an admin position in another department yesterday, and I have an interview for a teller position in Oakland, Friday. I'm pretty racked, but I know God will see me through. You know what? You're a good soul. That's the only way to describe you, considering you haven't mentioned the money I forgot to give you for the driving lesson and the fact that you fed my girlfriend, her child, and one of the other women that she went to the play with. I'll say it again. That pasta was the bomb! Everyone loved it. My girlfriend wants to reciprocate at her place. To tell you the truth, I didn't know that my girlfriend was bringing anyone back with her, and while they were at the play, I ate 3 more servings and my god son had 2. I had a really good time on Saturday, even though it was kind of rushed, and again I want to say how much I appreciated the practice.

As you already know, I definitely need it. I've been stalling to talk about it, but I've been thinking about that kiss. Was that something, or was that my imagination? ...I think we need to discuss this in person, but I just needed to put it out there, and this isn't something that can be talked about over the phone. I wish I could do it sooner than later, but my girlfriend is supposedly coming with the car this weekend, so I won't be staying in the city. Toooo Bad! I hope you been having a good week and I will definitely be in touch.

Stay Strong, Lisa

January 27, 2000

Lisa darling,

First, yes I'm taking liberties by calling you darling. After our driving lesson when I called you every endearing name I could think off and still be your friend, I guess it's OK. As far as payment goes, let's talk about this in person. I appreciate you appreciating me. That my cooking was loved by one and all makes me very happy. When we get together again there can be more of my cooking for you if you like. This is something that gives me great pleasure. I had a great time too, on Saturday. Aaahhhh, the kiss. Yes I stole a "real" kiss as I put it and yes it was "something" but only a "little something" as far as my kisses go. No brag, just fact. No, it isn't something we can talk about over the phone. I do think I can talk about it at least a little via this e-note. Here is where I am at. I like you, I'm enjoying getting to know you.

The good news for me is I got my boss at my **CCSF** administrative job to give me more hours which solves my immediate financial crisis. You know what a relief this is. So based on our current schedules we at least get to hang out twice a month till the conference. Let's continue to meet in cyberspace until we can meet in person. Think about what you want and where you would like our burgeoning friendship to go. I am. I don't want you to feel that I'm rushing or crowding you but I do like the angel that we're making together.

Warm, friendly and respectful regards, Spencer

February 3, 2000

Lisa,

I'm glad we could talk. Thanks for your honesty. I was reading last night before falling asleep and I wanted to share this with you and your girlfriend that you're going to see this weekend.

"...it is of utmost importance to our collective survival that women look beyond the hostility men display in order to see the truth of who Black men are. Black men are mirrors; they reflect a part of who and what we are. They are marinated in our wombs." quoted from - The Spirit of a Man: A Vision of Transformation for Black Men and Women Who Love Them by Ilyana Vanzant, Harper, San Francisco, 1996. This book was recommended to me by one of the people who run Marcus Books on Fillmore St. I do miss you. Regards, Spencer

February 10, 2000

Dearest Spencer,

First of all, thanks you for the lovely valentine. It really meant a lot to me. The truth of the matter is, is that I was going to ask you to be my valentine, but you beaten me to it. I just bought the card today and I was going to send it, but I lost the piece of paper with your address, and then I started talking with Lenora and lost all track of time. That's why I'm writing this so late at night. I had to reply after all the support that you have given me and my friends. I don't know why, but you've taken an interest in me the person, rather than only concentrating on that one thing. It's been a long time since that happened. To tell you the truth those nights on your couch watching TV with you on one end

and me on the other, made me feel that maybe you only wanted a hang-out partner, since you had a regular lover, and if that's the case, then I can deal with you on that level too, but that kiss let me know the deal, before you even said it.

Before I go, I just want to say thank you for keeping me aware. The articles you send me bring me back to the real world. You are very special to me. Your cyberspace Valentine - Hoping to make it a reality.

Lisa,

I do like you. Let's try for Sunday, during the day and spend some quality time together. I do have plans Saturday PM, an old friend I've known for years we're going to catch up on years gone by since we hung out and chatted. I do want to get to know you better in whatever fashion works for us.

Regards, Spencer

February 14, 2000

Hi Spencer,

I refuse to allow myself to let another day go by without getting in touch. How are you doing? Better than I, I hope. Things are basically o.k. I got a 90 on the test that I took yesterday. That made me feel pretty good. I've been in sort of a funk these last few days, which is why I didn't call you back, but it really meant a lot to me to hear your sweet voice. I've made some strides this past year, and met some very wonderful people, (present company included), I still feel like it can be

taken away from me at any moment, and I'll be starting over again. (I hope I'm not bumming you out too much)

What are you doing this weekend? I'm going to the city for a late lunch and a movie with my girlfriends, but my schedule will be clear after that? Want to hang? We'll probably be finished about seven. Maybe we can go someplace and hear some music. There's a place on Mason called Biscuit and Blues that I've heard about. It's on Mason and Geary. Or maybe some place you know of. I get paid tomorrow, so it'll be my treat. Not a problem. So let me know what's up. I really hope we can connect. Big Hugs and Sweet Dreams, Lisa

P.S. - Thanks. Just writing to you made me feel better. I'm going to bed now.

February 15, 2000

Let's get together. Let's talk one night this week to confirm. I'm up for fri/pm - sun/am if you are, your call? I've got plenty of food in the fridge. I understand about life, we'll talk.... warm and fuzzy regards, Spencer

February 21, 2000

Lisa dear,

I want to first say Thank You for letting me be myself again. I'm sorry I had to go on Sun. morn. I've thought about us and I like what we have. I trust that we will get together this week so I can let you see the Providian Bank jobs packet. What was your girlfriend's name? I want to send them a nice E-mail Thank You for their warm and wonderful hospitality. How did the ceremony

for their house go? I got some more work leads tonight at my writers' union meeting.

Let's take as much time as we need to really get to know each other better before we move to the next plateau too soon. I want us to be friends no matter what we decide to do later and no matter what happens. I can always use more friends I miss you tonight, now that you're definitely on my mind. Would you feel safe spending the night at my house one night? Consider it. Call me or e-mail me when you can.

Warm and fuzzy regards, Spencer

Lisa and I spent the night together, just sleeping at one of her best girlfriends' home. I thought it was her way of seeing if we could sleep together and not be sexual.

February 22, 2000

Hi Spencer,

Thank you for all the information. I will tell all my friends and send a reply myself. I feel that the monthly fees I pay now are enough. Thank you for coming on Saturday. I'm glad you enjoyed yourself. I think you're a gentle, warm and wonderful person and I look forward to seeing you again soon. So far, I have an interview scheduled on Friday morning, so maybe we can get together in the evening and I will consider your generous proposal for lodging. The Feng Shui consultation on Sunday was quite an experience.

The person calls herself a Feng Shui Master and she went from the outside of the house to the inside distinguishing Chi (positive energy) and Cha (negative energy) using a bagua table. When she found areas where there was more cha than chi, she suggested things they could do, such as putting up a mirror or adding a red tassel on the doorknob (she said that red is a protective color), to invite the chi in. The whole thing took about 3 hours, but it was very interesting. On a happy note, I was finally able to get BABMC and redwoodcitynews on the web. I'm so excited. It looks like a lot more work had been done on the BABMC site since Saturday, practically all the links came through. In closing, I just wanted to say that I loved the time we spent cuddling and I've been thinking about you too. I'm glad we're friends. Lisa

February 23, 2000

Lisa dear,

What time should I expect to see you on Friday? I'm looking forward to spending some quality time together Friday & Saturday. Warm regards, Spencer

March 1, 2000

Spencer,

Hope you're cold has subsided and that you're keeping warm and dry. I would suggest that you take some Echinacea. It really does work. I've been in Pacheco for the past few days visiting my girlfriend and her family. (I just found out that where they live isn't called Pleasant Hill after all. I thought so because she picks me up from that Bart station.) I guess you could say I've been shirking my responsibilities, but we really had a great time. It was important for me to do be able to do this, because after next month my schedule is going to change so dramatically. Her 23 year old son was also visiting, so I got bumped from staying in the guest house. Seeing him made me realize how old I really am. I've known him since he was 16. I'm so proud of the decisions that he has made for his life, and that he's not going off half-cocked like the rest of us did. Listening to his plans made me also realize that I never made any plans of my own. I thought that I would always have AAA to fall back on, so I didn't have a plan B. Going to school was a good idea, but I didn't "focus" on anything in particular, so basically I'm going to be 34 on the 9th and I have no trade to speak of (I really don't know why I'm telling you this again, it was just on my mind).To tell you the truth, I envy you. You can say that you're a professor; I've never been good enough at anything to make a profession of it. I'm really hoping that this Wells Fargo gig is going to teach me something that I can put on my resume as a skill.

By the way, I saw the Mumia protesters on TV. Why did it get so out of hand? I think I heard that almost 200 people were arrested. It was beautiful to see all of that support though. Were you able to be there? Did you still want to get together this weekend? Let me know. Maybe I'll call you tomorrow night and we can discuss. Remember when I told you that we'll all miss you at the meetings? It just dawned on me that I won't be able to attend the meetings after the conference either because I'll be working weekends. That's really disappointing. I'm going to see what can be done after I've worked there a few weeks. So that's all. Take good care of yourself, like only you know how.

Stay Strong, Lisa

Mumia Abu-Jamal and a rally in his support was what first drew me to meet members of the local writers union I had joined. The march and rally drew thousands of people and included people like Ed Asner and Joan Baez. Mumia Abu-Jamal began his teen years as Lieutenant of Information for the Philadelphia chapter of the Black Panther Party. Later his journalistic ability led him to work for four different radio stations in Philadelphia including reporting for **National Public Radio**. In early 1981 he was cited by Philadelphia Magazine as a "Person to Watch" because of his *"...bringing a unique dimension to his reporting..."* In his role as a reporter he was recognized as a "Voice of the Voiceless".

In late 1981 he was charged with the murder of a Philadelphia policeman and sentenced to Death Row. While still incarcerated he has written five books. Because of the exigent circumstances of his trial and conviction he has garnered support for a new trial and release. He has been honored by the city of St.Denis in France with a street named in his honor. He has become the most famous prisoner in the fight for abolishing the death penalty. Jamal is a journalist of the people who is an articulate and significant journalist even now though incarcerated and is a clear beacon for all political prisoners everywhere.

Mumia Abu-Jamal, although one of this countries longest held political prisoners there were others. Geronimo Pratt spent twenty seven years in jail for murder. When justice was served and he was released he later sued his captors and won a multimillion dollar settlement for wrongful conviction from the city of Los Angeles and the U.S. government. Last Man Standing: The Tragedy and Triumph of Geronimo Pratt by Jack Olsen recounts his ordeal.

Ruben "Hurricane" Carter a former professional boxing champion served nearly three decades in jail for murder and was tried twice and finally won release. His life was made into a powerful film called **The Hurricane** (1999) starring Denzel Washington. Carter upon release served a dozen years as executive director of the Association in Defense of the Wrongly Convicted. He has just published a book titled <u>Eye of the Hurricane: My Path From Darkness to Freedom</u>.

March 2, 2000

Lisa,

My health is good; my remedies knocked the cold bug out after a few days. With the addition of some Hunan hot food including their hot & spicy soup, the cold headed for the hills. The Mumia march was designed specifically to get people arrested to heighten awareness. I'll explain when we get together. Yes let's do get together. Is a Saturday-Sunday get together OK? I would take you home Sunday whenever you want.

As for being a teacher it was an accident and not as carefully planned as you might think. I've good news on the work front. I may be out Friday PM, not confirmed as of now. If so can we confirm our date Sat.am? I look forward to seeing and being with you. Warm and fuzzy regards your bright and shining moon at least today anyway.

Bright and Shining Moon eh? It fits. I'm glad to see that you're in good health and spirits. By the way, I finally spoke to the guy about the car, and he said that not only does it need a windshield, but it also needs a hood, and it's been raining, so we're talking a few more weeks before I can get it. Did you get the card finally? I hope so. I mailed it on Tuesday. I guess I understand the premise behind the march, but I wouldn't want to be the one to go to jail. I guess I'm not as radical as I thought. Anyway, I hope it works. Getting together Saturday would be cool, but I'm not going to be able to stay the night. It's a bummer, but I'll explain later. I'll call you after the meeting on Saturday. I'm looking forward to spending time with you too. Lisa

March 3, 2000

Hey babe,

First some FYI- A direct quote *"Say Hi for me and thank Lisa for being so good to me our first evening of meeting one another. You two must get together with Larry and I very soon. I suggest we look at our calendars for May dates - just stay clear of Mother's Day, ok? Until soon, Peg"*, end quote. I had a wonderful, extraordinary, special, original, sexy, happy, spiritual, time with you this past weekend. I'm glad it's been easy to share. Let's continue to share at levels that make us giddy with joy. So when we're not together in the same space we can think back on our joy and bliss together and feel warm and fuzzy all over. As I do now reminiscing.

Your special lover and friend, Spencer

March 5, 2000

Hey LOVER!!(I like how that sounds), Thank you so much for the poem. I really needed to hear that exact message at this point in my life. Unfortunately, I just realized that I don't know 5 people on the internet, but I'm going to make copies and give them to the people at work because my dreams have already started to come true. I hope that your settling into the new gig o.k. As for me, ever since the weekend, I haven't been able to get two things off my mind; one is your warm caress I thank you for reminding me that sex doesn't have to be mechanical, it can touch all of the levels that you described, and still maintain a wild and erogenous flavor.

You let me be me, big mouth and all. I eagerly await the opportunity to "share" again, if fact I'm getting "giddy with joy" just thinking about it. The second is that offer to work at Young and Rubicam. Both propositions are rather intriguing (and that's all I'm going to say on that subject). Please let Peggy know that I was really pleased to have met her and I do hope that we can all hang sometime. I think that would be fun.

Big hugs and kisses, Lisa

March 9, 2000

Spencer,

How's everything going? Fine I hope. I'm sorry that I've just gotten around to writing until now. I just got home a few minutes ago. I'm so happy I get home at a decent hour now. My class is going well. I was made team captain on my first day (Monday).Today I got some hands on experience and got to listen to real calls that come in. It was interesting, but scary too, that I'm supposed to be able to answer all those questions. There's so much I still don't know. I'm going to have to study this weekend because there's going to be an assessment on Monday, and I want to do well.

We tried to get the trainer to make it open book, but he wasn't going for it. Thank you again for a wonderful weekend and for taking me home on Sunday. It was great to wake up to Aretha. I knew she did, but I don't think I ever actually heard her sing gospel. Natural Woman was the first song I heard by her and that was because my mother bought the 45. I know I've just shown how young I truly am. But that's o.k. because in my training class, I'm one of the elders. I told them that today was my birthday and that I had turned 34, and these youngsters just looked at me. One the girls on my team said, "But you're so down?" I assumed it was a compliment, so I said thanks. Most of these kids never had a job before, and when I told them I had worked for AAA for ten years, they were like that's almost a lifetime. I had to agree. Well, that's all for now. You are a great guy. Keep in touch and let me know what's going on.

Stay Strong, Lisa

March 18, 2000

Hello Lover,

Hope everything is going well. I got good news and bad news. The good news is that my overtime request was approved today, so I'll be able to make my 40 hours this week; the bad news is that I told them that I would work tomorrow until 7:30 PM, so I probably wouldn't get to your place until after 9:30 PM. I'm glad to know that it was that easy to get the work, but I don't want to infringe on you either. The little time we get to spend together is precious enough. Anyway I'll beep you at 12:50, that's my lunch break. Maybe we can talk about it then.

Hugs & Kisses, Baby Girl

March 30, 2000

Lisa,

I heard you say it in one of our moments of passion, it felt good we'll visit that subject again soon I know... I'm overwhelmed by your affection for me, for us! Just so I'm clear- Wed PM we're together. Or are you getting tired of me. I'm getting more and more enamored with you. I tried to show you physically how I feel spiritually. I'm still glowing warm regards with the L -word, Spencer

May 6, 2000

Mi amour, I just read your email; after our experience these last few days I hope you know that I could never tire of you. You've showed me that being with someone doesn't have to hurt; if we take each moment as it comes. With you I don't feel guilt, regret, just safe!!! I am overwhelmed by the joy that emerges out of me when I'm with you. I hope we can get together next week for your birthday. Wednesday 5/10 PM really works for me. I can make turkey burger meat pies or something. Let me know what day is good for you.(I just realized that I fell asleep before sending this. I'm going to bed now and revisit these last few moments in my dreams. Hugs & Kisses, Baby girl

May 6, 2000

Lover, friend, and companion these are all part of being in relationship for me with you... I love what we have and continue to make grow when we are together. Wednesday is the birthday for my friend Sandy she asked if I would help her celebrate. I

agreed suggesting that if you were interested I would like you to join us. It will make it easier for me and her. Anyway let's plan a Tues-pm to Fri-am. With all my love respect and admiration with warm and hot regards, Spencer

May 8, 2000

Hey Lover man,

We grow as two mighty oaks, never overshadowing the other, each willing to nurture the other and share our comfort...(to be continued..)I'm paraphrasing but you get the gist. How ya doing, Sweetie? I've missed you lots. Thanks for telling me that you e-mailed me. The flesh was willing, but the body to tired to answer last night. The computer was the last thing on my very long list of things to do, but talking to you on-line is no chore.

Matter of fact, it's become my favorite pastime, 'cause you write good enough to make me excited reading your e-mails! My goal this week is to juggle my bills so I'll have enough to pay my mortgage, clean up the house, and get somewhat organized, so that by Wednesday PM, after my driving lesson, we'll be able to be together to bring your birthday in with a bang and help cheer up your friend. Then on Thursday, I'll wait for you to come home, so we can bring your birthday in with a bang again and again, and go to work Friday AM. I just got an idea of what we could do, so I'm going to go call you now so I can hear your sweet and sexy voice. Love and whole lot more, Baby

May 13, 2000

Lisa darling,

I've opened my heart to you and I'm a better man for it. I miss you. Please know that we must not let the external forces of things we have no control over, day to day life insecurity, friends, fear, prevent our being open to great possibility in our relationship. What I have learned being in relationship makes me cautious with an open heart. I'm never, higher, stronger, smarter, braver, and more passionate than when in relationship. I know, Yes! I am in two relationships right now. We are in a consensual non-communal polyamorous relationship.

True "polyamory" is where three, four, five, six, etc. People live communally. No one introduces or has sexual liaisons with any new members to the group without the consent of the other members. Safe sex rules apply for new, outside the group romances. If a new member is to be introduced to the group medical exams are required. I say all that to give you something to think about. I'm as serious as a heart attack. I love you. I love Louise. You both love me.

What's any right thinking man to do? No! This is not polygamy!!!! If you met a man and thought he could live with our group that would be a choice you or any other member of the group might consider. Or it could be a closed group of just the three of us. If you were happy would you care what other people thought? What I'm describing has a whole sub-culture that exits within the so-called norms of society.
Visit: http://lovingmorenonprofit.org/,

With all my love, Spencer

May 15, 2000

Hey Big Daddy, I think of what we have created; our own little world to which we invite others to participate in our joy. No one could possibly condemn us. Louise is a very special person in your life and I hope nothing comes between your love. I think that your way of thinking is a practical approach to the situation that we have allowed ourselves to get entangled in. I have no qualms about the rules, because as you already know I've made the men I'm with protect themselves. As I've told you, I have my friendships, but I do want a "relationship" with genuine passion, in which I feel that I am a part. You make me feel wanted and appreciated, which in turn, makes me want you all the more. I agree that open relationships can work as long as the insecurities are discussed and left at the door, and at this point in my life, since I'm not able to be with you as much as I'd like, I'm glad that you're not lonely when I'm not there. It's all good. Hope to see you the week of the 22nd. Love & Kisses, Baby

May 16, 2000

Baby, I love us and all that we may become...I'm very happy for us I miss you a lot, I look forward to the time when we can embrace again, let me know your schedule, do you have e-mail at work? I'm just trying to keep the connection going by the way your pictures you know that special pose I like it a lot and I love what you're saying to me when I look at it, warm, special, loving regards, sealed with a passionate embrace, your Big Daddy

May 21, 2000

Hey Big Daddy, Thanks again for getting those pictures done for us. By the way, I can't send or receive emails at work. I really, really, really missed you this week. God is Sooo Good and so are you!! Love, Baby P.S. Reminder: The girls are coming in on Thursday for lunch, if you're available.

May 22, 2000

Baby girl,

I miss you more than you miss me. I'm glad you realize that you need to do things for you. The more you listen to yourself and be yourself the better it is for us in relationship. Tell me the truth always I want that as much as I want us to succeed. I will do likewise. Let's grow old and wise together like two trees. I trust you baby, I really do. I also treasure us. See you Wednesday at my office. I look forward to our weekend together.

Love always, Big daddy

May 28, 2000

Baby girl,

I love you. I know you know that. I want to let you know that despite our own individual and personal misgivings and trepidation's about falling seriously in love with someone else in our lifetime, we've done it again. Even though you've said this is your First serious relationship, I know you know what love is. And if you didn't know before you know now. I love you. Let's promise to be together at every opportunity that presents itself. I promise to always be there for you if and when you want me. I

have been totally satisfied in so many ways since last we were close. your favorite, Big Daddy

Big Daddy,

My turn to share with you. *To everything there is a season, a time for every purpose under heaven: A time to weep, a time to laugh; A time to mourn, and a time to dance.* Ecclesiastes 3:1,4. It's not WHAT you have in your life, but Who you have in your life that counts. For we will all have eternal life, it is just a matter of where.

June 17, 2000

Baby girl,

"...now you are not only the lover I remember and miss you are the home I am longing for in my memory..." a borrowed line but my real sentiment all my love and my heart your, Big Daddy

June 18, 2000

Big Daddy,

Your 1st e-mail was a great turn-on, your 2nd one was right on time. It must've been you who was calling me so frantically. I'm sorry I was on the phone talking with mom; some serious shit has gone down this week. So much, that my nephew has moved out of my sister's house and is staying with mom.(The same damn house that I paid partial rent for the last 4 months so he could stay... Anyway, that's another story, I shouldn't have ignored the beeps... sorry darlin') Your news is right on time too,

because I didn't tell you this before because I didn't want you to stress (and because I was a little envious), but my friends are going to the Monterey Jazz Festival this week-end and I can't go. But even when I got the worse news in my life tonight, you were there for me, making me feel loved. I know that that was the original intent. But your "I Love Yous" make it all good! Every stroke of the key echoes in my heart and I feel genuine joy. Thank you for being a "real" man. You are my rock, my angel, and a love like no other. I'll pray that you have a safe journey and a fruitful event, and I will call you on Tues. PM. I'll miss you, my one and only love, Hugs and Kisses, Baby Girl

June 27, 2000

Baby girl,

I love you so much it hurts. I'm happy for us. I know how much you love me. I'm going to treat you right baby. You deserve the best. The week is moving slowly. I live every day for us as the weekend when I come alive arrives.

Your, Big Daddy

June 29, 2000

Hey Big Daddy,

Hope the rest of your week has been going well, considering all the sh-- that you have to catch up on. I've just been organizing my emails, and I've discovered that our entire history is chronicled in here. From our first the sunrise at the beach on 10/9/99, until now. It has the emotion and the humor and inner

most thoughts that were developed since the very first real hello, when you picked me up from BART.

I'm going to make a folder just for us and when you come, you can see the progression of a true love/love relationship. It's a trip. So far I have 6 months of us tucked away. It's been a blast to see that we really have made every moment memorable. I am looking forward to Sun. Can't wait to see you and show you how much love I feel for you. You are the best everything!!! Baby

Baby girl,

Of course we will have Sun.am through Tue.pm together I would consider nothing less, save what you want....I am yours body and soul....I'll try to get cut loose early Mon., my boss would probably go for it. Keep collecting the pages darling they are the first book that we are writing together. You are wise and wonderful. Smile darling I love you I can't wait until we're together again. all my love, Big Daddy

July 27, 2000

Hey Big Daddy,

It broke my heart today to hear you so sullen. I wish I could've jump into the phone to smother you with kisses; to be there with you too, to make you feel safe and sexy and happy. The thing to remember is that no matter how long the separation, our hearts still beat as one and our rendezvous is phenomenal. More to discover. More fun to share. More love to make. I never knew how to feel love until I met you. See you soon my love and I'll call you later, Your Baby Girl

MY Baby girl,

You must know that your visit today really touched the deepest part of my heart & soul, I felt your love. I am very happy when I'm with you. You fulfill ALL my desires. If the only thing you take from our relationship in your lifetime is learning the true meaning of love then my life surely has not been in vain. I am a better man because of you. I can't wait (although it appears that it will be awhile) until we do live together. I always want to make our time together happy and filled with love.

I know that when we do get it all together physically, financially, etc. it will be wonderful and wonder filled. I love you baby and I do want to spend the rest of my life living with and loving you. Stay as sweet as you are all my love Big daddy. P.S. - I'm going to make a special dinner Sunday, just for you, be hungry, and get there as soon as you can.

July 29, 2000

Hey Big Daddy,

I was glad you were still up tonight so I could hear you say Darling. Our souls are in synch, we've just got to get the rest of us in check. I think I will get my hair done next week after all, but I'll call you for sure about tonight. All I want to do is be with you. Love, Baby Girl

By this time Lisa and I had become a monogamous couple. I was working full time as an office manager for the **National Writers Union/West**. I was commuting by mass transit train from San Francisco to Oakland. Lisa was in a cycle of office jobs. At one point she had a dot.com job that was walking distance from my job. So on occasion we shared lunch together or spent

time just talking while she would take a break and we would meet in front of her office while she took a cigarette break.

Eventually we made plans to live together. Lisa owned a condominium in Antioch, California. A sixty minute train ride from San Francisco, then another forty minute bus ride to her place. I was still in my apartment. I had lived there on Hayes Street since Bonnie and I had separated. By November we had decided to live together. She rented her condo and moved into my apartment in San Francisco. I was also without a car, as the Honda had died.

Later Lisa was hired by Welles Fargo Auto Finance Division, Walnut Creek in December 2000 as a Lease End Sales Consultant. She was able to get public transit bus and train to get to her job which was closer to Antioch.

November 2000

The journey continues, I've found the love of my life. She is young, beautiful and black, my sweet blackberry pie. This is my last relationship, barring the always unexpected. I will die with her my last true love till death do us part. It's taken me over thirty years of relationship trial and error but I'm happier and more satisfied than I've ever been. I look forward to our life together with great anticipation. My goals now are health, long life a solid evolving relationship, prosperity and continued happiness. Being a black man of a certain age gives me insight into the vast unknown that is called American life. I've had a variety of trials and tribulations but having achieved and accomplished all that I have what I'm not sure.....

My journey low these fifty odd years is one that has both mystified and amazed me at times. I'm not your average black man. In my neighborhood in San Francisco where I've lived for twenty years, the local neighborhood "boyzs 'n tha hood" tuffs call me *"white boy"* when I'm within ear shot. I try not to be within earshot too often.

Because I spend no time on the corner just hangin' they see me as trying to be "white". My friends are a multiethnic mix of black, white, Asian and Hispanic. I come home, I don't mix with them. I cross the street to avoid contact with them and my life is either in my home or with friends. My blood family is all back east. Being a for sure left coast kind of person I've made the San Francisco Bay area my home now for twenty four years, almost as many years as I lived in Detroit. So you say what have you done with your life and what do you feel you might have done with your life? Now as for what I might have done, that is the rub, what might I have done instead of those things mentioned in my shopping list of achievements?

My list does not include any of the myriad of jobs which are not so much accomplishments as necessity for survival. What makes my life any more important, interesting, worthy of chronicle? The answer lies somewhere in the myriad of things already mentioned jobs notwithstanding.

I've been a student of the cinema most of my life and with many articles and now two books about film have turned a corner it seems now on art and my efforts to make it a more integral and cohesive part of my life. It is a great challenge to see myself as more artistic than not. An artist whose work I've discovered and know now in a more profound way and have great admiration for is Man Ray.

Man Ray: Prophet of the Avant-Garde, 1997, 60 min. Color, documentary, from the PBS American Masters series. Produced & directed by Mel Stuart, written by Neil Baldwin based on his book Man Ray: American Artist The program is narrated by Stockard Channing. " They say I'm ahead of the times. I say no, I'm never ahead of the time. It's the others who are behind the times." Man Ray Ray created a significant body of work as a painter, photographer, object maker, and filmmaker.

He was a unique, provocative, innovative and original American artist. "Just be yourself and you will be original." Ray told his students. He was born Emmanuel Radnitsky in 1890 to Russian émigrés in Brooklyn, New York the oldest of four children. Although a bad student he was a distinguished artist at an early age. After high school he seriously pursued art and changed his name to Man Ray. He became an adept photographer photographing his own art work. Ray had good technical training and while living in his studio in Manhattan became a book illustrator and draftsman. He made illustrations of everything from anatomy to machinery. Early American influences on his art and aesthetic include photographer Alfred Steiglitz, whose gallery provided a place for Ray to meet other artists.

In 1913 an International Exhibition of Modern Art brought the art of Cezanne, Pablo Picasso, Georges Braque and Marcel Duchamp to America for the first time. The influence of seeing this work deeply affected Ray who then adopted a cubist approach in his own art. Another early influence on Ray in America was radical feminist Emma Goldman whose magazine Mother Jones used several of his illustrations. In 1922 Ray moved to Paris. While living in Paris, Ray photographed his friends which included Igor Stravinsky, Erik Satie, Arnold Schoenberg,

Georges Braque, T.S. Eliot, James Joyce, Pablo Picasso and Henri Matisse among many others.

Ray expanded the art of photography creating his Ray-o-graph. He took an object and put it on photographic paper exposing the object and paper to light. Then he developed the photograph avoiding using a camera and having no negative. Later he used this technique with motion picture film. When the film he created using this technique was exhibited in Paris the audience responded with shock and disbelief and it created a riot in the theater that required the police to intervene.

Ray said, 'My works are designed to amuse, bewilder annoy and inspire reflection." In his life, he never achieved the critical or financial success of many of his artist peers. His work did not sell well until he died in 1976 at age eighty-six. His major works now sell for millions of dollars. In the DVD there is an essay by Neil Brown that describes that Ray was a man influenced and inspired by the women he loved. Ray lived with and loved four women in extended relationships.

Adon LaCroix a Belgian poet became his first wife. Kiki of Montparnesse, a dancer. She and Ray lived together for six years. Lee Miller who was a fashion model met Ray and asked to become a pupil and they were together three years. His last love was Juliet Browner who was a dancer. She lived with Ray more than thirty years until his death.

All his lady loves were models he used in his work as subject, inspiration and muse. Ray saw the women in his life as desired, erotic, companions and sometimes colleagues. For more information on Man Ray visit: http://www.manraytrust.com/

Man Ray/Lee Miller Partners in Surrealism is an exhibit in the **Peabody Essex Museum** in Salem, Ma that ran from

7/11/11-12/4/11. The exhibit chronicles and codifies the power of their relationship as teacher/student and lovers. The exhibit feature work by both artists' created during their affair in love and the arts. Their art work together produced powerful contemporary art and photography. The exhibit combines rare vintage photographs; paintings; sculpture and drawings. Their art work is considered some of the most important in *European Surrealism*.

I realize now at this point in my own life that the women in my life have had a major influence of my life and work. As I entered the relationship with Lisa Grant I had no way of knowing the profound influence she would have on my life. Lisa although eighteen years younger than me was very worldly and wise in ways that made me more mature by being with her, being inspired by her and deciding to pursue our dreams together.

Lisas' mom Eliza Grant passed (1928-2001) and we attended her funeral in Florida. I met many of her family.

My love and life with Lisa is rewarding, challenging and satisfying, yet I feel there is much yet for us to do/achieve together. My life with Lisa my wife to be is grand and a challenge to my very being as she becomes more and more my reason for being. George Hill came to visit and spent the night. Funny how time and space help to give perspective on friends. His four children all now grown are his reason for being with that he can be proud. What will I leave besides a more experience worldly

and wiser wife behind when I'm gone? Lisa dislikes looking ahead to what time will do to our relationship and our eighteen year age difference. When I look back at my life I marvel at all I've done, where I was, where I've gone and what I've come to and what might be. My years of living in Detroit compared to my years of life in San Francisco are like two unmatched bookends.

July 7, 2002, 3pm, Las Vegas

Our visit to the land of dreams and riches has yielded a mixed bag of emotions and ideas. The up side, Lisa has taken our personal investment and belief in each other and asked me to marry her. This is the real McCoy- license, ceremony and friends, the details are partially sketched and will be filled in, set once we get back to San Francisco.

On the flip side The Bell Family Reunion which was our original reason for being in Lost Wages has proven to be a mixed bag of notions. Nia, Lisa's' friend invited us to attend her family reunion and a chance for us to meet and greet her family. They are a close nit group of Bells' and other extended family by marriage, were fun and funny. I envy the fact that their closeness has been almost annually and grows with each new generation. Nia aka Bernadette is a thirty something with grand desires and ideas that she focuses on her currently chosen profession of jewelry-maker.

I love Lisa and look forward to marriage and life till death does us part. After many years of being on the edge it's over the cliff we go into the wonderful unknown of time, space and being with the unlimited potential of two people in search of harmony and fulfillment.

July 16, 2002 6am

Plane trip on behalf of **NWU** Delegate Assembly. My trip through the neighborhood produced visions of street memorials to fallen members of the community felled by violence. Lisa is solemn and sad at my departure, expressing her love and deep affection for my essence and being, departing for a week of lonely separation. My ability to travel as I please whether it is for work or pleasure it seems to me was built on the backs of my ancestors.

Just what does the contemporary 21st century Black American owes to his ancestors besides genes strong enough to survive from the 16th century to now? When I watch parents with children I have a sense of envy tempered by the reality of what it would mean to be a parent. Could I, would I be of a mind to scribble streams of consciousness with children near or dangling from my neck or arms.

July 19, 2002 day 4 NWU D.A.- Hampshire College, Amhearst, MA

Funny lines overheard, "...my room reminded me of jail...", "...I can't share a room I didn't bring any panties or pajamas...". The staff worked till 2am yesterday prepping material for the start of the day's sessions. Last night besides that, there was a tremendous and wonderful storm with much needed rain, thunder and lightning.

July 21, 2002, 7:45pm PST

Somewhere over America on a Continental flight from Cleveland to San Fransico. Thank goodness the NWU DA is over. Each year, and this is my third DA, it seems to get harder.

My weight is my shield when I'm encountered on the mean streets brothers say, *"... hey big man..."* then whatever petty rap whether it's for change or to sell me some hot goods. They recognize that with my size if they challenged me to a fight my size alone would create a challenge for them. So my weight is my shield against all the oppression and injustice, potential unwarranted or unwanted attacks of life, people, the US way of life. Is it really living, my weight is my shield.

Lisa and I were married on September 15th, 2002. One of her friends made the pool cabana in her condo complex available for the event. Lisa and I got decorations and a public address system. Lisa and her friends decorated, we invited probably between her friends and mine about thirty people.

We had a mutual friend take pictures and he produced two wonderful albums of photos of the entire event. One album was for my mother in Detroit. Lisa decided we would honeymoon in Detroit and take my mom her album personally.

October 4, 2002

Waiting in NW Air terminal in Detroit Lisa and I have spent an event filled week here. Mom got sick. We took her by EMS to the hospital and she is thank goodness on the mend. I was able to introduce Lisa to my long time Detroit friends.

October 9, 2002

What a long strange journey my life has been. I'm now happily married. I did not think that was something that would be for me. I did not know if the right person came along

convention or no I would take the plunge, I've jumped the broom with a woman young enough to be my daughter. My choice comes after a decade long search for a real soul mate she is that and she is all that the transgressions and travels of my youth led inexorably to her now we are two but as one.

I spoke with Mom today who is home from the hospital. All is well she has neighbor as caregiver, Lucille who knows her and loves, her as a friend, for whom she is, my mind is at ease. I committed to having mom and her sister Constance come for an extended visit come summer 2003. The goal is for mom to have a companion while she adjusts to California and by 2004 or 2005 at the latest for her to live with Lisa and me. A tall order, no matter what I envision.

October 17, 2002

Three days before the biggest move of my life moving from San Francisco to Antioch. Moving from an apartment where I lived longer than any other place in my life - twenty-two years and quite a few relationships later it's time to move on.

It is all together fitting that I get married and begin a new life with my bride in a home she was buying before we met. Antioch also fitting as Antioch College opened doors to a new life in San Francisco when I graduated from their San Francisco center in 1977. Now twenty-five years later the city of Antioch offers prospects for a new life with my wonderful wife Lisa.

October 23, 2002 8:15am

Pittsburgh/Bay Point Bart station, second day of commuting the trips is long and boring, AM express bus to BART yesterday PM bus ride from hell. Two sets of BeBe's kid's, a one hour ride interrupted by three ten minute stops along the way what a drag. Weather turning cold making commute a lot less friendly, leaving house at 7am to get to work by 10am.

October 20, 2002 2:45pm Oakland

I've been given notice by e-mail that my job will be gone soon. I'm overwhelmed. I'm being given moral support by Joel Washington a member of the Executive Board.

December 08, 2002

12th St., BART, Oakland, Its official my office is to be closed 12/31/02 with my last payroll on 1/6/03. A relief and a big drag. Have I been so unwise it is this I gotta' get a job thing blues again, new vistas, new horizon and opportunities, never the same twice. If there is a lesson to be learned then it is that change is a constant of life. My blessings are Lisa, Lisa & Lisa and the house and her job.

December 20, 2002

Bought Lisa her holiday gifts. My e-burst to friends and foes produced enough job leads for a minute. Using final comp day today, next week is the end of the National Writers Union/Oakland office. Dec.31, being my drop dead day to have

the office packed and closed. A door closes a window opens god grant me the strength and intuition to find a good solid well-paying reasonably interesting long lasting job. I've been up since 4AM.

December 27, 2002 4pm Marriott, Oakland

I've spent the better part of this day closing the office. Clearly the end of an era. I have regrets recriminations, bitterness, remorse and angst and stress in general now that I'm UNEMPLOYED. I met with my pal Kenn Graddick last weekend. We had been incommunicado for the better part of five months. It seems the stresses in his life had lain him low an unable to communicate to anyone, family, work, and friends. I was more than concerned. Until his stress related disorder we had been close as friends, buddies, homies, for many years. The good news is he is better.

January 7, 2002, 10:30pm PST, San Francisco Fritj Cafe, Hayes St

Simple expression by the working like, "... *payroll is once a week or every other week*?" one employee query to another brings on the angst of being gainfully unemployed.

Yesterdays' **OPRAH** focused on the story of an individual's life. She visited a small town in Louisiana at the request of an audience member. Oprah flew in her plane to visit the town. Within an hour of Oprahs' arrival the Mayor and half the town showed up. Oprah wanted to see if as the woman had suggested, "... *my town lives you*." Indeed before Oprah left she and her hostess had become the Grand Marshall in their local college pep rally and Oprah succeeded in finding out more

about "...*the town that loves her.*" We learn more about the town and the woman's family. The best story was of an individual who was an African who though born in Africa was educated and grew up in Cuba. It was there he developed his reason for being which was to become a doctor like his mother, which he did. He married a Cuban woman and moved to Chicago to practice medicine and give something back to the community because of his good fortune. Compelling and heart-warming. My life pales by comparison.

Antonio Carlos Jobims music has an inexorable quieting, soothing, reassuring ennobling, and energizing quality.

January 24, 2003 11am Jack London Square, Barnes & Noble Cafe

I got up with Lisa and the chickens, around oh dark hundred. I took the bus and BART to San Francisco. I checked my bank balances. I had Chinese food for breakfast. I took BART to downtown Oaktown. San Francisco still has its scores of begging homeless. I gave a weeping crack ravaged woman a dollar and twenty feet away another homeless person immediately qued up and asked for money.

I've got a phone interview with the City Car Share organization of which I am a member. I feel fairly confident. If I must return to physical form after death let it not be a pigeon. Human existence is full of unimaginable twists and turns, foibles, follies and foolishness.

I wonder as I wander will this book of meanderings ever tell the whole story that is the miasma called life which has liberty, adventure, happiness, sorrow, pain, woe, joy and finally death. Is death the end or the beginning, I think probably another beginning. Will death be a continuation, echo, extension, reflection, or a completely different form of life.

4:45pm Atrium Bar, Marriott, Downtown Oakland, I watched **The Lord of The Rings: The Two Towers** (2002). It moves faster than part one. There is more action as the trailer said two great armies in the battle for Middle-earth and it spares nothing in terms of action. The battle scenes both live action and computer enhanced are vivid and energetic. The most interesting character was a pale skinny computer generated character named Gollum. Gollum is conflicted from the time we meet him until the last frame leading of course to Part 3. Gollum's conflict albeit an age old one seemed very natural. His superego and Id are conflicted between the poles of being good and being evil. He spends much of this film verbalizing his inner demons bouncing from trying to do good and the right thing to being overwhelmed by his inner demons, much like man today.

On BART to San Francsco, Lisa and I have come to an important juncture in our relationship. We are at odds regarding the return visit with intentions of staying journey to California by her sister. I vociferously disapproved of her using our home as a port of entry and return to California. Last night we exchanged harsh words. Today Valentine's Day we kissed and made up and we agreed no sister living in our home and using it to get back into California dreaming. She will be back but not at our house blues again.

My life now is series of sweaty fitful nights, not the good sweats of hot steamy intercourse. All wishful thinking on my part. Unemployment insurance has kicked in with the first check. The big surprise was a money order from an assortment of **NWU** Officers and Board members as a way of acknowledging my past quality work for them. Lisa and I both agreed it was a nice gesture. My solace is in knowing the organization increased membership and is better and more efficiently run, thanks to all my hard work.

Now it's on to the next job until my retirement at 62. My new magic number I'll be 55 this year so in seven years 2010 a nice round number. My life goes on like this journey to San Francisco which is a two hour commute in the AM using an express bus that takes 45 minutes then a train ride of an hour. Today is my day for me to dig and be dug in return. I'm meeting Lisa later in downtown Oaktown for dinner and a drive home courtesy of Rideshare.

March 6, 2003, 4:30pm, Atrium Bar, Oakland Marriott hotel

Hangin' in Oaktown Blues again! The movie of the day was Michael Moore's disturbing documentary **Bowling for Columbine**. A scary look at violence and our love of guns. The epiphany of the film comes when we meet two of the young men who were shot in the Columbine High School massacre both carrying bullets in their bodies that could not be removed. One young man was a quadriplegic the other walked with great difficulty. They along with Moore confronted K-Mart regarding the sale of ammunition over the counter much as it was available to the two young men who shot them. Within a few days of their timely visit to K-Mart corporate offices the company stopped the

over the counter sale of ammunition through their stores. That is using media to make effective social change.

March 28, 2003, 3pm, Nordstrom's shopping centre, basement

I am waiting patiently while Lisa visits the doctor for a yearly exam. We are in San Francisco in preparation for a bus trip to Reno, NV. The trip was organized by some of Lisa's friends. Life in Antioch temporarily has, Lisa's' woe begone sister living with us. That girl is a drama queen. The most innocent thing becomes drama. I believe it comes with her being a native New Yorker. New Yorkers generally have drama as an innate part of their personality, mores the pity. I guess the good news is she has a job, she just got paid and I hope in the next week to see her move into her own place. My own psyche suffers both physically, emotionally and spiritually while I'm trying to find myself again in relation to work.

March 28, 2003 6:30pm on the bus to Reno, Waiting patiently.

The odyssey was getting there. We started waiting at 5pm on Mission & 5th for a bus till 5:30 missing two buses in the process trying to get to 1st & Market. Finally we walk to Market each with two shoulder bags, a suitcase and two bags of food for the trip.

We get to the point of departure about 5:45p and now are waiting for late arrivals and I hope we depart soon. Now moving even as I write, Thank goodness!

March 29, 2003 12:30pm Baldinis Casino, Sparks, NV

So far the trip has yielded some cash rewards, Lisa winning on the slots the cost of our trip including her sisters' fare. We

won $55 on the bus with one of the little bus lotteries run by the hostesses of the trip. The ride up last night was filled with lots of alcohol hard and soft. So as a result the bus riders who were a mixed load of mostly black, some white and a few Hispanic is a real American bus ride. The driver was great in his abilities on the road and in his good humor and care for his passengers. After a half hour of slow traffic and alcohol the din of noise aka conversation rose significantly at times the louder they got the louder they got. The raffles were a pleasant break in the high school and sophomoric alcohol laden behavior. I say this all in great good humor and admiration for our collective resilience as our country wages war with Iraq and we are on the verge of World War 3.

3pm Cal Neva Casino, Reno, NV,

Americans have become inured of war and its consequences. Television makes the war seem much like a video game, except young Americans and young Iraqis will die because of it. I and ashamed now more than at any time in my life to declare I'm American. I was never fond of expressing that under any circumstances but now more than ever I'm ashamed to be an American. Will Lisa and I and our families live through the darkest period of American history being led by His Fraudulency and his gang of war mongering thugs.

How to survive and do more than that, which is what the powers that be want, is that we only survive and not thrive and make love and art and try to make this sordid world a better place to live and do more than just live. Gambling the poor man's stock exchange. It's less complicated then the real stock investment portfolio equation and produces faster more

immediate results. That's why the rich and powerful have made gaming clearly one of the fastest growing industries in the U.S.

July 16, 2003 10:30am
Jack London Square, Oaktown, Barnes & Noble Cafe

Mom arrives for a lengthy 22 day visit on Friday in two days. I've finally made arrangement and am getting a medical/physical exam this PM. Prior blood and urine tests for insurance revealed no known problems. Let's hope this pattern continues with/after today's physical. Lisa and I have done mostly all we could to get the house ready for mom's visit from a physical perspective.

The last bit left is storing things away and some cleaning. I've applied for a teaching job with a new charter school being started by the S.F. Sheriffs' Department. I hope my prior contacts and the video we produced **Art From Jail** (1991) at least serve as entree to an interview at least.

August 8, 2003, 8:30am, Momi Tobys Cafe, San Francisco

Mom has come and spent twenty-two days with Lisa and I and it was memorable. Mom and I spent most days just hanging out watching the tube and being. She had a chance to meet Lisa's sister and her sister's lover and even Keith, her sisters son, Lisa's nephew. All in all it was a very good visit. We bought a Van while she was here. She was there with us as two bruthas' who were salesmen got us a deal on a Burgundy color, Dodge Caravan with 49K miles for $9K plus financing with no money down with me as buyer and no co-signer.

Mom had a good opportunity to see the character and nature of Lisa, her sister and her lover. So, she has a good understanding of what I have to go through dealing with them individually and as a group of women. The low point was a day long excursion to Santa Cruz that ended with Mom and I stranded on the beach alone in the dark and cold wondering when Lisa, Lisa's sister, her lover, and one of her sister's friends would remember us, the food, blankets etc. and bring us the key to the van. We had trauma going, we got lost and more trauma coming home ending in us going back via Highway 1, the long way around through San Francisco, Oakland and home a long ignoble day.

Mom is definitely up for the move to the coast and no snow and warm weather. I said eighteen months, she thinks longer. Moms' adopted daughter Lucille is also up for moving with Mom so this will make the transition easier as she will have a full time care giver/roommate, which I like a lot. Mom said she will tell Lucille what her impressions were and believes Lucille is as ready to leave Detroit as she is this is a very good thing.

August 28, 2003, 2pm Antioch, Marina Park

We're financial solvent now that second mortgage has produced money in liquid equity. In law blues as Lisa's' sister and her lover try to use and abuse me as their personal chauffer while they resolve personal transportation issues. It took Lisa days to finally see through their scheme. I knew from jump what they were up to...

Lisa's sister has been missing for a week or more and her sister's lover is frantic. When she does emerge, Lisa has told me she no longer has interest in helping her sister ever again.

2004

January 30, 2004 3:30pm, Nordy Plaza, San Francisco

I arrived early for brother Marvin Xs' *Book Fair and Poetry University* event being held today and tomorrow in the Tenderloin of San Francisco. Participants scheduled to appear included world class writers like Ishmael Reed, Amiri Baraka, Sonia Sanchez, Kalamu Ya Salaam and a few dozen other local and international writers. Things were moving slowly, only a few authors and vendors were set up. There was no open mike with poets as scheduled. From now until 5:30p or so authors are signing books and networking, I left and will go back around 6p for the dinner stay awhile and split.

San Francisco is enigmatic and colorful especially in the Tenderloin where the event is being held in the basement of St. Boniface Church. For those unfamiliar the Tenderloin is home to the outcasts of society, every corner is another life filled with trauma and much drama. The effects of drugs and alcohol can be seen everywhere.

I met one of the filmmakers in my book **Reel Black Talk** at the fair, Allen Willis. He has a table full of literature that he has written under the nom de plume of John Allan. He has and does write extensively on socialist ideas and reviews books by authors not generally known to the general public. I had some nice chats with a few of the vendors. Marvin is to be commended for pulling a rabbit out of a hat with no hat and no rabbit but there it is a world class book fair produced by black people with world

renowned authors from all over the country participating. I feel like such a poser even attending.

I met Marvin X through the **National Writers Union**. Marvin X is a writer who was/is part of the Black Arts Movement that emerged in the 60's civil rights era as the artistic expression of black people. The aims and aspirations were/are for a unique and original aesthetic that reflected the black experience with a more revolutionary fervor following the assassination of Malcolm X. The east coast writers Amiri Baraka, Sonia Sanchaez, Nikki Giovanni, David Henderson and Calvin Hernton were some of the writers who took the time to make institutions that encouraged publishing, theater production, poetry readings and created a foundation for black writers and artists to survive and thrive in their own community.

Marvin X was part of the west coast group of writers who saw the emergence of their fellow artists as a clear clarion call to take up the cause of making a foundation for a unique black aesthetic. Ishamael Reed, Ed Bullins, Ron Karenga, Askia Toure worked their ideas into plays, novels, poetry and visual art. The impact of all of these writers certainly can be said to have influenced writers who emerged to more national prominence like August Wilson, Ntozake Shonge, Maya Angelou, Toni Morrison and Alice Walker. I am indebted to their groundbreaking and path making work of all of these visionary artists from both coasts.

Lisa died March 1, 2004 I'm devastated. The week finds her family and some of her friends believing I had something to do with her death. The coroner told me if there was even a hint of suspicion I'd be talking with the police and not him. Cause of death is listed as a pulmonary thromboembolism, a blood clot. I cannot describe my terror and shock as she went from breathing one minute and not breathing the next, I'm calling 911 talking with the first the operator then an Emergency Medical tech on delivering CPR and by that time an EMS truck, a fire emergency unit and the police are there.

They spent quite a while trying to revive her then finally decide to take her to the hospital. I follow in panic with the police assuring me they would lock up the house. I arrive they tell me to wait in the chapel. Around 2am they say they got her heart going but could not get her to breath. It was over I was more shocked and stunned than I've ever been in my life. My life, I have it she doesn't. Funeral services are one week from today, followed by cremation as was her wish.

My big worry, debts with no money forth coming from insurance because the coroner is spending six to ten weeks trying to figure out why she had a blood clot thus all insurance policies are on hold and the bills pile up. I've resorted to begging via the internet and e-mail to my family and friends. So far some money, some promises of more it is hard to fully grieve with the drama of suspicious family and friends all around. My friends are going the extra mile to help me. I'm waiting at SFO for Mom she will stay two weeks possibly longer that is the best news of this very sad week I can't believe this is/has happened to me.

March 6, 2004 10:30am SFO

Mom comes to California and helps me regroup. The plan is Mom and I will live together in Atlanta to be near family. We have a few dozen relatives there.

April 3, 2004 10:15am

BART, My wife has been dead for more than a month I still am too stunned to believe it's real. Various family (hers) and friends (hers) have made my life a living hell. First there were innuendos and accusations that I killed my wife. Now the struggle is over blood money of insurance and who should get how much. If that isn't hell on earth then I don't know what is. Then the van has had a plethora of repairs a battery and charger then brakes and just this past week a new transmission. Everything that could go wrong has.

The light through all this has been our true friends who gave enough money so I would not go homeless and loose the house and could pay bills till insurance money arrives. I'm never sure from day to day just what to expect and how to handle it. The true friends and there are many and my mother and our family have held me up with prayer and good wishes. Lisa I miss you so much it hurts!

April 4, 2004 11pm

Home, What is a home when there is nothing to come home to....All alone writing at home all alone? Meaning in my life I have to put meaning back into my life right now it has no meaning.

April 17, 2004 1pm Jack London Square

Lonely so lonely, I could die. Words that have a much more profound meaning now than at any time in my life. My financial house is somewhat in order, with half the insurance policies having paid off, so as a result I've paid Lisa's sister and put her and her lover on a short leash. Her son does not care about the money one way or the other. But I will send him some money by month's end when the checks clear. I miss Lisa soooooo much.

What meaning does my life have now? I lost the most precious thing in my life aside from my own life. I lost my wife, why, why, why! Why me, why now, why her, why? I cannot at this time make sense of her death I may never make sense of it. What did I do to deserve this?

Sat. May 1, 2004, 7pm Antioch

Its' been two months since Lisa died I cannot believe I am writing these words to say that this has been the most unreal two months does not do justice to my daily struggle with various and sundry different aspects of the estate of a loved one. It's a full time job and one hellava struggle every day since none of the things I do regarding my late wife's estate will bring her back to me. I've cried some but life's challenges keep me so pent up with frustration that I feel blocked from my depths of grief.

May 12, 2004 2:30pm
Jack London Square Oakland, Barnes & Noble Café

The latest distraction is one of Lisa's' girlfriends exhibiting signs of jealousy. She called and castigated and upbraided me

for "...inviting a strange woman into Lisa's house..." and that "...I was doing damage to her memory..." because I'd "... invited someone into Lisa's' house..." Because in my latest e-post to family and friends I'd mentioned that I had invited Lucille Lightfoot a dear friend of my Mom and our family to stay with Mom for half the time Mom will be here. She was very upset and by telling her a lie and apologizing was I then able to get off the phone.

I'm overwhelmed. This is unbelievable I'm not making this up. If one of Lisa's' girlfriends feel this do others on my e-post list also feel this angry as well or is she so far out in left field, she's playing some other game. Some people Lisa and I were nice to have turned on me.

May 31, 2004

It is transition time, I'm selling the house and moving to who knows where. Lisa help me?

June 4, 2004 5pm Antioch

I'm at a loss for words, my heartaches, I'm frustrated, mystified and just overwhelmed by the loss of my wife. People tearing at me and sniping at me during my time of grief. I'm set free and chained by life and its inexorable variety, pain, pleasure, mystery and unfathomable qualities, when you lose your wife of only a few years. I hope people understand I'm not myself now, I'm not sure who I am and what I'm doing.

June 6, 2004 9pm 2200 Peppertree Way #2, Antioch

Why am I here now in this place at this time having gone through so much and there is yes, still so much more that I cannot put here what it does, has done, is doing to me at every hour of the day and night and with every breath I take! 28 year cycles, 1948-1976/28, 1976-2004/28, my life at 56.

July 12, 2004 7am
Jack London Square, Oakland Garage, level E, 5th floor

Here I sit facing an overcast grey sunrise with a view of downtown Oakland and the harbor. I miss my wife so much I'm still very numb from Lisa's' death. I can't describe the inexorable pain I feel and the great sense of loss and so much unrealized potential. My wife would have been 38 had she lived. I still do not believe that this has happened to me. I seem to be out of my body watching this person trying to make their way in the world.

I'm excited in a muted kind of way about the move to Atlanta. My cousin Michael Simmons had a real estate agent contact me so I responded to her e-mail query with a question of my own. Can I get a house without a job but with a down payment and money to pay the note? I'm feeling optimistic about things in some moments but in other moments my belief, my faith in myself, in humanity, waivers and I tremble with fear.

Every day is still the most difficult day of my life. I cannot explain the hurt and anguish I feel. My choices now will go a long way towards making the process which will be creating a path for the rest of my life are very important significant and key choices. In this so called great land of ours now at war with the

Arab world in the beginning of Amerikas new hundred years war with the Arab world.

It seems oddly beyond coincidence that we are fighting for liberation of oil for the sellers in this country to be making some of their highest profit in years. I'm angry; I hope the rest of Amerika gets angry at the Bush crime family.

The Michael Moore documentary **Farenheit 9/11** which has stirred so much protest because it indicts the Bush crime family and regime for its shameless acts of greed , destruction and avarice. I hope America runs the Bush crime syndicate right out of the country. I wonder as I watch children play what kind of world we are creating for their future. What kind of a world indeed!

Michael Moore has earned $187.3 million dollars with his films a total of 7. On average he earns $26.8 million per film, his Fahrenheit 9/11, earned $119.2 million. (18) He makes documentary films. They all have his distinct point of view. The films all address the social and political issues of our time.

Sicko (2007) our health care system or a lack of it as I write. **The Big One** (1997) the environment. **Canadian Bacon** (1995), cold war politics. **Roger and Me** (1985), General Motors destruction of the infrastructure of Flint, Michigan which presaged GM's own ultimate demise and resurrection with government bailouts.

He had a short-lived (1995-1997) television series titled **TV Nation**, a magazine format program that addressed the issues of the day and put a satiric and poignant twist on issues and ideas of our time, social, political and other wise. The program won an EMMY (1994) and was nominated for several others.In 2002 his book <u>Stupid White Men...and Other Sorry Excuses for the State of</u>

the Nation, had reached #1 on the New York Times non-fiction list. On the day after his infamous "Oscar Backlash", where he attacked both George W. Bush and the Iraq war, attendance for his movie **Bowling for Columbine** (2002) went up 110%. The following weekend, the box office for the film was up 73%. Here is a man of both convictions and actions. He stands up and he stands for something.

Moore was interviewed by television host **Tavis Smiley**, **PBS** (2010). Moore expressed disappointment and despair on these contemporary American times. He sees fear being used to control people. Which we know from our past is a very dangerous social pattern. Moore elaborated that people are being dumbed down, especially with forty million people who can be classified as illiterate, seven thousand young people a day dropout rate for high school. These things make the American people easy to manipulate. Capitalism has failed and the American people need to create a non-violent citizens movement to stop the forces of destruction of our way of life. Moore went on to describe how the banks are still unregulated despite their failures; people with the money are still controlling the fate of our nation. There is a growing chorus of progressive voices that includes working class whites, Blacks, Hispanics, gay & lesbian people who are discontented with the Democratic congress.

Moore won an Academy Award for **Bowling for Columbine** (2002) he has been nominated for another nineteen awards and won thirty three awards nationally and internationally for his films, including the Freedom of Speech Award from the US Comedy Arts Festival in 2003.

Sunday Aug 1, 2004 11pm Petaluma

I've spent most of the day and evening laughing with my old Detroit friends Lynne Prather, George Socha, Jerry Silhanek and his wife Michelle Glead. Jerry and Michelle have been very gracious hosts all day and evening. My throat aches from the laughter, this time with friends is just what I need now more than at any time in my life.

August 9, 2004 9pm Antioch

Thank You Lisa, without your love and foresight I would be nothing. A journey begins to the south and home till the end we shall see....

Now on to more timely matters namely our new Atlanta house. I'll be speaking/writing in plural as Mom and I will inhabit the new domicile. Today I met the agent at the house for an inspection and the better news is the price has come down $2K. The best news is the California house has a serious bidder.

Noon, November 8, 2004

Greenbriar Parkway Mall, Picadilly Cafeteria, Atlanta, GA,

The topic of conversation amongst the staff and patrons is the film **Ray** starring Jamie Foxx as Ray Charles. The script and performances are excellent. My pick for Best Film and Best Actor. The women in the film are also very good. It's now two months plus in Hotlanta. I met with Ayoka Chenzira another filmmaker from my book **Reel Black Talk**. She invited me to her birthday party and introduced me to a variety of Atlanta's best, Black and brightest. I've begun a fictional memoir based on someone I knew who left me their journals, memoirs, stories, articles and diaries. This is a challenge for me on a lot of different levels. Not the least of which is the rights and clearances conundrum. Time will tell but as usual it's not talking.

For my first Thanksgiving in Atlanta, I invited Mom to come to Atlanta and spend time with my cousin Linda Simmons and I in her home. The day before Thanksgiving I told Mom we were going to lunch with a friend of Linda's'. When Cheryl Kinsey arrived we got in my car and drove to a building and walked in together. Mom was a little confused as it was not a restaurant but an office building, but the distinct aroma of food could be smelled as we waited in the lobby after being told the person we were there to see would be with us shortly. I told mom, " You better sit down girl we're about to buy a house." She sat and almost started crying right then. I said, "Don't cry now Mom it's too late, we're buying a house today." Ms. Kinsey, my Real Estate agent had made these arrangements at my request. After we signed all the papers and gave them a check, the four of us went and had lunch. Now Mom and I are officially residents of Atlanta. The reason the office smelled of food was they were doing so many closings that day and as a special treat for staff they had catered the lunch time meal for staff.

December 19, 2004 Atlanta, GA

I arrived August 30. I had a room in my families' house. I had a phone, I got a P.O. Box, I bought a car, I bought a house, I moved Mom in with me and I have no wife. My pain is still great. I'm incapable of expressing in words my deep sorrow at the early and it seems unnecessary death of my wife **Lisa Rhenette Grant Moon (1966-2004).**

New Year, 2005

Mom and I adjust to living together again. I am now a son again. She is now Mom again as we live together. "...parents and children can only walk side by side, never together; there is a deep ditch between them across which they can pass to each other from time to time a little love." (19)

January 18, 2005 8:30pm Atlanta

With Fela on the box pounding his relentless African beat accompanied by horns, guitars and voices my brain throbs and seethes. My pain and anguish over the death of my wonderful and special wife Lisa has not abated it has ebbed and flowed like the cycles of the moon. I feel drawn to my future untethered but buoyed by the earthly things my love did for me before she left this hard, harsh and sometimes horrific existence we call living. Please forgive me Lisa for all the pain and suffering I caused you in this life. In the next life where I know you are with family and at peace.

Thank You, Lisa for all you did to make my Mom and our lives as good as it is right now and it is full and rich with great potential. Thank You Lisa, I miss you so much.

March 7, 2005

I miss Lisa now more than before our lives, my Mom and I are different now that we live together again as man and chief

provider my role is different from when Mom and I lived together with roles reversed. The pain and angst of Lisa's death has dulled some of my intuitive senses I cannot here really reveal all that has gone on with me mentally, psychologically, physically. I know I want to be true to my one true self for the remainder of my life....

March 16, 2005 Noon EST, Atlanta

What lesson in life and living do I need to learn from my current situation? Of course I do not have an answer at my fingertips, but I do know that there is much to be learned from what I have and am going through mentally, spiritually, physically, psychically. I need to learn that my happiness should not be based on making others happy with me.

March 24, 2005 10am, Atlanta

If as is if as indicated there is a divine plan the laws of karma and reincarnation are true.... Why me, why now, why Lisa?

September 13, 2005 8pm EST

I've been in Atlanta a little more than a year (Aug.31, 2004). I've moved my life and my Mom to a very different environment the weather, the people, the ideas, the economy. I'm trying to find work using Gladwell's "Tipping Point" theory. So far I've had many introductions.

October 15, 2005 3pm Picadilly restaurant, Greenbriar Mall

Life has seen fit to open doors for me/us. A new friend Angela Knox introduced me to people and I've done a guest lecture at a local high school.

November 8, 2005 3:30pm

The Black Mans' Film Festival and the three films I saw were like an oasis in a desert. The oasis of documentary films in the Festival quenched a very thirsty man....Sometimes I feel lost in a wilderness as I adjust to life anew.

My dreams of late included my late wife for the first time. The dream with her was pleasant and reinforces my yearning for consciousness.

Saturday, November 19, 2005 8am
Oakland, CA, Lynne and Mikes house

The journey from Atlanta to Oakland to bury and remember my friend **Kenn Graddick** (11/30/49-11/10/05) draws to a close. Thusday PM at the wake seeing his son Chandler and grieving wife Francee was difficult. It was there she informed that she had put me in the services as one who would remember Kenn to family and friends in my own words. My sleep that night was intermittent and very tearful.

When my time to speak came to speak about our great and wonderful friendship I do remember I said, "*Today is one of the saddest days in my life, today is one of the happiest days in my life...*" I was barely able to get through with my words between sobs and tears. At the post wake repast that followed the service,

people made a point of telling me how touched they were by my own personal expression of grief and how heart felt it seemed to them. This was a great relief for me. I will miss you Kenn and I will always remember you.

December 21, 2005, 12:30pm

I've survived the death and funeral of my best male friend. I've continued to network with people here in Atlanta. My heart is full at year's end and holiday time with the pain of missing my wonderful, special and brilliant wife. She said to me so often I can hear her say to me that, "... you're so brilliant." My brilliance was in marrying her because had I not done that which was one of my most selfish acts, marrying someone who loved the sight and sound of me despite my flaws and made me a better man I would not be here in this moment with my mother and I both safe and secure with home and hearth at this holiday time of year. Thank you Lisa, I miss you so much it still hurts.

December 28, 2005 7:30pm

The end of my second holiday season here in the deep south. I end 2005 in a new home with Mom, both of us widowed.

CHAPTER SIX

The challenge now was learning to be the son of my mother who was seventy-two and me being fifty-six. We had not lived together since I was in my late teens. She was very supportive as I tried to recover from having my life turned up-side down and now transplanted to the South meeting and being with and our old yet new family. There are no words that can describe the major shift in every pore of my being down to the smallest molecule of my existence.

Mom cooked, cleaned, did laundry and stayed active within the house. I cleaned my area downstairs where I had taken residence. She had the whole house upstairs to herself. This worked and allowed me the necessary space to take stock, breath, grieve and try to make sense of life. Being alive, losing my young wife so quickly and tragically. Now as I continue to relive that moment of her leaving the earthly plane I still fell a deep indescribable chasm in my heart and soul that will never go away. Such pain, it hurts beyond words.

Mom did comment later that when I was in my space I played the music rather loudly initially. She let me and never complained. She said I later, *"...toned it down...".* She knew some of what I was dealing with being twice widowed herself. Both her husbands died slow deaths from illness. She stood by their side

until they passed. I always admired her great courage. I know I acquired some of her courage and that helped me through this sometimes awful time, to get through it to the other side.

After my first step father (Howard Finley) passed I saw what it had done to my mother, she was clearly worn down, but a survivor. After my second (James Jackson) stepfather passed she was even more worn down because she was older. My quest in the first year included seeing that Mom got to an assortment of doctors, a general practitioner, a gastrointestinal specialist, an optometrist. Her health issues included glaucoma, Crohns disease and emphysema. I found all these doctors through the Crawford Long Medial hospital, it was recommended by my family here because of its connection to Emory University and its proximity to our home. Once we had established her medical care that was now part of things I needed to stay up to date with medicines and doctor visits.

Finding a job and establishing a new life here in Atlanta also became an immediate concern.

Through the efforts of a woman I met, I secured a Guest Lecture at a local high school. It turned out to be a lesson in what I know, what I needed to know and how I am perceived. A spin on a bad experience ultimately. It did not lead to another guest lecture. For me America and all that, that word conjures both real and imagined was a conundrum. Thinking about America was a challenge.

America beyond the color line: Los Angeles, Black Hollywood (2004), 60 min. PBS, hosted and presented by Henry Louis Gates. Gates a well-known Black scholar visited the entertainment capital of America searching for a Black perspective on the industry. One of the tenets that he examined was – Has Hollywood become color blind in pursuit of profits at the box office?

Gates begins with a visit to Chris Tucker a star in the film **Rush Hour 2** which grossed 241 million dollars worldwide. Tucker is now paid around 20 million dollars per movie to appear and perform. He has moved from Atlanta and now lives in the Hollywood Valley, a sanctuary for the rich and famous. Tucker says, "Hollywood is tight." But adds, "Once you are famous color is gone." Tucker acknowledges that his religious faith keeps him anchored. Later we see Tucker in church where we see Stevie Wonder who is a member of his church and is seen singing in the choir. California is the fifth largest economy in the world.

Samuel L. Jackson says, "Yes, institutional racism exists. If it doesn't make money then they don't want to be bothered with it, it's all about business." Then Gates spoke to Arnon Milchan. Milchan said, "...3 of 10 movies make money, 3 of 4 break even and 3 of 4 lose money. The A List actors get $10 million dollars per film performance, the superstars get $20 million per film performance." He described black superstars as people like, Denzel Washington, Will Smith, Samuel Jackson, Halle Berry, Chris Tucker, Martin Lawrence and Eddie Murphy. An example of

Hollywood excess is the film **Daredevil** (2003), based on a Marvel Comics character. The budget for the film was $80 million dollars it needed to make $225 million dollars to be profitable, it only made $102 million dollars so it was unprofitable, Milchan produced this film.

Milchan said, "I'm Jewish and yes there is a form or racism. But people are too selfish and arrogant for a conspiracy. It is a disassociation by community. The film about the guy or girl next door, blonde, with blue eyes is the easiest movie to make." He says the problem is educating the consumer. While waiting for an interview with a Hollywood power broker Arnon Milchan, Gates encountered the pop music sensation Alicia Keys who was next door making a music video. After speaking with Milchan and during a break from filming her video Keys spoke frankly to Gates. She wants to write scores for films and theater. She sees the people behind the camera have control, that's what she wants. She wants to tell stories about people like Angela Davis and Lena Horne.

Later Gates spoke with a group of black actresses and they describe a color line not only within the race but a color coding in Hollywood. The color coding in Hollywood goes from light to dark. In the Hollywood industry especially amongst white people, black is not beautiful in Hollywood. Cafe ole as a color is in, all else is out. Gates then spoke one on one with Nia Long a black actress with some wide exposure and cache. She says, "The politics is unfair. The A List for Black people has more men than women. If I was white I'd make four million dollars more per

movie. The lighter skinned you are the less threatening you are compared to being dark skinned." She feels she has suffered more because of race vs. sex.

Don Cheadle a well-known black actor says its racist and more. Most movies are bad. Mediocrity is rampant, excellence is rare. Stories are the key and race is always a factor. Reginald Hudlin a black director of note says there are no black people who can green light films i.e. give the money and word for a film to be made. He further enumerated the Hollywood system is controlled by agents, managers and studio executives. These people have a complicated skills set to do what they do. It is black and white. Whatever is the last hit movie is what is - it. black movies do make money and that success is unheralded by the press. The problem is the international gatekeepers, distributors, marketers, are just lazy that's all, because to promote and market a black films requires them to think in new ways. So has, Hollywood become color blind in pursuit of profits at the box office? Not yet! What would Stepin' Fetchit and Hattie McDaniel think of today's black movie stars?

I began for the first time in quite some time to keep a diary of my dreams. I had not done this for many years.

"...dreams are today's answers to tomorrow's questions..."
Edgar Cayce (1877-1945), Seer

November 4, 2005

Dreamt about my deceased wife Lisa. We got together and she wanted to go to a store for something. I asked why I had not seen her sooner as I wiped smudges from her face. She was happy to see me as happy as I was to see her.

November 7, 2005

Dreamt of attending a consciousness raising music festival. Event had a multi-generational audience.

December 18, 2005

Dreamt about working doing manual labor and being paid.

January 13, 2006

Midnight. Tonight I went to the Auburn Avenue Research Library for a literary event called *Freedom Riders to Freedom Writers*. The event sponsored by Hands On Atlanta and it featured Abiodun Oyewole, one of the original **The Last Poets**. **The Last Poets** are Black and Puerto Rican poets who created unique spoken word performances with instrumental accompaniment. They produced several albums as the group and were part of a film that highlighted their performances. They made waves throughout the literary community that were sometimes lauded by the mainstream press and were the

vanguard in spoken word in the seventies and eighties. They were progenitors of spoken word/performance art in the communities of color. Every time I go to an event at this library it has been like an oasis in the desert. "Dune" was totally down and completely uplifting in his words, ideas, autobiography and message. I made a point of taking a copy of _Reel Black Talk_. I bartered a signed copy with "Dune" for some of his work. I got two CD's, a DVD and a signed copy of his poem <u>For the Millions</u> that he read at the 1995 Million Man March which also had some brilliant drawings and graphics in it by a black artist, Ademola Olugebefola. I told "Dune" to let me know what he thought of my book so I gave him a card and got his phone number in New York city, he doesn't do e-mail. A night to remember.

February 7, 2006, 12:15 am

Today was as good an example of the heights and depths I've encountered here while trying to make a home for myself and mom. I met the editor of a new (Fall '05) film trade magazine, Southern Screen Report. The meeting with the editor/publisher Pam Cole was another oasis of ideas and information. This afternoon I was called for a job interview where I was offered $10/hour to tutor nine to sixteen year old children. Tonight I went to my second meeting with the SankofaSpirit group. This past Sunday was the first exhibition of the "Movies with a Mission" film series and we talked about all that happened and made plans for the next program in March. (The organization exhibits free to the general public quality

contemporary Black cinema, mostly social issue and historical documentaries.)

February 17, 2006, 11:30 pm

I've taken steps to improve my potential job prospects. I'm volunteering with Sankofa Spirit a film exhibition group and I'm writing for the Southern Screen Report. I'm also volunteering with a local church producing and directing a half hour program of religious content designed for the local religious broadcast channel. I've lined up a Guest Lecture at a local university, American Intercontinental University for next week. Saints and angels are praised.

February 25, 2006

Dreamt about the notion of perceptions and how often people have mistaken perceptions. I'm on the back of a bus that is not moving. A guy taps on the window several times to get my attention and ask for the time. I finally turn and eventually turn my arm so he can clearly see the time. He goes to the side window of the bus and is waving goodbye to someone. I can't see who it is because the bus is crowded, he then walks away. The bus has not moved. I then see him begin to collapse with convulsions like he is has a heart attack. People surround him, the bus drives away. I learn later people thought he was a junkie but he was not he just collapsed near a methadone clinic so people assumed he was an addict but I learn later he was not.

March 19, 2006, 10 pm

I'm no closer to employment. My guest Lecture at American Intercontinental University went well. The letter of reference from Ms. Sue Rinker joins my CV package. I'm more disappointed in my interactions with people than before. I meet people tell them what I do, what I have, what is available, send cover letter with CV package and never hear from them again. It's discouraging; I try to remain positive despite making only slight headway. I have two stories in the new edition of SSR magazine. I am doing another story for the next issue. My work with the Black cinema exhibition group SankofaSpirit goes well.

Southern Screen Report: your local film and video production news source,

March 19, 2006, Vol. 2 # 2, print edition. *SankofaSpirit Screens "Movies with a Mission"*

A new Black cinema program has taken up residence at the Apex Museum of Black History on historic Auburn Avenue in Atlanta. The program, "Movies with a Mission", is being run by a volunteer organization, SankofaSpirit. Theresa Noni Charles, the founder is a graduate of Clark Atlanta University with a B.A. in Marketing and Management. She and her hard working volunteers have created a monthly film schedule for the Apex Museum that runs until July of this year.

What does SankofaSpirit mean? Sankofa is an Adrinka symbol that comes from Ghana. Loosely translated, it means to

look at our past (our history) as we move towards the future. We added the word "spirit" because it is our ancestors that we give thanks to as we look back to move forward. I created SankofaSpirit in 2003 as a community-based organization working as a collective to reclaim, rekindle, and reconnect with our great legacy.

How long has the "Movies with a Mission" film series existed? This is our third season. For 2006, we have partnered with the Apex Museum of African American Culture on Auburn Avenue.

How many films have screened since the inception of the program? We've shown eight films over the last two years, so 2006 is our largest screening series yet with nine films scheduled this season. "Movies with a Mission" is a community service and all screenings are free and open to the public.

Why have you put so much time, money, and energy into this film series? It's about consistently creating something of value and community building. "Movies with a Mission" is the vehicle. You walk away from each film with a sense of appreciation for those who came before us, and we hope it inspires you to pick up the mantle and move forward. (The program now runs year round, 2010.)
http://www.sankofaspirit.com/

July 12, 11:30 pm

The summer has included a visit by a two different California friends, first was Henry Calhoun. He stayed a week in a nearby

hotel and we had some quiet good time together. Later Louise Connors came to visit our relationship is now a platonic one. We spent lots of time seeing the sights of Atlanta. Mom was not interested in getting out and seeing the sights, which was part of our original plans for the three of us.

September 9, 2006 12:30 am

Today Mom and I saw the film **Idewild**. It brought back memories of Idewild, Michigan which were pleasant memories. Mom was surprised at how much I remembered from that time in early childhood. The film was an excellent musical film that was set in the thirties and the dance numbers combined the lindy hop and hip-hop. I gave it my highest rating for execution and its original and deft panache. We both enjoyed the film. Idelewild, Michigan memories include the long drive to get there usually three hours. We stayed in a house that was in the rural section of the city.

The house we stayed in was owned by a near relative of the family we lived with at the time. As I recall the house was very nice with stylish furniture and exquisite bric a brac and chotskies. I remember a porcelain black panther that fascinated me with its design. There was even a swing put in the trees surrounding the house in my honor. The mornings in summer always seemed chilly that was certainly a time of innocence for me in my life.

September 30, 2006, 7:30 pm

55 ½ hours worked on my new job! I'm working for Manpower at the USPS as a casual mail handler/clerk. Lots of bend and grunt. My tenure should be good until Jan.07, then its anybodies guess based on the politics of the work place. Life in Atlanta really begins now that I am working. I hope my next income generating position is able to make better use of my ability.

November 18, 2006, 11 pm

Gwinnett County QT Station on Satellite Blvd. The job for the USPS is really about earning money to pay the bills and keep a roof over our heads. Lucille Lightfoot arrived from Detroit this week and has begun to transform the house with her cleaning frenzy. Mom is content to have someone to talk to and be with while I'm working and sleeping which is all I seem to do lately.

The best news is Ian Young of Toronto, Canada a bookseller who I've ordered books from and began an e-correspondence with, thinks my next book idea is a good one and says keep him posted.

Televised sports have always been one of my great escapes from everyday life. This is true for many millions of Americans. I was a lousy athlete in school and did not try out for any teams on any level. Two excellent sports films from this period are **Coach Carter** (2004) & **Glory Road** (2006). **Coach Carter** (2004), color, 136 min. Inspired by the life of Ken Carter. Directed by

Thomas Carter (No relation), written by Mark Schwahn & John Gatins, starring Samuel L. Jackson. Ken Carter was the leading scorer on his basketball team in high school. After graduating from college and making decisions about what to do with his life he chose to go back to his community and teach basketball and a whole lot more. He took his Richmond High School basketball program and indeed taught basketball but he also made players sign personal contracts that also required a parent's signature.

The contract addressed social behavior, a dress code and included a good grades requirement. His contract required that the players keep a minimum 2.3 GPA to participate on the team. When many players did not achieve his academic requirements he closed the program down after the team had gone 13-0 for the first time in their history. They were on the verge of playing for the state championship. The community was upset, the parents were upset and the Board was upset. Because of his actions and the interest it generated Coach Carter appeared on the **Today** program on **NBC** and caused a firestorm in his community that echoed around the nation. Then Governor Gray Davis lauded his efforts and supported his ideals and had his picture taken with Coach Carter. His story its impact on Richmond, California and around the nation is told in this film about life with basketball as a metaphor for achievement. Coach Carter wanted his players to see beyond the court of dreams. His players from that team have all gone on to college and careers and some have done as he has, come back and helped to make their community a better place to live.

A historic moment in sports history is chronicled in the film **Glory Road** (2006). In 1966 the year I graduated from high school, I along with millions of others watched on national television a sports event that forty years later was such an important moment that it led to the production of this exemplary film. In the NCAA Men's' College Basketball Finals the past met the future. An all-White team played an all-Black team, a first in NCAA College Basketball Finals.

The men of Kentucky were led by the legendary basketball coach Adolph Rupp. Rupp felt that Black players were inferior to White players. Kentucky along with most Southern schools of that time was completely segregated. Don Haskins of then Texas-Western (now called the University of Texas - El Paso) wanted the best players for his team regardless of color. His team was a mix of twelve Black and White players. Against all odds this small school took on the powerhouse Kentucky team and made history in the process.

Glory Road (2006), 118 min. color; Directed by James Gartner; Written by Chris Cleveland and Bettina Gilois; produced by Jerry Bruckheimer, Starring Josh Lucas, Derek Luke, Austin Nichols and Jon Voight. The DVD features interviews with coach Haskins and his players in their own words. The salient points of the this significant sports event as told by the people who participated in it were – it freed Black and White people to think in new ways about Black participation in sports; it was the most important game in college basketball history; Coach Haskins changed the game of basketball and sports throughout the

South; the racial pressure that the Texas-Western players experienced changed the game from recreation to something entirely different; the immediate response of both Black and White communities after the game when viewed today looks jaundiced.

Jackie Robinson is remembered and revered for his play on *"the field of dreams"*. Joe Louis is remembered and revered as a *"credit to his race"*. Jack Johnson is remembered, reviled and admired for his *"...unforgivable blackness"* and being the first Black boxing Heavyweight Champion. Muhammad Ali is revered the world over not only for his boxing prowess as the self-titled *"The Greatest"* but for his spiritual and religious practices that he stood up for all the way to the Supreme Court. Ervin 'Magic' Johnson and Micheal Jordon are remembered for making basketball a sport that millions of young men want to play and emulate their accomplishments. After retiring from sports both men have achieved great success in the business world. Sports in America is a metaphor for life in America. Sports provide a place where you can be poor while playing as an amateur and a multimillionaire when you become a professional. There exists a slave-owner relationship in sports. The owners, managers, front office staff, agents, fans are majority White. Over time there are now a few minority owned sports franchises and people of color are as rabid in their support of their teams as anyone.

The 1966 NCAA Championship game was described by Pat Riley a member of the Kentucky team. Riley went on to a career as a successful NBA player and then as a multi-championship

winning NBA coach with two different teams first in Los Angeles and then Miami. He said, "...the game was an Emancipation Proclamation for sports." As you may recall from history the Emancipation Proclamation did not totally end racism. Today we still battle racism on every front despite having a Black President. So sports can help with understanding we are one people on one planet but the answers to the troubling social and political issues of our time are mirrored in the arenas and fields of dreams. Both of these films of important sports history are part of our American history.

In 1988 while pursuing freelance journalism opportunities whenever possible I was assigned a story by a San Francisco magazine called *Media Review*, Summer,'88 issue. My assignment grew out of the remarks by Jimmy "The Greek" Snyder and Al Campanis that got them both fired from their respective employers **CBS** and the **Los Angeles Dodgers** because they made racially insensitive remarks regarding Black athletes. I was assigned to interview two prominent Bay area African Americans to respond to their comments. One of the people I interviewed was **Harry Edwards**, PhD. Edwards is a Professor of Sociology at the University of California at Berkeley. Dr. Edwards while an amateur athlete in track and field was one of the lead organizers of the Black Power salutes of John Carlos and Tommy Smith while on the Olympic podium in protest of treatment of Blacks in this country at the **1968 Olympics**.

Edwards said in my interview regarding Black athletes, "Paradoxically and ironically, it is racism in the larger society that

is responsible for Black athletic dominance in sports. But this success takes place at a tremendous price, at the price of some of our most aspiring and competitive young people being channeled in disproportionately high numbers into an arena where the overwhelming majority are doomed to failure. Where do you go when the NBA is the only game in town and you're not part of that 1.6% of guys who make it to college and then into the NBA? For Black society, the problem and the price is gross underdevelopment. They drop all the way to the gutter nine times out of ten because the big game is the only game in town; and if you don't make into that game, you don't make it."

He further enumerated, "The mass media is the most segregated aspect of the sports institution in terms of racial configuration. There are 28 black beat sports writers out of 658 writers covering basketball, football and baseball. The situation is media is directly responsible for a Jimmy "The Greek" Snyder-not just the ideas he harbors after twelve years at **CBS** but feeling comfortable enough with those ideas to enunciate them with cameras rolling, and be surprised at the reaction."

In 1992 the multi-award winning and preeminent sports documentary filmmaker **Bud Greenspan** (1926-2010) wrote, produced and directed a documentary which was hosted and narrated by the best-selling author James Michener titled **The Black Athlete**, 59 min. color. Athletes and scholars of the day were interviewed on the role of Black athletes in American society. The list of those interviewed today shows us a great historic import with the comments and the list of those

interviewed including Muhammad Ali, boxing; O.J. Simpson, football; Roy Campenella, baseball: Lee Elder, golf; Arthur Ashe, tennis and historic Black athletes like Fritz Pollard. Pollard was the first African American to play pro football and later to coach. Pollard was the first Black coach in pro sports.

Dr. Edwards was interviewed in this film and his ideas were more adamantine than when I interviewed him four years earlier. When queried by the program host James Michener, about the Black athletic experience Dr. Edwards was very clear. "I believe it's true in American society where Whites suffer, the Black suffers more and athletics is no exception. Blacks have believed adamantly in the mobility of sports as a mobility escalator out of the degradation of Black society and it has simply not come about. Because they have not prepared themselves and because there are no opportunities readily available Blacks tend to suffer more than Whites. Of the several million amateur Black athletes in intercollegiate sports there are less than a thousand jobs available in pro sports. Given that NASA has several Blacks being trained for their astronaut program a Black person has a better chance of going to the moon than making it in pro sports."

Things have not changed and seemed to have become more entrenched overtime especially in the press. John Cherwa an editor and sports coordinator for the Orlando Sentinel and Tribune published the <u>2006 Racial and Gender Report Card of the Associated Press Sports Editors</u>. His report indicated that 94.7% of the sports editors, 86.7% of the assistant sports editors, 89.9% of the columnists, 87.4% of the reporters, 89.7% of the

copy editors/designers are white and for those positions 95, 87, 93, 90, & 87 percent are male. "We clearly do not have a group that reflects Americas workforce."

William C. Rohden a black sports reporter for the New York Times in his 2007 penned book <u>Forty million dollar slaves: the rise, fall and redemption of the Black athlete</u> makes the case that Black athletes still find themselves on the periphery of true power in the multibillion-dollar industry their talent built.

In 2011 on **PBS Frontline** a segment of this magazine format documentary program focused on "*$ and March Madness*". The NCAA Men's' Basketball Tournament has in excess of 140 million viewers it is a multi-million dollar business. 1100 colleges and universities participate in a non-profit that generates 700 million dollars a year in revenue from contracts with the **CBS** & **TBS** networks. Additional revenue includes money from shoe companies like Nike and sales of video games depicting the players who receive no money from the sales of shoes or video games. The players mostly Black are indentured servants receiving very little of this revenue.

My moms' health began a roller coaster ride of ups and downs and in and out of the hospital. I was never sure from week to week what her health was going to be. Near the end of 2006 she went into the hospital. She convinced the doctors she would get better more quickly at home. A physical therapist came several times. I hired a local neighbor lady to be in the house at night for Mom when I was working.

Florence Edna (Moon) Jackson
(September 18, 1931 - January 18, 2007)

February 1, 2007, 4am

Mom is gone now; she passed away in her sleep at home after many weeks of pain and suffering. Our family friend Louise Connors came from California and was here during the last two weeks of Moms life. I could not have gotten through it without her help and support. I'm back with the USPS Air Mail Centre working, six days. It is an answer to a prayer. Why have I had the two most important females in my life die in the last two and a half years what lesson am I being given? Will I learn anything from this struggle; I'm at a loss for words.

March 3, 2007

Mom has been deceased a month. Lisa died three years ago this week. My week started with a dream/nightmare where I repeated a line from the **Elephant Man,** *"I'm a man not an animal."* I awoke from that nightmare and I am living a nightmare. I feel so depressed by my circumstances, but I must count all my many blessings.

Recently while watching television a reporter introduced a story describing the five stages of grief. The 5 stages of grief are denial; anger; bargaining; depression; acceptance. I'm going through the most challenging and difficult period in my life. I had no idea that grief could be so all consuming. I had never

experienced anything like this process of grief in my life. I realized that in my adjustment to the most momentous changes in my life I was going through the five stages of grief. This book is my acknowledging in some way that despite the pain when I think about my wife and mother writing this book has helped me to deal with some of the grief and anguish.

I heard more talk about God and religion in the work environment at the USPS than at any job ever in my life. The irony is that the people exhibited the most antithetical behavior to the words that came out of their mouths as to be best described as devilish behavior.

June 30, 2007

Dreamt of going along a path that led into a house. I chose the path as a shortcut. The people who lived there chased me thinking I had stolen something. Once they calmed down and saw I had not, they walked away. Ran into a Black woman that resembled my late wife Lisa. Hanging out with Martin Scorcese. Met a group of Arabs with arms full of books. All of this was in the one dream.

March 16, 2008

Dreamt of returning to Wayne State University bookstore. I dreamt of the Native American trail of tears exemplified by the film **Cheyenne Autumn. Directed by John Ford** (originally

released in 1971, revised & updated in 2006), directed & written by Peter Bogdanovich, narrated by Orson Welles. **John Ford** (1895-1973) is described by Clint Eastwood as the granddaddy of all American directors and said that Ford was afraid of nothing. Other directors who lauded Ford included Steven Spielberg, Martin Scorcese, Walter Hill and Orson Welles. Welles said as a filmmaker he studied the classics, *"...John Ford, John Ford and John Ford."* Ford made over one hundred films from the silent era through to the later part of the twentieth century.

He won six Academy Awards for his films. Actors who talked about Ford and their work with him included Harry Carey Jr., James Stewart, Maureen O'Hara & John Wayne. Ford likes to get his work done with one take, he felt the actors are more spontaneous and energized for the scene. Ford worked in and succeeded with and through the Hollywood system of production. His work was authentic, he was a great painter with his visual style, he also liked a sparcity of words, his work was well staged for the camera, and his work seems very organic.

Fords cinematic style changed over time, his films made during the silent era was one style, the 30'- 40's represented one style and in the 50's-60s his style changed again. Ford in his films showed the irony of American legends cinematically. Ford told great stories, his films are a collection of rituals, he was not afraid of sentimentality, he was very patriotic and his oeuvre chronicles over 100 years of American history within his films. The social fabric of the family is the protection for his characters against the

challenges of life in his films. Ford also had a great sense of spirituality and he did not see death as the end of life.

Cheyenne Autumn (1964), script by Mari Sandoz, James R. Webb & Howard Fast, cinematography by William Clothier who was nominated for an Academy Award for his work. Music by Alex North. Produced and directed by John Ford. Starring Richard Widmark, Carroll Baker, Karl Malden Sal Mineo, Deloris del Rio, Gilbert Roland, Ricardo Montalban, Edward G. Robinson, James Stewart and Arthur Kennedy.

In 1878 for 197 days 286 members of the Cheyenne tribe that was now no more than a thousand members walked 1500 miles from an Oklahoma reservation back to their traditional homelands in Montana. They were being pursued by the U.S. Cavalry. The chiefs who led them were Little Wolf and Dull Knife.

The idea of making a film of this incredible profile in courage began in 1957 but did not reach production until 1963. **John Ford** directed 113 films of these 54 were westerns. Fords westerns defined this genre in American cinema. Ford realized at age 69 when he made this his second to last film that he had made an entirely uneven and in some ways negative portrait of America's indigenous people.   Ford wanted to make a film that assuaged his feelings. As an Irish American on some level he understood prejudice and its impact on people from his personal perspective. Conscience, guilt, Ford's love of the past, shooting the film in 70mm to give depth and breadth to his story all are part of a film that in many ways presage later westerns images of Native Americans. The best example of what Ford wanted to do

with is images is really exemplified in the film **Dances with Wolves*** (1990) a film that won critical, financial success and seven Academy Awards.

Fords film was not well received, loss money in its American release, but did better financially in Europe. The film is Fords visual poem albeit a schizophrenic one. A for effort and C for execution. Even with this grade it stands as a valiant attempt to right the wrongs of too many negative images of Native Americans including the bulk of Fords now legendary westerns. This story shows the plight, the resistance and decimation by government forces of the Cheyenne tribe. Ford does as only Ford could show the humanity of indigenous people in the face of overwhelming odds. The DVD is choked full of information on Ford, the film and the times in which it was made.

The New Jim Crow: Mass Incarceration in the Age of Colorblindness by Michelle Alexander. The author has done a copious amount of research. There exists a clear and dangerous double standard of law enforcement in our country. The facts in this book show you how justice is not always evenly balanced as some would have you believe. Don't be fooled learn all you can about America and why it does and does not work for some, often based on the color of your skin.

American Violet (2008) color, 102 min., directed by Tim Disney, Produced and written by Bill Haney. Starring Nichole Beharie, Tim Blake Nelson, Will Patton, Michael O'Keefe, Xzibit, Malcolm Barrett, Alfre Woodard & Charles S. Dutton. This film chronicles our current justice system that allows local district

attorneys and local law enforcement agencies to exceed and abuse their authority. This story is based on fact. During the time of the 2000 local and national elections in a small town in Texas, a local D.A. with the aid of the local police initiates a police raid on an all-Black housing project. The raid is spurred by a police informant who is facing drug charges himself. In the raid a young mother of four is arrested. This young mother has no prior drug convictions or any police record.

Everyone including the young mother who is arrested is given a choice, either plead guilty to the criminal drug charges and be set free or fight the charges and risk serious penalization if they lose their court battle. Most of those arrested accept the felony charges and become part of the criminal justice system. For the young mother it would mean the potential loss of her family. She decides to fight and not plead guilty in face of over whelming odds and circumstance mounted against her. She shows great courage and begins with getting the support of the local ACLU. Her courage and perseverance goes a long way in showing her community, her children and her mother who does not believe she can win, the true cost of freedom in America.

I live in Atlanta, Georgia while I am writing my cinemoir. Georgia was one of many states that did not want a Black president. Georgia is the number one state in incarcerating people at a rate of 1 in 13 adults (18). I've spent a good portion of my adult life in fear of police, living here now does nothing to alleviate those fears. CNN has just reported that the FBI has had more than a 1,000 cases in the last 3 years of misconduct. This

information was from internal e-mails to staff regarding people involved in these incidents and their punishment. It is alleged that 500 cases of misconduct occur each year in the agency. Allegations include misuse of position, fraud and entering secret government databases, 1/30/11. How can I be protected from this even if I don't break the law?

I look at the images of the upheaval in the Middle East and North Africa and see that freedom comes at a very dear and costly price for some people. Life is such a precious gift. This lesson is lost on leaders in some countries who are willing to kill their own people rather than even consider talking about social and political change. The world stands by and does nothing. Life is so sweet and so short. There is a film that is on the pulse of the changes in the Arab world.

The Stoning of Soraya M (2008), 114 min., color, directed and co-written by Cyrus Nowrasteh, co-script Betsy Giffen Nowrasteh, based on a book by Freidoune Sahebjam. Starring Shohreh Aghdashloo (Zahra), Mozhan Marno (Soraya M.), James Caviezel (Freidoune). The film is set in 1986 Iran. A French/Iranian journalist stops in a village in the hills of Iran after his car breaks down. In the short time he is in the village a local woman named Zahra surreptitiously gives him information about events in the village that she wants the world to know about.

A local man has his wife stoned to death as is the custom of this village because of her infidelity. There is more here than meets the eye. In the course of time waiting for his auto to be repaired the reporter learns that there was a conspiracy to cover

up the truth. The truth of the matter is the husband falls in love with a younger woman in another village. So the husband fabricates the story of his wife's infidelity. He also is assisted in this lie by the local religious leader called a mullah and local civil authorities.

This is a great lie with a profound impact on Soraya M.'s two young sons and the local people in the village is indelibly etched by the performances, the story and the fact that this is a film based on a real incident. These customs of Iran are still part of the social/political/psycho-sexual conditions of women throughout the civilized world in many countries not just Iran. In an interview with the Hollywood Reporter the director said, there's a quote in the beginning of the movie stating, *"Beware the hypocrite who hides behind the Koran."* The underlying theme is that the Koran has been hijacked by people pursuing their personal agendas, whether it's the husband or mullah in the film, or terrorist. http://www.hollywoodreporter.com/; see also http://www.thestoning.com/.

This film is a very compelling, tragic, timely and insightful because the film was produced, directed and written by Iranians who are familiar with the customs and practices of the Mid-East. There is the real potential for social and political change with the dissemination of this film. The current Iranian revolution-in-progress, after elections, is the tip of the social/political iceberg. Iran is a country in a region of the world still in the throws of becoming part of the new millennium. This film addresses some of those issues and ideas of change.

In July 2008 a Jonesboro, Clayton County, Georgia - man Chaudry Rashid a fifty-seven (57) year old Pakistani pizza parlor owner killed his twenty-five (25) year old daughter Sandella Kanwai. It is described by police as an *"honor killing"*. His daughter no longer living at home but married wanted to divorce her husband. Mr. Rashid felt that for his daughter to divorce her husband would bring shame and dishonor to his family. Eighteen (18) countries including the US in 2004 according to a United Nations report had honor killings inside their borders.

What **image** compels people to see <u>**life**</u> as anything less than sacred?

Two films that generated a significant buzz in the film community and at the box office were **Precious** (2009), 109 min. color & **Avatar** (2009), 162 min., color. **Avatar** is the most successful film in history topping $2.7 billion dollars in world-wide box office receipts. **Precious** on a paltry budget of $10 million dollars has made over $63 million dollars world-wide. The real story of these two films is not in their box office returns but the images and ideas they both convey with compelling acuity. The 3D images of **Avatar** has produced a revolution in Hollywood filmmaking that now has any movie that has any form of fantasy associated with it that makes it a must to be produced and released in 3D. **Precious** because of its success has people

sitting up and taking notice of this little film that could about the black experience.

There are only going to be less than a handful of films released through the Hollywood idiom that deal with the Black experience exclusively. If the subject is pathology and not the overriding everyday hard working aspects of most Black family life then mores the pity. The list of African Americans who deserve a film based on their contributions to America is a long one W.E.B.DuBois, Dorothy Height, Marian Anderson, Chester Himes, James P. Beckwourth, J.A. Rogers, George Washington Carver, Coretta Scott King, Johnnie Cochran, John Coltrane - you get the idea.

In America can life be only pathological if you are not free, White and 21? It troubles me that very few people are willing to tell the truth about art reduced to being the excuse to lower our expectations of ourselves while perpetuating negative images and ideas.

In 1977 I had the good fortune to meet **Lester Cole** (1904-1985). Mr. Cole spoke to our under graduate film studies class in California. Cole was one of the co-founders of the **Screen Writers Guild** in 1933. Cole was a member of the *"Hollywood Ten"* prosecuted for un-American activities and contempt. He served a year in jail for his writings and beliefs and could not get work as a screenwriter for many years. He is screenwriter for the film **Born Free** (1966) under the pseudonym of *"Gerald L.C. Coppley"*.

He later taught at the University of California at Berkeley. He was retired from working at the time of our meeting. He described the stupidity and lives destroyed by the Congress led House Un-American Activities Committee (HUAC) hearings. He wrote his memoir <u>Hollywood Red</u>, in 1981. I could not then and cannot now find any solace in the facts that lead to such a dismal period in our American political history. People who did testify for HUAC and who were considered friendly witnesses and *"...named names..."* included well known individual's like director Elia Kazan; author Dashiell Hammett; actor Howard da Silva; athlete Jackie Robinson and there were others as well. This chapter in American social politics deserves our collective memories lest we forget. This documentary is a lasting tribute to people like Mr. Cole who stood for something.

Dalton Trumbo, (2009) 60 min., color, **PBS American Masters** series. Directed by Peter Askin. **Dalton Trumbo** (1905-1976) was an original and prolific writer who had written his first book by 1934, had three novels in print by 1940 and until 1945 was a very successful screenwriter in Hollywood. This documentary is based on his son Christophers' stage play about his father. Dalton Trumbo's early success in writing came through free-lance magazine articles written for the top magazines of the day, McCalls, Saturday Evening Post and Vanity to name a few. His 1939 novel <u>Johnny Got his Gun</u> received what is now called the National Book Award. His work in Hollywood as screenwriter began in 1934. He became with his mastery and skill a very successful screenwriter.

In 1947 HUAC began to call Hollywood actors, producers and writers to testify before Congress. Trumbo was among a group of nineteen who refused to testify, Trumbo cited his First Amendment rights. This list was reduced to ten and became known as the *"Hollywood Ten"*. This group was black-listed and not allowed to get work through the Hollywood idiom. Many also did some time in jail. Trumbo served a year in a Federal penitentiary. Four writers and their families from the group of ten moved to Mexico and wrote under many different pseudonyms and a friend took their scripts around and they were able to seek out a small living this way. Martin Ritt's film **The Front** (1976) that starred Woody Allen and Zero Mostel chronicles that period and tells the story of one black listed writer.

In 1957 a script by Trumbo for the film **The Brave One**, won an Academy Award. He was listed as Robert Rich in the films' original credits. In 1960 Kirk Douglas hired Trumbo to write under his own name for the film **Spartacus**. In 1975 Trumbo picked up his Academy Award for **The Brave One**. Trumbo's journey to redemption and recognition is chronicled in this excellent documentary. The story is made more compelling by using his own diaries of the time read and enacted by actors Liam Neeson and David Straithairn. Donald Sutherland reads from Trumbo's acclaimed novel <u>Johnny Got his Gun</u> which Trumbo turned into a film that he wrote and directed in 1971. The film won two awards at the Cannes Film Festival, including the Grand Prize of the Jury.

This documentary film shows how the hysteria of the fight against Communists, which at its peak only had around eight thousand members in this country, destroyed lives and families completely and utterly unnecessarily. There is a point in the film where children of the "ten" described being shunned by classmates, so the effects of HUAC and their destruction of their parents' lives shattered the lives of their children as well.

The Hollywood Ten were – Alvah Bessie; Herbert J. Biberman; Lester Cole; Edward Dmytryk; Ring Lardner Jr.; John Howard Lawson; Albert Maltz; Samuel Ornitz; Adrian Scott; Dalton Trumbo.

April 23, 2010

Lynne Prather my long time Detroit friend arrived and I picked her up from MARTA. Later we picked up Marianne and we drove to my Cousin Linda's home in South Fulton County. We stopped in at Linda's long enough for the ladies to have a glass of red wine and lemonade for me as the designated driver. Linda met Lynn three years ago when she first came to Atlanta and stayed in my home. After drinks I then drove us to Johnny Carino's in the Camp Creek Marketplace mall. The meal was very good.

Lynne and Marianne Connor are staying here in my home as they are the Facilitators for the **Artist Conference Network** Conference, which begins tomorrow for two days here in my home for the second year in a row. I have been participating in

the coaching techniques for a year with the local group that calls itself - *"Atlanta Fabulous"*. **ACN** has chapters in nearly a dozen cities nationwide.

"The Artist Conference Network is a unique coaching community for people doing creative work. The Network is comprised of small groups throughout the US. Members are trained to coach and be coached. The Promise of the Artist Conference Network - We guarantee that practicing these coaching techniques results in breakthroughs in focus, momentum, and empowerment in your creative work." From their website, http://www.artistconference.net/.

To participate in the ACN group I was asked to write about why I wanted to participate in their program and got this reply - "I am very happy to welcome you into the Conference you answered your questions with such clarity." Kristen Anacker, ACN, Feb.09. I can say without equivocation the ACN work has provided focus, momentum, empowerment and clarity for me. This book would not have been possible without the work I've done in the group with their process. So I look forward to the weekend event. The ACN process has been a significant impetus to me in writing my memoirs and as a result, <u>the door to creativity is always open.</u>

Out of this years' conference I came away more focused and energized to complete this book. My vision is − I am a fountain of understanding with empathy for discovery who values the diversity of life. My quarterly goal is - to finish the first draft of my memoir. My one year goal is - to get a draft of my memoir to

Ian Young of Toronto, a Canadian book store owner. My breakthrough is – I am a book lover, I love them so much I have to write them. It comes from this context - I am a dedicated writer creating a new genre.

The following weekend was a reunion of friends from Detroit. Lynne Prather, Victoria Campbell and Maketa Groves worked with me in organizing and planning this event. The idea for a reunion of people from Detroit came about last year when Lynne was here after last years' **Artist Conference Network** Conference. Lynne and I were reminiscing and she suggested that, "Wouldn't it be great to get all our friends from Detroit together here at your house for a reunion?" I was reluctant initially but was won over by her enthusiasm. We started with a list of about forty people to invite and sent e-mails to most of the people on the list. Eight people including yours truly managed to get together for three days April 30-May 2, 2010 here in my home. Over the course of the weekend we listened to music, ate, drank, talked and relished the dance of life with friends, some of whom we had not seen for more than thirty years. Thank goodness for **Facebook**, e-mail and the internet.

The three day weekend exemplified that despite our having been socialized separately and sharing growing to young adulthood at roughly the same time, our shared experiences at the Hancock House (945 Hancock Street) in Detroit provided a social cement of love, care and concern for each other that we still have today in 2010. Remarkable! The people who participated included Lynne Prather, Jerry Silhanek, Bill & Diane

Byland all from northern California; Victoria Campbell from New Mexico; Jerry and Larry Kaplan from Michigan. We celebrated Larry's birthday Friday evening and we celebrated my birthday the next day.

Saturday afternoon some of us went to see a photography exhibit at a local Atlanta gallery the Jackson Fine Art Gallery. Lynne had read in the local newspaper that Andrew Moore a photographer had taken photographs of *"Detroit Disassembled"* and they were on exhibit. We were saddened and exhilarated by his artistry in telling Detroit's story of sharp economic decline in still images. They were very large photographs that filled a wall with their size and were in color. The detail he captured in his photography is phenomenal, visual poetry.

While there we had the gallery manager take a picture of our group in front of one of his photographs. I sent her a copy so she can send it to Mr. Moore a picture of the *"Hancock House Lives, Detroit Reunion, 2010"* group viewing his work in Atlanta. Mr. Moores' amazing work can be seen at: http://www.andrewlmoore.com/.

Many people who could not come to the weekend event expressed regrets, as our current economic conditions in the country have affected virtually everyone. For the people who were not able to make it some checked in by-email to send regrets, and I made an effort to follow up with certain people I wanted to reach out to. I got some replies which I will share, because they reflect the life and time of fellow - Baby Boomers.

I just learned today, that I have been accepted into graduate school. So, a lot has been going on! I have wanted to attend graduate school for some time now, and with all that is going on, with my sons grown up and doing well, and with the President's attempts to overhaul the education system, I feel this is the right time! I am going for a Master of Arts in Teaching/single subject, English/Creative Writing. This way, I continue working with junior and high school teenagers, as I have with poetry writing- yay, few want to work with this age, but they're my favorites! Anyway, I will be there with you in spirit if not in essence. Maketa

Don't know if you remember me. I didn't hang around for a long time at 945 Hancock. Sorry, I'll have to pass on the get-together this month. We had made other plans for that time and can't easily change them. I'm living in rural northern Vermont near the Canadian border. Married. 3 adult kids + 2 stepchildren (they've moved all over the country). 7 grandchildren. Retired in 2002 (54 yrs old) and enjoying it. K.L.

A memoir, eh? Didn't know we were the kind of people that could do that. I remember the times very well. You and the others of your circle were very kind to me. 'Appreciate that greatly in retrospect. One of our largest alumnae groups is in Atlanta, and we were there for an event over the winter. My wife and I met about 8 years ago, right after I was let go from the last regular job I've had. No reason for it except budget cuts. Hard to re-enter the employment stream in your 50's, as I'm sure you know. Either you're overqualified if the position is in your field or under qualified if not. Even if you're willing or able to shift your

paradigm and become a system analyst, florist, chiropractor, or whatever, the clock is ticking and the train is moving. More people left at the station than really want to be there. So, I'm back to playing music as a thing to do. Rural Virginia doesn't have the population density to make this easy, but I'm making the best of it. Speaking of which, I have to get back to working on some songs for a demo one of groups I work with is cutting this weekend, so I'll wrap this up with a Best Wishes, Stay in Touch and let me know if there's anything I can do to fill in the memory blanks from our time together 40 years ago. Say that slowly - 40 ... years ... ago. Doesn't seem possible, does it? Take care bud. And that's the latest ...Rick

I was able to view the pix on Facebook once you friended me. Thanx for the e-mail list. Only a few people that I recognized. I guess I didn't hang around 945 for very long. It was 1969. What could you expect? I didn't get my draft refusal charges cleared up until 1972. At least I didn't have to do jail time. There's a story there also. Wow! You're a published author? I'm impressed by anyone that has the drive and patience to see writing thru to that point. Thought about it more than once. It was an exciting time. K.L.

I sent a follow up e-mail explaining how the list of about forty names was derived - I moved from the Hancock House with the last group to live there into a house 1/4 of a mile away called the Commonwealth (street) House. The first meetings of the group called the Detroit Film Collective were there. Some of those people knew people who lived in a house on the Eastside

of Detroit in Indian Village. Occasionally the DFC met there. The residents of that Iroquois (street) House, most of those ladies worked for WABX-FM. Later some of those people including yours truly moved into a bigger house near Belle Isle called Seyburn (street) House. My lady at the time became co-owner of a second hand clothing store with one of the radio people. They merged their small shop with another lady who was owner of Fabulous Second Hands which had inspired their store, and opened a bigger store together the three of them. The FCH lady her boyfriend was in the DFC. And friends of those people, that's who is on the list.

While in Atlanta a variety of opportunities to Lecture presented themselves. None produced anything other than a one or two shot opportunity. Recently through the help of family I got one more opportunity to begin to Lecture again. The program is a facility for men in recovery from drug and alcohol abuse. I did two Guest Lectures separated by a week one month. The response I thought was good from the people who were present.

So I made arrangements to do the lecturing on a more permanent basis. I created a course that was titled *American Life: Yesterday, today & tomorrow*-An Africentric perspective on life in the United States. We will watch a variety of films and programs that deal with the American experience. Discussions will focus on material screened in class. We will also discuss books from the Recommended Authors Reading List. Four pages of contemporary and historic African American writers. You are

asked to read one book a month. The Instructor has an undergraduate degree in film making with a minor in sociology & a graduate degree in film and television production. He has forty years' experience in virtually all phases of media.

I had an opportunity after I had done a few lectures to sit down with the Pastor who founded and runs the program. In our very frank discussion, he said they could not and would not pay people to work for them and that anyone who works for them is a volunteer. That the men had told him that the material I had presented to this point (four separate lectures with films and discussion) "...had no value for the men. The exception was one white guy."

So I thanked the Pastor for his time and accepted that once again my efforts to connect to opportunities to showcase my abilities have been thwarted. I found out in my conversation with the Pastor his staff person who brought me in had paid me out his pocket. It is ironic that the only person who thought my presentations had merit was white. I am of course hurt and disappointed. So I continue to write and hope that this memoir is more than an exercise in futility.

Lena Horne: In her own voice (1996), **PBS, American Masters**. Ms. Horne passed on May 9, 2010, two days before my birth day this year she was ninety-two (92). Executive producer and director, Susan Lacy. PBS re-broadcast this program a week after Ms. Horne died. This compelling, revealing and lasting tribute to a great artist and great American deserves your time and interest. The program is filled with interviews with many of

her friends Joe Williams, Alan King, Bobby Short, Ossie Davis and her daughter Gail Lumet Buckley. In addition there are some frank conversations with Ms. Horne. In America because of her genetic inheritance Ms. Horne was blessed with an over-abundance of good looks. She spent her teen years developing her talent as a singer in cabarets. Later in her life she developed skills as an actress and because of her social conscience became a political activist.

She made her debut in the legendary Cotton Club at age sixteen in New York city. Her time there were years where she learned how to perform and over time become part of the family of performers who worked there. At sixteen (16) she learned to accept that the audiences at the Cotton Club were exclusively white and that as a black person she was relegated to just the role of performer. This had a very lasting impact on how she saw herself as a performer and person trying to do what people do in show business, stay employed and keep working. She described that experience as "indentured servitude" and left to tour with the legendary musical ensemble of Noble Sissles' Orchestra as their singer.

From touring she married and had two children. At twenty-one (21) in 1938 she made her screen debut in the all-black cast film **The Duke is Tops**. This film can be found as one of the many "race movies" of the period that have survived. Ms. Horne honed her burgeoning abilities by settling down to perform in the first New York city area club to offer black artists an opportunity to perform to integrated audiences, Cafe Society.

Ms. Horne described music as a refuge and salvation from all the issues that black people faced in America at that time. Because of her exposure in this setting she was able to meet Paul Robeson who became a friend. She also met the then head of the **NAACP** Walter White. Because of her beauty with pressure from the **NAACP**, Hollywood called. Once there she auditioned for **Metro Goldwyn Mayer** and was signed to a seven year contract a first for a Black female.

She was the first Black female artist to be fully glamorized like white female movie stars. At MGM she always had bits parts in their films that could be cut from the films, without destroying their continuity, for southern audiences that still rejected images of blacks in anything but stereotyped roles. During the time of World War II many Hollywood stars and performers did USO shows for the soldiers. The military at that time was still segregated. Ms. Horne refused to sing for white soldiers and German prisoners of war in a segregated audience where black troops were put behind all the whites. She was thrown out of the USO. This led to her eventual loss of work for a time with MGM. At MGM she met Lenny Hayton a staff music arranger for the studio, he was white. They decided to get married.

Their marriage caused a national sensation. In 1947 interracial marriages in some parts of the south were still illegal. This did not change until the Supreme Court overruled this ban by a ruling of 9-0 in a famous 1967 case of a black woman and a white man, *Loving vs. State of Virginia.*

Ms. Horne did produce some memorable roles while in Hollywood but they were generally in all-Black cast films such as **Stormy Weather*** and **Cabin in The Sky** both made in 1943. Tiring of the roles and lack of opportunity Ms. Horne moved on to solo performing with her husband now as her musical director. She talked about her marriage to Hayton in very practical and loving terms. She knew that as a white man he could open doors of opportunity for her at that time that a Black man could not. She toured and with the rise of television, doors opened there because of her talent and beauty. Ms. Horne embraced the civil rights movement. She met civil rights leader Meadger Evers and did a concert in Mississippi. His death by assassin was very cathartic for her. During this period she eventually divorced Hayton. She described this period in her life as a watershed time for her. Later there came a time when her son died, her dad died and one of her long-time friends and fellow artist Billy Strayhorn died.

She went into a virtual hibernation from everything. Eventually her friends coaxed her to begin to perform again. Her triumphant return to public performance was heralded by the 1981 one woman show **Lena Horne: The Lady and her music** which was a critical and financial success as well as being recorded for the **PBS** series **Great Performances**. People saw in that show which was part performance and part autobiography a different Lena. She said she let people see the whole of herself which she had not revealed to any one for many years. She described herself at the time of the production of the

documentary on her life as a black woman who with family, children and grandchildren was not alone but free. Ms. Horne will be remembered as an original, important and significant contributor to American arts and history.

In thinking about relationships from the past I remember being told by women over the years....

"You were the first person who made me feel like an attractive woman."

"You were the first person to really show me what real love is all about."

"You were the first person who loved me for myself, just for who I am."

"You see me as I really am as a person."

This is not about self-congratulations, it's about trying to see myself in context of relationships and take a measure of myself as a man who cherishes quality interpersonal relationships.

My belief system is influenced by the way in which I was brought up which was as a Christian. From the age of five or six until I was in my late teens I attended Baptist, Methodist, Lutheran and Seventh Day (when I attended it was called Sanctified) church services as a result of my mother and other family members insistence and encouragement. Before I left Detroit a friend introduced my then partner and I to Buddhism. We attended one meeting.

I also recall that at one point my mother's lover in my early years and my mom visited the home of Muslims, followers of Elijah Muhammad. I listened from the other room while adults talked. I learned more about the Muslims after I reached my late teens and early adult years. Later in my life one of my friends introduced me to the practices and services of Catholics. In America we can worship as we please. I am a spiritual person.

As Oprah has described it, it means I "have an open heart". I know there is a power greater than man. Because of my understanding of history I do not believe that it is necessary for me to go to a church every Sunday. My faith in things greater than man leads me to see the sacred aspects of everyday life and in the power of people to manifest certain aspects of the spiritual and divine in how we live. My life is my meditation. Man does not have the answers and fools himself by believing that he does to the mystery of life and existence. Because we have lost sight of whom we are and where we are in the universe and on this planet we struggle to find the light of truth. I encourage people to question why the more religious practices and divisions we have based on religious beliefs the less we seem to have a peaceful and organic relationship with ourselves, people and the planet.

Martin Scorcese has made many films that can be best described as profane. The most well know of these are **Raging Bull***, **Taxi Driver***, **Good Fellas'*** , **Gangs of New York** and **Casino**, these films deal with aspects of life in America that leave you overwhelmed by their graphic, powerful, poignant,

passionate and often times painfully truthful renderings of the subjects depicted. He has made two films that look at life from an entirely different perspective.

The Last Temptation of Christ, (1988), 163 min., color. Directed by Martin Scorsese, script by Paul Scharader who won an Academy Award for Best Adapted Screenplay based on the novel by Nikos Kazantzakis, produced by Barbara De Fina, Cinematography by Michael Ballhaus, music by Peter Gabriel. Scorsese was nominated for a Best Director Academy Award for this film. Starring Willem Dafoe (Jesus), Barbary Hershey (Mary), Harvey Keitel (Judas).

The film was on many Top Ten Films of 1988 Lists. Because of the story and the way in which the ideas were presented the film generated controversy even before many of its critics had seen it. The author of the novel Nikos Kazantzakis on which the film is based chose to take a combined traditional and non-traditional approach to his subject as fiction, not a strict religious history or biography.

Any critique of the film needs to begin with the original source material. Novels use a great deal of artistic license to convey characters, ideas and plot. Because the subject is one of the most well-known men in history people make assumptions and have a misplaced pre-conception of the who, why, when, where, what and how of Christ's' life. That does not help in either viewing or understanding this film. The first time I saw this film was in a movie theater. I went with a group of friends and we were met by a picket line of people protesting the existence of

the film. We had as a group decided because of the controversy surrounding the film before and during its first run we wanted to see for ourselves what the film had that made people so passionate in their condemnation of the film.

The film begins with this caveat, "This film is not based upon The Gospels but upon this fictional exploration of the eternal spiritual conflict." We see Jesus the carpenter making crosses for the Romans. Their cruel and unusual punishment of nailing people to crosses provides work for this carpenter. We see Jesus assisting with tying people to one of his crosses. In the process he is splattered by the blood of one of the victims of Roman justice as he assists them while they nail someone to one of his crosses.

Of all the Scorsese films I've seen this is the least violent and bloody. This is ironic given the period and subject. Scorsese chooses to focus on his characters and story to his credit. Judas confronts Jesus, "Jews killing Jews, coward." Jesus replies, "I'm struggling". Judas replies "I struggle, you collaborate."

Throughout the course of the film Jesus has fainting spells, hears voices and sees visions that confuse, confront and challenge him and his belief system. He wonders is this God or the devil who is speaking to him, a dilemma he spends the better part of the film trying to resolve. Jesus has some very profound words of wisdom as he says, "Everything is a part of God. Death is not a door that closes, it opens and you go through it. I want freedom for the soul. The foundation is the soul. We can change with love." Along the way with Judas as his first disciple he meets

and converts John the Baptist, James, Andrew, Peter, Phillip and later the other disciples. Over time more disciples and converts are added to their group. The film takes us on a journey of discovery of Jesus as a man clearly in conflict, not unlike modern man today. At one point in the film we see Jesus with a wife and family. I found the film challenging and rewarding. I end this look at a man whose life still resonates many centuries later with a line from the film, "Harmony between earth and the heart is the world of God." Jesus the man can be described as a first century spiritual activist.

Kundun (1997), 135 min., color, directed by Martin Scorcese, written by Melissa Mathison, produced by Barabara De Fina. The film was nominated for four Academy Awards. Overall the film received thirteen national and international film nominations and won five awards, three for Cinematography by Roger Deakins and two awards for music by Phillip Glass. Scorcese has made these two very powerful experimental films **TLTOC** and **Kundun** that are clear clarion calls for an understanding of the more sacred aspects of life. This story based on recent historic fact is about the country of Tibet its people, their religious practices and beliefs and the life and times of the 14th Dali Lama. Through the course of the film we learn about the death of the 13th Dala Lami who is the spiritual and secular leader of this country. Thus begins the great search for the 14th Dala Lami. The customs and social mores of this little known country known for many years only by stories and some books is reveled in a fashion that is

clearly homage to the spirit of man and a people with an indomitable spirit.

Finding the 14th Dalai Lama is a journey that holy men with a deep and abiding understanding of their society, its customs and people is both as educational and exhilarating an experience as you can present in cinema. Scorcese triumphs with this masterwork on spirituality. Over time the new Dala Lama grows from child to young adult hood. Into his life, the countries and history marches the Chinese Revolution. Tibet was a sovereign nation for centuries. In 1950 the Chinese annex Tibet and make a claim for the land and its people. The Dala Lama a man of peace eventually is forced to leave his people and country to survive. His survival and story told so eloquently in this film is a tribute to spirituality and truth. Scorcese makes films that appeal to popular sentiments. This film appeals to the higher nature of us all, no matter what your belief systems.

The 14h Dali Lama whose religious practices are Buddhist calls for a renewed sense of personal ethics and interfaith harmony. The Dala Lama is in exile in India. His plight and story with this film and the work of people from all over the world have taken a concerted interest in Tibet and their leader. In 1989 the Dala Lama was awarded the **Nobel Peace Prize** and in 2007 he was awarded a **U.S. Congressional Medal**. He fully supports the efforts of an elected parliament-in-exile to regain the rights of the sovereign people of Tibet.

Mohandas Karamchand Gandhi (1869-1948) is revered and remembered for his life and work in India where he was born.

Throughout the rest of the world he is acknowledged as a superior but humble individual who spoke truth to power. His principle of *Satyagrha* was resistance to tyranny through mass civil disobedience. The foundation of this philosophy was *ahimsa*, total nonviolence. With these principles firmly understood he was able to force the British which had ruled India for many generations to willing leave India and let India attain democratic self-rule after World War II ended. Dr. Martin Luther King recognized and understood that ahimsa was the crucible for the fire of the burgeoning civil rights movement in this country. In the King Center for Non-Violence in Atlanta there is a room devoted to the life and work of M.K. Gandhi. Gandhi was born and raised as a Hindu but when asked later in life about his religious practices he said, *"Yes I am Hindu. I am also a Christian, a Muslim, a Buddhist and a Jew."* His life and words inspired millions in his time. His life is still a great beacon of light in the world today when we look at his life read his words and understands his principles and practices as a flesh and blood man. In a recent interview Syrians who are in the throws' of the Arab spring and their quest for democracy, they have invoked the names of Martin Luther King, Jr. and M.K. Gandhi.

Gandhi (1982), color, 191 min. Produced and directed by Richard Attenborough, script by John Briley. Starring Ben Kingsley, Candice Bergen, Martin Sheen, John Gielgud, Edward Fox, Trevor Howard, John Mills, Saeed Jaffrey & Roshan Seth. Music by Ravi Shankar and George Fenton. Winner of eight Academy Awards for Best Picture, Best Original Screenplay, Best

Actor, Best Director, Best Film Editing, Best Costume Design, Best Cinematography, Best Art/Scenic Design & Direction. It was nominated for eleven Academy Awards.

The film was nominated internationally for fifty awards and won twenty six including the Academy Awards. The DVD is a two-disc set with the second disc making it very worth the purchase price. The second disc of information and interviews give you a complete and fairly comprehensive perspective on the making of the film and adds immeasurably to the overall appreciation of this must see film.

Gandhi saw all religion as needing a more holistic and contemporary reform to match contemporary man and his times. His faith in the principle of truth led him to stand up for himself after he passed the bar exam in England and then later for fellow Indians in South Africa where he began his early adult life as a lawyer defending the rights of fellow Indians. Because he himself experienced racism and bigotry first hand in the England and South Africa his passion for social change was fueled by a personal fire and dedication. Those experiences with political organizing became the foundation for his philosophy of non-violence. When he later returned to India he has was already acknowledged as a very important political and religious leader. On more than one occasion Gandhi was jailed for his actions against injustice. He said, "I am always prepared to go to jail, I am a soldier of peace."

Gandhi's' own words tell some of his remarkable story, "Non-violence is the greatest force at the disposal of mankind. It is mightier than the mightiest weapon of destruction devised by the ingenuity of man. Truth, purity, self-control, firmness, fearlessness, humility, unity, peace and renunciation, these are the inherent qualities of a civil resistor. Love is the strongest force the world possesses and yet it is the humblest imaginable. Truth is God and God is truth." <u>An autobiography or the story of my experiments with truth</u> by M.K. Gandhi.

The film produces a nonpareil view of this little man with such great power with words and ideas. The film opens with the funeral of Gandhi where nearly half a million people actually participated in its recreation. Today films are so busy adding people to scenes with computer generated images this spectacular opening scene serves as a reminder of the power of "true" epic film making in the hands of skilled craftsmen which can produce an elegiac sense and wonder with cinema. Gandhi's life and his social and political work inspired Bishop Desmond Tutu and Nelson Mandela of South Africa; Martin Luther King Jr. and President Barack Obama of the United States all of these great men of peace publicly acknowledged their debt of inspiration to Gandhi. They are all winners of the **Nobel Peace Prize**. Gandhi's birthday October 2nd is a National Holiday in India and the United Nations has made that day an International Day of Non-violence. If you have not seen this film why would you not want to see this film?

July 17, 2010

After watching a **CSPAN2/BOOK TV** panel on *"Religion"* from the Harlem Book Festival, I came away more resolute in my belief system as it relates to being a spiritual person versus a religious person. The panel has written these books which expressed their views on religion, 'The alter of my soul' by Marta 'Morena Vega; The Politics of Jesus' by Obrey Hendricks; 'God is not a Christian, nor a Jew, Muslim or Hindu' by Carlton Pearson. I came away with these ideas that they expressed and with which I agree.

Religion is about conformity, i.e. I am you're not; religion is one of the most divisive forces of our time; some aspects of it are a dead and nearly meaningless ritual; ritual vs. true spirituality i.e., sacred ritual; the issues of rights, rituals and rules propelled on some level by fear vs. faith; religion has gone from a relational to a doctrinal orthodoxy; some concepts of God are based on fear; spirituality vs. religion; religion as an institution and its social political implications; religion today is a political force, i.e. moral vs. political conservatism; Jesus' teaching vs. Christianity; interior vs. exterior consciousness. They even quoted Malcolm X "...enslaved by The Bible and the bullet...".

> *"...anyone who says he knows what God is or isn't doesn't."*
> Rob Brezsny, Pronoia

My experiences in California and Michigan draw a sharp contrast to my life now here in the South. In California I was presented opportunities for understanding and learning that I

see now as very formative in my current perspective on myself and the world. California's diversity had a very lasting and profound impact on me.

Hispanic Hollywood: Then and now, the changing images of Latinos on Film (2007), 124 min, color. Executive Producer Dante J. Pugliese, written by Stephanie Bianca & Henry Stephens, narrated by Henry Darrow. This film independently made and found by yours truly on the internet is as informative a lesson in Hispanic images past and present as you will find. The documentary film begins with the big picture of Hispanic culture and people.

The world of Hispanic culture incorporates a multi-ethnic mix of Cuban, Mexican, Spanish, South American and Central American cultures. My walks on Mission Street in San Francisco along the section of this street known for its Hispanic restaurants cooperates this fully. Virtually every variety of Hispanic cuisine is represented in a several block section of the city known for its cuisine. The film gives us a rich history of individuals and films. Some actors are better known today than others who none the less not only opened doors but made large contributions. Myrtle Gonzales made forty films at Universal Studios; Ramon Navarro a silent film star was a lead in the original silent version **Ben-Hur**. Gilbert Roland appeared in films for sixty years from silent to sound films. Caesar Romero had a film and television career that lasted thirty years. Rita (Cansino) Hayworth was a pin up girl for World War II soldiers and a very well-known movie star. During World War II, half a million Hispanics served and during World

War I Hispanics won more Medals of Honor than any group. Leo Carrillo appeared in over a hundred films.

On broadcast television in the fifties he and Duncan Renaldo as the Cisco Kid with Carillo as Pancho his side-kick together they were the "first" Hispanic pop culture heroes as a sort of Mexican "Robin Hood". Desi Arnaz was the "first" Hispanic television star in prime time television in **I Love Lucy** which he produced with Lucille Ball for their-own DesiLu Productions. To date there have been only two other Hispanic stars to be the lead in their own television programs in prime-time broadcast television Freddie Prinze, Jr. and George Lopez.

Rita Moreno was the first Hispanic to win an Oscar, Grammy, Emmy and Tony. Anthony Quinn in his fifty year long career won two Academy Awards and Benecio del Torro recently became only the second Hispanic male to win that award. The stars who participated in this film are legion Raquel Welch; John Gavin; Martin (Esteves) Sheen; Academy Award winner Penelope Cruz; comic/Paul Rodriguez; director/Robert Rodriguez; Antonia Banderas; Jimmy Smits; pop music star/Ricky Martin; Edward James Olmos; Andy Garcia.

The film makes abundantly clear as we will see when the numbers are all in from our recent census, it will show there are great disparities in the roles for Hispanics in films and television versus the actual demographics for Hispanic Americans. The smoke screen of immigrant reform cannot save us from dealing with the reality of America which is and will continue to be a multicultural society and Hispanic Americans who are a leading

poli-socio-cultural-economic force in America and the world in this century.

Hollywood Chinese: The Chinese in American Feature Films (2009), **PBS American Masters** series, 90 min., color. Produced, directed, written and edited by Arthur Dong. This tremendous documentary chronicles the Chinese experience in American feature films. The film begins with historic cinematic antecedents. We see images of China Town from newsreels of 1902. The Chinese civilization one of the worlds' oldest was now seen for the first time in cinema.

Early images of Chinese were influenced by stories from newspapers that described the Tong organizations in a negative light. The Tong organizations were originally formed to work as beneficial organization to assist Chinese immigrants in the transition from China to America. Over time criminal elements created groups that fought with each other in what was called the "Tong Wars" and this was what created early negative images of Chinese.

Another influence on the image of Chinese was the work of religious missionaries who postulated a notion of their superiority necessitating the need to convert a culture which they little understood or really cared to understand. We are blessed that Mr. Dong has done a copious amount of research and gives us the benefit of this. We learn about early silent filmmakers whose work was unknown and unseen until this film resurrected the work of Marion Wong.

Her work was the first well-crafted images of her community made completely outside the Hollywood idiom. Her surviving family members describe her efforts and struggles as an early independent filmmaker. Ms. Wong also worked in theater as well as film and made films despite their not making money. Another filmmaker resurrected and discovered in this treasure trove of information is James B. Leong who worked as an actor to get money to do Asian motif films.

Hollywood images of Chinese are discussed by actors and directors both Chinese and non-Chinese. Nancy Kwan; Christopher Lee; Luise Rainer; David Henry Hwang; Stephen Gong; B.D. Wong; Tsai Chin; Jackie Chan; Ang Lee; Wayne Wang; Justin Lin; Keye Luke; Phillip Ahn; Joan Chen; James Shigeti; Jet Li; Chow Yuon Fat; Gong Li and many others. High water marks in Chinese images include **Flower Drum Song** (1961), **The Last Emperor** (1987), **Enter the Dragon** (1973), **Crouching Tiger Hidden Dragon** (2000). This film won four Academy Awards including Best Picture and was nominated for another six Academy Awards. It received another ninety one nominations both nationally and internationally and won seventy three awards.

Another level of discussion was the differentiation between Japanese and Chinese culture with many Chinese actors playing Japanese during Hollywood's World War II anti-Japanese films of the period. Charlie Chan a fictional character created by writer Earle Derr Biggers was one of the most popular in literary history. Films of his novels made 20th Century Fox one of the most

lucrative studios during their production and distribution. The films in some ways chronicled the rise of Asian upward mobility but created stereotypes that persist to this day. Asians want what all communities of color want an ability to tell their stories from their perspective with films they write, produce, direct and star. This documentary goes a long way towards dispelling myths, telling the truth and letting the Chinese community express their version of their story, highly recommended.

I lost my job with the USPS in July of 2008. By late August I was collecting unemployment insurance. By Fall 2008 I was sixty years old and eligible for my wife's Social Security. In December of '09 a first cousin Micheal Simmons moved in with me as a roommate. After the Presidents' speech and the opening of the makeafforable.gov website to help millions of people like me, I began that process of trying to get my mortgage modified, based on hardship and need. I applied for a Loan Modification with the Wells Fargo owned Mortgage Company called Americas Servicing Company, in spring of 2009. I got into the Home Affordable Mortgage Program. In that process I used a ream of paper that was both mailed and faxed to them.

In that Kafkaesque nightmare process I spoke to people in their offices from California, Iowa, Minnesota, Texas, North and South Carolina. I finally had one person who was assigned to work with me after almost a year. Over the course of two weeks we worked out a Loan Modification based on my financial needs. I signed and submitted papers changing my mortgage interest from 6.5% to 2.3% for five years with an escalator that goes up to

4.3% by the seventh year. I also sent a certified check with the notarized paper work.

In the week after having done what I though was a Loan Modification I got a call from their Texas office saying it had been denied. I said check your records. She found my Loan Mod papers and the check were in their system, but said I was being denied because I had not submitted the paper work in time. The next day I got another call from their California office at 9am EST. She repeated what the lady from Texas had said. I said check your records again. She agreed that my paperwork was in the system.

She insisted that my Loan Mod was being denied because my paperwork had not arrived in a timely fashion and would not get off the phone until I gave her an electronic check. Today I got an e-mail from who knows where saying that my Loan Mod was being denied because I had not submitted my paperwork. Exasperated beyond belief I called my contact in South Carolina who had set up the Loan Mod. She put me on hold and when she came back said all was well and moving forward in a positive direction but to call next week to check on my status. The ride was not over, nor had I come into the station. I continued to get harassing calls for another month. I did get the Loan Mod.

August 3, 2010, 3:30 pm, ATL

Today is **James Baldwins** (1924-1981) birthday. I went to my personal library and listened to a radio interview with Baldwin I

recorded from 1984. I then watched the **PBS American Masters** series documentary on him titled **The Price of a Ticket.** While listening and watching I had an epiphany. Baldwin said at one point in the film, "...as long as you see and call yourself white, I have to be black...". That comment inspired thoughts of a time many years ago in the Hancock House days of the late sixties. The house was situated on Hancock Street, three blocks from Wayne State University where all of us who lived in the house attended school. The eight bedroom house was an eclectic mix of people whose parents were working class families from in and around the greater Detroit area. We got together in this house by accident and some by design. We learned to live together as people despite our social programming and America which did not understand hippies and alternative lifestyles. Our commune like house epitomized and represented certainly something different with a mix of single men and women and couples, Black and white. All of the Black people were in interracial relationships.

The men in the house always showed the women in the house a good deal of respect as they were all very strong and independent. Jackie who was white and the shortest person in the house could sometimes be the loudest. She always seemed to have a new boyfriend. At one point she had a guy from the immediate area as boyfriend. One day he got first verbally and then shortly physically abusive to her. Many of the men were home at that time so she came to us. We asked him to leave.

He was like all bullies. He was not willing to stand up to men. We outnumbered him anyway four to one, he left the house. Later I explained to the other guys that I felt bad because I thought that I was somehow the person who should have thrown him out, Jackie's room was right next to mine. The other men all of them white let me know that, Asa which was this guys' name and who was black, was a "house" problem, not a race problem. That stuck with me today.

Something else Baldwin said in the documentary when his assistant asked, "Why do you have so many people over every night to talk and drink and stay up late?" Baldwin replied, "That is what truly living life is all about for me and it is what I need so I can write about people and life…". He would then proceed after everyone left to go write until late in the day. I am struck by Baldwin's artistic philosophy.

August 7, 2010 11:30 pm

This year of my memoir is such a journey of discovery and personal mining. Rediscovering and resurrecting my past to put it in a story that others will read gives me some concern. FACEBOOK has been like Jiffy Pop popcorn, people keep popping up from the past. Tonight it was Bryna another former Detroiter. We also worked together as well at the Studio Theaters, she was a cashier. She is remarried and has grandchildren. I brought her up to speed on my journey these last six years and on my life in general. She surprised me with her

frankness and openness in telling me about her life from then to now.

Her former husband and I also worked together in the Studio Theaters he was an usher. He later became an Assistant Manager. Her former husband Gary was also a budding musician who played piano and he I shared a love of jazz. My memory of him is the time we went to Ann Arbor one day to see the Dave Brubeck Trio with Gerry Mulligan. We left Detroit early to avoid the Friday evening rush hour traffic. Gary drove and we got to Ann Arbor in less than an hour. Once there Gary said he needed to make a phone call. We stopped at a hotel in downtown Ann Arbor, he parked got out and went in to make his call.

He seemed very excited and had a big grin on his face when he got in the car. He began immediately to laugh and talk at the same time. He was beside himself with both joy and excitement and almost could not speak. When he did manage to tell me what happened he said was very happy he had chosen that building to make his phone call and not a phone booth. It seems this was the hotel where the artists we came to see were staying. He saw Gerry Mulligan in the lobby and they had a conversation and he got his autograph. He always felt that the evening concert was made more special because of his encounter. As I remember it was a very fine concert. There is wonderful recording of their collaborations during this period. The recording is titled Dave Brubeck Trio with Gerry Mulligan, Live @ the Berlin Phiharmonic, 1970. The one particular number I enjoyed that is also on this recording is a track called Blessed are

the poor (The Sermon on the Mount). This tune and their performance display the passion and fire of Brubeck and Mulligan.

August 17, 2010 4:00 am

As I was falling asleep after being up late anyway reading, I reached that in between state. Partially asleep, partially awake. I dreamt about my mother and felt her presence so powerfully that I thought in my dream I was dreaming that she was alive. I dreamt that someone was in the house. I kept asking my mother, "Why won't you talk to me?" and caught myself and heard myself saying that over and over to my mother. The whole experience was so vivid it woke me up completely and brought me to a heightened emotional state.

When I leave my Artist Conference Network group meetings recently I've been saying, "Happy Trials" and everyone in the room knows what I mean. Recently some people have even begun to sing the song as I leave. **Roy Rogers** (1911-1998) & **Dale Evans** (1912-2001) left an entirely original iconic image of themselves and what they stood for and believed. Separately and together they appeared in nearly one hundred feature films made from the thirties to the early fifties. They were known as the *"King of Cowboys"* and the *"Queen of the West"* in feature films, radio and later on broadcast television. Rogers' background includes one parent who was full Cherokee. Rogers & Evans had a radio program from 1944-1955. Their television

series aired from 1951-1957 & 1961-1964. Their series was produced by their own production company.

They had a blended multiracial family composed of their own birth children from prior marriages for both and adopted children of color. They became advocates for adoption and helping homeless children through their charity work. In their many feature films, radio and television programs they had and exhibited a strong patriotic sense and a belief in right over wrong and showed good always wins vs. evil. They understood the power early on of merchandising of their names and images. In 1940 a clause in a feature film contract kept that power. They have between them five stars on the Hollywood Walk of Fame, for radio, television and films.

When they retired they opened a museum in Victorville, California and later moved it to Branson, Missouri. Baby boomers such as the members of our ACN group know them and their song. Their museum run by their children closed in 2009, because it has fallen on the hard economic times of today and that many items were auctioned.

The film **Under Western Stars** (1938)* has been recently added to the National Film Registry of the Library of Congress. The LOC wrote about the film - "Under Western Stars turned Roy Rogers into a movie star. In the film, Rogers plays a populist cowboy/congressman elected to champion for small ranchers' water rights during the Dust Bowl. He and his golden palomino Trigger appeared in nearly 100 films and a long-running television series. Known as "King of the Cowboys," the popular

Rogers had an enormous impact on American audiences. Rogers was perceived as the almost perfect embodiment of what a cowboy should be in appearance, values, good manners, and chivalrous behavior."

Only a website with merchandise will continue to be run by their children. http://www.royrogers.com/. Roy and Dales' good bye and good luck theme for their television series that they sang as the shows closing credits scrolled over their faces singing, was the song called *"Happy Trials"*, written by Dale. The song ends with the words *"...happy trails til' we meet again."*

There are moments in my life that make me feel - Why was I born to die? The other moments and much of the time I am doing all I can as a homosapien. I know in my heart we all want to make peace, love and happiness for everyone on the planet. Humanity must make this our life's mission. Our morality based in fear cannot help us to reach a greater understanding of humanity. The mortal coil is a dream from which we will awake.

THIS MOON IS AIMING FOR THE STARS IN THE NEXT GALAXY OVER

ENDNOTES

*(Publishers and dates in **Bibliography**)*

1. <u>Unforgivable Blackness: The Rise and Fall of Jack Johnson</u>, G.C. Ward.

2. <u>Race in the American South: From Slavery to Civil Rights</u>, D. Brown & C. Webb

3. Black-Labor Issues of Radical America, Vol. 5, no.2, March-April, 1971

4. T. Rafferty, N.Y. Times, 5/11/08, Arts & Living sect. p. 21.

5. <u>A book of the film by Alexandro Jodorowsky, El Topo</u>

6. <u>Cassavetes Directs: John Cassavetes and the Making of Love Streams</u>, Michael Ventura

7. <u>Samuel Fuller</u>, Nicholas Granham.

8. <u>Orson Welles: A Biography</u>, Barbara Leaming

9. <u>Ousmane Sembene: dialogues with critics & writers</u>, ed.by Samba Gadjigo

10. N.Y.Times, 8/23/09.

11. Facet Features, 6/7//92

12. *"Shifting amid and asserting his own cinema"*, N.Y.Times Manohla Dargis, pg.8 &10, Arts & Living section

13. Black Progress: Reality or Illusion?, Carol C. Collins, 1985.

14. New Age Politics: The emerging new alternatives to liberalism and Marxism. Mark Satin

15. San Francisco Quake: A matter of seconds (1999), documentary, prod. by N. Katzman 1999

16. *The Independent*, "African American film makers", June, 1991, S. Moon

17. Reel Black Talk: A Sourcebook of 50 American Filmmakers

18. http://www.boxofficemojo.com/people/.

19. The Poets guide to Life: The Wisdom of Rilke, ed. & trans. by Ulrich Baer

20. N.Y. Times, 8/21/11, "Capturing the idling Motor City" by Mike Rubin, p.19 Arts & Leisure section

21. "Prison spending out paces all but Medicare" by Solomon Moore, March 3, 2009, nytimes.com

AFTERWORD

We are being bombarded by some of the most repressive forces ever conceived by man. Sure media is an easy target. But it surely is the target on which we must focus. There's nothing wrong with the weather after generations of nuclear underground tests world-wide. The ozone depletion has nothing to do with so called erratic weather patterns world-wide. Do we believe these statements? Media perpetuates these lies. The facts are Antarctica is melting so fast it has created a first, ice quakes. The capitalist economies are at war for oil in the Mid-East. We know for a fact there are enough resources for everyone on the planet.

The means of production and distribution have not achieved a symbiosis that makes all that we need - food, clothing, shelter supplied in quantities sufficient for everyone on the planet. Basic poli-socio-psycho-cultural-economics.

Yes, it starts when we are born. Remember when you were young. All that mattered were you and your peers. You grew together and you grew apart. Time, money, chance, stupidity, good sense and age got you through it. At 63 I'm still here. I'm an elder now. I give you the benefit of nearly forty years of media experience.

I've have seen the face of media up close and personal and those in it changed it inexorably for the worse. It has not in my estimate changed for the better because of the golden rule. Those with the gold - rule. A small number of media

conglomerates control everything we see and hear in any form of media. Whether it is radio, print, cable, broadcast, video games, music, web use. News is governed by the basics which I got from working with one of the leading news directors in the country. Tits, tots and pets, if it bleeds it leads.

The recent approval of the mega-merger of NBC/Universal and Comcast is very troubling this merger will create a company that will control twenty (20) percent of all US network and cable television viewing habits. This mega merger was approved by the Federal Communications Commission a government agency paid for by our tax dollars. *"...when regulator like the FCC become more concerned with pleasing corporations than protecting the public, we're all in big trouble."* (1)

How many people still remember the jingles to television ad campaigns we were forced to hear and see as we grew to adulthood? How many generations now have seen this every broadening array of media since they were small? Do you watch TV or does it watch you? George Orwell in his futuristic and prophetic novel published in 1949 titled 1984 tells us brilliantly about media, war, and propaganda. Are we not under the watchful eye of "big brother"? Eves dropping sanctioned in the United States from the level of the presidency down.

Average people need to control media, disseminate better quality media and generally use it for the tool that is it and not the diamond studded bobble it has become. In 2006 movies about average people that looked like, acted like and talked like average people won the major awards that year. Three Oscars each went to **Crash**, **Broke Back Mountain**, **King Kong** and **Memoirs of a Geisha**. This must surely be some kind of record for movies that audiences could relate to about average people.

Geisha is about a girl who goes from being no one special to just one more geisha. **Kong** is about average people yelling and screaming. **Crash** is a slice of the lives of average people in urban America today. **Mountain** is about two people who are gay. All very average stuff .

The Academy Awards in 2011 has zero people of color in the Awards race this year. People of color still find it difficult to get jobs in an industry whose members vote for the nominees. There are no Hispanic, Asian or black executives in Hollywood's top producers, people who can authorize the production of a film in the Hollywood idiom. Among last years' forty top money making films there was one directed by people of color. Tyler Perry has the best track record for money making films about black people. His films make very little money overseas, which is where Hollywood looks for a larger and larger share of their profits. In a multicultural country like the US with a black president Hollywood is color blind. *"In view of recent history the whiteness of the 2011 Academy Awards is a little blinding." (2)*

Media is what we have let it become and encourage it to be. It is a trinket in our society. It's as yet unrealized ability to educate, illuminate, transform and act as a social change agent is part of the big lie about media. Yes it can become what I've described and overnight. There has to be a will of the people on a conscious and deliberate level to implement and make the changes in media and its corporate controlled mechanisms. Both the owners and consumers have to do it consciously together. It won't happen soon or without more impetus from the consumers.

I recommend the following. More conscious use of all media for yourself and your family. More calls, letters, protests around content and community service issues to the stations, networks and advertisers. Appoint an organization that is international and include media theorist, educators, and citizens and be accountable to the citizens of the world. Funding all junior college and above film and media programs to improve access to historic information of all subjects. Citizen Oversight - by an international electronic voting process. This is an idealistic presentation but it is easily workable through international citizen participation.

"There is but one true light in the universe: namely the light of understanding, a trait in which humanity is woefully deficient. The presence of hope, belief, and fear is definite proof that the world lacks knowledge and adequate spiritual perceptions." Manly P. Hall, Lectures on ancient philosophy

Media has the power to change perceptions. Newspapers, magazines, radio, television and cinema can change humanities perceptions. This book focuses on cinema that is transformative. This book is a personal tribute to individuals who take cinema and other media and create work that makes a positive difference.

Cinema is sometimes known as software has evolved from an art form that includes - painting, drawing, architecture, photography, acting, music, and now there is a new emphasis on computer generated special effects. Today cinema can be seen not only in local film theaters but the Internet as a source and resource for cinema and cinema is even available for download to our cell phones.

In the 13th Century the Portuguese began the slave trade from West Africa. Later in that same century the profession of book publisher emerges. The 14th century saw the entrenchment of the slave trade with sanctions by the Catholic Church. Later in the century we see the first newspapers appearing. The 15th century saw the spread of slavery from South America to North America. In addition the 15th century saw the first public advertising being displayed. In the same century the first projection lantern was constructed and demonstrated.

The 16th century after over 200 years of international slave trading saw the first written protest by an American of the slave trade. The first slave revolts in North America occurred in the early 18th century. The 19th century saw the first Black newspaper *"Freedoms Journal"* being published in New York City. That same year on July 4th, 1827 slavery was abolished in New York State.

During mans' evolution, like all other living things man responded to his environment by adapting biologically. Many of the characteristics such as skin color and body build that we recognize as associated with race, represents adaptations evolved by man living in widely differing environments. A key to human global success has been the ability of different human populations to evolve variations in skin color, body structure, blood chemistry, and physiology best suited for survival in different environments.

The notion of race is statistical and describes the characteristics of populations. Any attempt to predict intelligence, body build, blood type or even skin color of an individual from knowledge of his racial population is hopeless. All northwest Europeans are not fair-skinned, all blacks are not

black, and all Japanese are not short-statured. The general characteristics of the population tell little about the specifics of an individual in that population. We can put members of the human species into groups based on physical characteristics that will overlap to some extent. The three main groups are Mongoloid, Caucasoid, Negroid with some smaller groups being Australoid (aborigines), Capoid (Bushmen of the Kalahari), Native Americans, Polynesians. In reality the larger groups are really racial conglomerates each containing a diversity of breeding populations. So in reality there are approximately two dozen racial varieties of man. When we compare this number to other species we see that there are on the order of 150 different varieties of the pocket gopher, there are a hundred distinct breeds of dogs, dozens of breeds of cattle and literally countless varieties of fruit flies or leopard frogs. The question then to consider is why are there so few rather than so many readily distinguishable races of man?

For me the definition of media today is an all-encompassing word which incorporates many varieties of communications. Print, radio broadcast television, cable, satellite, computer, digital, telephone, etc. Today a few companies, mostly large multinational conglomerates control and operate the existing media that we use. The imperative for these companies is profit, it just so happens that information and idea storage and retrieval is the new "electronic revolution" comparable to the late 19th century and early 20th century "industrial revolution" in terms of jobs, money and power. Can these companies be trusted to provide the best, most informed presentation of news and information and the widest variety of perspectives?

I don't think they can or ever will. So we must find the widest variety of perspectives and differing views of news and

information. There clearly is a media silence regarding some issues, people and ideas. The information is being held hostage by the profit motive.

We are entering our eighth generation of "videots". People who have grown up with television and now computers as an important part of how they interact and see the world. My parents were raised on radio which during its time stirred the imagination because it was merely one dimensional, sound only. Television and computers with their two and three dimensions, sight, sound and touch have created "videots" and "nerds". I embrace the advances in technology but I don't embrace the "powers" that control the delivery systems.

The first person to achieve one million contacts via the Internet on Twitter.com the newest way to electronically communicate was actor/activist Ashton Kutcher. Twitter.com allows the sender/receiver the ability to send short ideas, less than 140 characters via the Internet or cell phone. "This is a commentary on the state of media.

I believe that we're at a place now with social media where one person's voice can be as powerful as a media network. That is the power of the social Web. It was almost like an uprising of the Internet. On top of that, you can really rally people around different causes. Kutcher as been working to stop the disease malaria. World Malaria Day is April 25, 2009, and Kutcher is encouraging his Twitter followers to donate mosquito nets to African countries and join the malaria elimination effort. To help the cause, Oprah Winfrey says she's donating 20,000 nets!" http://www.oprah.com/, 4/18/09

In many other parts of the world today the social and political revolution-in-progress in the Mid-East and other parts

★ 327

of the globe is fueled by electronic cyberspace communication. The death of music legend Michael Jackson (1959-2009) created a virtual cyberspace traffic jam with it being reported that upwards of 65,000 messages per second were being transmitted regarding his death.

Images have the power to help and hurt the developing social mores of civilization. Nichelle Nichols in her book <u>Beyond Uhura: Star Trek and other memories</u>, tells of wanting to leave the fabled series in its' initial season. A fan came to the set, much to her surprise, that fan was Dr. Martin Luther King, Jr.. In their private conversation, when she explained that she wanted to leave the show he told her she could not. He convinced her to stay by saying, *"Remember you are not important there in spite of your color. You are important there because of your color. This is what Gene Roddenberry has given us."* NASA's first black female astronaut Dr. Mae Carol Jemison says, "*Uhura of Star Trek",* inspired her dreams to be an astronaut. Ronald McNair joined the NASA astronaut program with a PhD from MIT in physics. As a child he also watched **Star Trek**. His brother Carl in remembered his late brother during the many memorials to the shuttle Challenger disaster. McNair perished along with other NASA astronauts in his second ride into space. Carl said as a young child he saw **Star Trek** as simply science fiction. Carl McNair said his brother Ron McNair brother saw **Star Trek** as science possibility.

"...the bias perceived by African-American journalists and other minorities is not just a product of their collective imaginations." DigitalJournal.com.

"Black social problems and criminality are played up while white problems are minimized." <u>Mixing it up: taking on the media bullies and other reflections</u>, Ishmael Reed.

The image of violence in our cinema, television, video games, and over the Internet, clearly has a deleterious effect on civilization. Because you believe you are not affected negatively by these images does not mean you are not affected. You interact in society with people who are affected negatively by these images and filtered ideas. The facts are; that empty nooses have been hung in trees in Louisiana, in Secret Service headquarters and the office of the National Transportation and Safety Board; there are a plethora of hate-mongering websites on the Internet; a Neo-Nazi attacked the Holocaust Museum and killed a black security guard; Dr. George R. Tiller a Wichita physician was killed in his church because he was a doctor who ran an abortion clinic; bombings of churches and synagogues; child abductions; sexual slavery of young women throughout the world. Despite the prevalence of religious institutions society is spiraling in bad directions.

The media monopoly creates a cash cow of media for profit and not as a media that has the potential for major social consciousness change. Witness the trend in this country towards doing things about global warming that some say began as Al Gore's slide show. It was later turned into a book and then an Academy Award winning film. Now we have an international movement regarding global warming.

The main stream media has been responsible for helping to disseminate the information about the impact of global warming on the planet. President Obama has set forth his *Green Initiative* that he hopes will help the planet and create millions of new

★ 329

environmentally sound jobs. There is a sacred and profane aspect to media. We need to have more media that helps the planet and civilization to live without war. War makes man more religious, which makes man more war like, which makes man more religious.

The wars in Iraq and Afghanistan have over a million and a half troops deployed. Twenty percent are battling post-traumatic stress disorder. In 2004 there were 143 suicides in the Army. As of May, 2009 there are 64 reported suicides in the Army, a pace likely to create a new and tragic record. Source, ABC News, 5/27/09.

"...entertainment is our single largest export in the United States."

Richard D. Parsons, (then) Chairman and Chief Executive Officer, Time Warner Inc., in a speech presented on 12/06/05 in Los Angeles, CA.

We have a Black president, who has a multicultural heritage. He was elected because of a number of different factors. Some of the factors are a more diverse voting populace, the overwhelming numbers of young people who participated in the campaign and election process, with a more enlightened view of race, the use of the Internet in the national election campaign process and the worse economic conditions since the U.S. financial crash of 1929. Diversity is the watchword of the 21st century.

America is a diverse multicultural majority nation. On the 2000 U.S. Census, for the first time, multiracial individuals were allowed to indicate more than one race. Nearly seven million Americans did so. Diversity from a sociological perspective has

been examined by Scott E. Page in his book <u>The Difference: How the power of diversity creates better groups, firms, schools and societies</u>. Diversity is its own reward. We celebrate Hispanic Heritage Month and now we have the first Hispanic Supreme Court Justice, Sonia Sotomayor.

FILMOGRAPHY AND BIBLIOGRPHY FOR AFTERWORD

FILMOGRAPHY

Race: The Power of an Illusion (2003) – 3 episodes, 56 min., each. Produced by California Newsreel, Executive Producer: Larry Adelman; Episode Producers: Christine Herbes-Sommers, Tracy Strain, Llewellyn Smith, co-producer: Jean Cheng. Available on VHS & DVD from California Newsreel. www.newsreel.org.

This documentary series questions the very idea of race as biology. Part 1 reviews the science of race. Part 2 cover the roots of racism. Part 3 shows the politics of the concept of race. Seeing is believing, don't be fooled by your current beliefs held on race. One of the most important programs ever produced on the subject of race.

Meet John Doe (1941), b/w, 122 min. - story written by Richard Connell and Robert Presnell Sr., screenplay by Robert Riskin, directed by Frank Capra. This film depicts the power of media from a very individual and humanist perspective. The cast all well-known stars in Hollywood films are at their best. Barbara Stanwyck is the newspaper reporter out to seek revenge and stir things up at her newspaper, after being fired. Gary Cooper is the ordinary man who down on his luck answers Stanwycks fake story in her newspaper because he needs food and shelter. Cooper then becomes the pawn, setting in motion a tidal wave of political and media frenzy. This film chronicles perfectly the control media can have using the then prevalent dominant media of radio and newspapers. One of the best early examinations of medias affect.

A Face in the Crowd (1957)*, b/w, 125 min. - directed by Elia Kazan, written by Budd Schulberg. The film stars Andy Griffith, Patricia Neal, Lee Remick, Walter Matthau and Anthony Franciosa. Larry "Lonesome" Rhodes another drifter down on his luck, becomes a local radio star in a small town with the aid of a young woman looking for local colorful characters to interview for her radio program. In time television beckons. His success in television is meteoric. He goes from Memphis to eventually New York, the number one ratings and ad revenue market in the country.

"Lonesome" Rhodes lives high, wide and handsome. Andy Griffith was never better than this performance as "Rhodes" who lets his unscrupulous nature get the better of him. This film is as compelling a reason to scrutinize who we make into iconic and sacred, the people from the manufactured world of television. The sponsor always has the very last word.

Network (1976) *, color, 121 min. - written by Paddy Chayefsky, directed by Sidney Lumet. Academy Awards went to Chayefsky for his screenplay, Faye Dunaway for Best Actress as a television executive gone ratings crazy, Peter Finch for Best Actor as the alternately mad and sane nightly newscaster, and Beatrice Straight for Best Supporting Actress as the long suffering wife of embattled television executive William Holden. The cast also features Robert Duvall and Ned Beatty delivering quintessential performances. This is the television of today, forecast in this film almost twenty five years ago. Witness our consumption of programs like Maury, Jerry Springer, soap operas, worlds wildest police videos, reality shows and games shows, Dog the Bounty Hunter. This film is more compelling today than when it was originally released. This is more of what television is all about ratings and revenues, nothing more, nothing less. If you think

otherwise you've been watching too much television. The DVD version features extras on the filmmakers and the films lasting impact on society.

An Inconvenient Truth, (2006), 100 min., color. This documentary is narrated by former vice-president Al Gore began as he says, "... as his little slide show..." and went on to win two Academy Awards. Best Documentary and Melissa Etheridge won and an Academy Award for Best Achievement in Music Written for Motion Pictures, Original Song for the song "I Need To Wake Up". This film explains the effects of global warming and illustrates our need to address this issue. 50,000 copies of the film were given away to teachers in the United States via the participate.net website between December 18, 2006 and January 18, 2007.

Frontline: Digital Nation (2010), PBS, 55 min., color. A follow-up to a program titled **Growing up on-line** (2007) Dir. By Rachel Dretzin & Douglas Rushikoff. At MIT students electronically multitasking is the norm. Teachers have to adapt to this because grades are affected by this multitasking negatively. A Stanford University study of what goes on in brain imaging multitasking vs. not multitasking - results show multitasking is not effective, "... *worsens analytical reasoning...*". Technology is changing what it means to be human. Dr. Gary Small, UCLA, studies brain activity while being digital, analogous to studying harm of smoking, "...*it is addictive...*".

In South Korea, which is a digital culture, PC Cafes offer cheap 24/7 digital access. People died in PC Cafes from extended stay without food & water. In a three year study in Korea, who are the first to treat digital addiction as a psychiatric disorder, where 90% use of digital domain among young people, 10% are

at high risk for addiction They now have internet rescue schools, nationwide sites, low tech activities oriented approach to recovery from i-net addiction learning I-net etiquette/netiquette. Young people describe *"....technology is like oxygen..."*, its use in school is efficacious, *"...the world has sped up education has not..."*, *"...I never read books...."* says one student. *"The Korean government commissioned Dr. Dong-Hyun to conduct a three-year study on the growing question of Internet addiction. His findings helped Korea become one of the only countries to treat it as a psychiatric disorder."* Mark Bauerlin, wrote the book <u>Dumbest Generation</u> his conclusion is - students basic skills are worse today than in the past, print replacing the oral culture is a sure loss.

Drone pilots with no flying experience are trained at the USAir Force base in Las Vegas, NV 7500 miles away from Afghanistan. The Drone Pilots are used in actual combat in war in the real battlefield. Predator Drone Pilots have combat stress, Post-Traumatic Stress disorders. The U.S. Army has set up 13 gaming centers to replace recruiting centers, Army experience centers soft selling to underage includes real simulations of aircrafts and weapons gaming. *"Technology is not good or bad but powerful..."* <u>http://www.pbs.org/</u>

AFTERWORD BIBLIOGRAPHY

Bauerlein, Mark
<u>The Dumbest Generation: How the Digital Age Stupefies Young Americans and Jeopardizes Our Future or Don't Trust Anyone Under Thirty</u>, Penguin, N.Y., 2008

Borjesson, Kristina, editor
<u>Into The Buzzsaw: Leading Journalists Expose The Myth Of A Free Press</u>
Prometheus Books, Amherst, N.Y., 2002

Chideya, Farai
<u>Don't Believe the Hype: Fighting Cultural Misinformation About African Americans</u>, Penguin Group, N.Y., 1995

Moore, Michael
<u>Stupid White Men and Other Sorry Excuses for the State of the Nation!</u>
Harper Collins Publishers, N.Y., 2001

Nichols, Nichelle
<u>Beyond Uhura: Star Trek and other memories</u>
G.P. Putnam's Sons, N.Y., 1994

Packard, Vance
<u>The Hidden Persuaders</u>, David McKay Co., Inc., N.Y., 1975

Page, Scott E.
The Difference: How the power of diversity creates better groups, firms, schools and societies Princeton University Press, Princeton, N.J., 2007

Reed, Ishmael
Mixing it up: taking on the media bullies and other reflections Da Capo Press, Philadelphia, PA, 2008

Tapscott, Don
Growing Up Digital: How the Net Generation is Changing the World
McGraw-Hill, N.Y., 2008

Vidal, Gore
Perpetual War for Perpetual Peace: How We Got to Be So Hated Thunder's Mouth Press, Nation Books, N.Y., 2002

X, Malcolm
The End of White World Supremacy: Four Speeches Merlin House, Inc., N.Y., 1971

OTHER SOURCES

1. "The era of the mega merger"...by D. Saldana, Commondreams.org

2. "Hollywood's Whiteout Year Few Blacks on Silver Screen", 2/13/11, N.Y. Times

"Center tries to treat web addicts", Associated Press, N.Y. Times, 9/6/09. "...many psychiatric experts say it is clear that Internet addiction is real and harmful."

"Hollywood's Whiteout Year Few Blacks on Silver Screen", M. Dargis & A.O.Scott, 2/13/11, N.Y.Times

"Is there racial bias in the media?", Forsloff, Carol, digitaljournal.com, 9/09

"Astronaut's brother recalls a man who dreamed big", NPR, 1/28/11

"The era of the mega merger...", D. Saldana, Commondreams.org

MUSIC – THE SOUNDTRACK

OF MY LIFE

Writing about my life includes writing about music and its profound impact on me, Live and recorded music. I write about concerts and special artists in my estimation and some of the leading lights of music as recognized by their audiences and their significant contributions to music. In editing the first draft of this book I realized that music I liked and listened to was the Soundtrack to this Cinemoir. Many of the artists/performers I mention I have seen perform. What's a movie without music? The ideas in this section grew out of a series of phone conversations and e-mails with a musician and friend from Detroit I reconnected with this past year, Judy Adams. We have known each other for many years. Please check her out at http://judyadamsmusic.com/.

From the first hour of my day and as I am falling asleep at night I am listening to music. This habit goes back to my teen years discovering pop music radio and portable radios. The I-pods of my day. I cannot tell you how many times I fell asleep with my portable radio literally laying on my ear as the battery wore down and I wanted to fall asleep in the music or vice versa. On more than one occasion I lost a radio because I had fallen asleep and the radio ended up on the floor never the same again. Radios and nine volt batteries were my teen year's addiction. As a young adult I had the advantage of living during a time when radio provided through what came to be known as

"free-form radio" as wide a spectrum of music genres as are still heard today in one musical set by the host DJ. You might hear blues, reggae, rock, Indian or classical in one musical set. Some artists of this era produced music that mixed genres. Music is the soundtrack of my life.

"Music is a great metaphor for human relationships. We are all one really big orchestra trying to find the perfect harmony. May the muse help us create a truly joyful planet."

Oscar Castro-Neves

In his liner notes for his CD - **All One** (2006). Neves acknowledges his musical influences as including Charlie Parker, Heitor Villa-Lobos, Ravel, Debussy and Sergio Mendes with whom he worked for many years. My undergraduate degree in music listening was from the ***Ann Arbor Blues and Jazz Festival*** Lineups - 1969, 1970, 1972 & 1973 all of which I attended.

Friday Night, 8/1/1969

Roosevelt Sykes; Fred McDowell; J.B. Hutto and the Hawks; Jimmy Dawkins;
Junior Wells; B.B. King

Saturday Night

Sleepy John Estes; Luther Allison; Clifton Chenier; Otis Rush; Howlin' Wolf; Muddy Waters

Sunday Afternoon

Arthur "Big Boy" Crudup; Jimmy "Fast Fingers" Dawkins;
Roosevelt Sykes; Luther Allison & the Blue Nebulae; Big Joe
Williams; Magic Sam;
Big Mama Thornton; Freddy King

Sunday Night

Sam Lay; T-Bone Walker; Son House; Charlie Musselwhite with
Freddy Roulette;
Lightnin' Hopkins; James Cotton

Friday Night

Roosevelt Sykes; Bukkha White; Mighty Joe Young; Jimmy
Dawkins;
John Lee Hooker; Howlin' Wolf

Saturday Afternoon

Harvey Hill; Hound Dog Taylor; Lazy Bill Lucas; Juke Boy Bonner;
Luther Allison; Albert King; Fred McDowell

Saturday Night

Robert Pete Willliams; Johnny Shines with Sunnyland Slim;
Johnny Young;
Joe Turner with T-Bone Walker; Eddie Cleanhead Vinson; Bobby
Blue Bland

Sunday Afternoon

John Jackson; Papa Lightfoot; Little Brother Montgomery; Carey Bell;
Buddy Guy; Otis Rush

Sunday Night

Mance Lipscomb; Little Joe Blue; Lowell Fulson; Big Mama Thornton;
Junior Parker; Son House

@ Otis Spann Memorial Field
Friday Night
Howlin' Wolf; Jr. Walker & the All-Stars; Sun Ra & his Arkestra;
Contemporary Jazz Quintet; Seigal-Schwall Blues Band

Saturday Afternoon
Muddy Waters; Art Ensemble of Chicago; Hound Dog Taylor & the House Rockers;
Mighty Joe Young with Lucille Spann

Saturday Night
Bobby "Blue" Bland; Pharoah Sanders; Dr. John; Little Sonny
Sunday Afternoon
Archie Shepp; Freddie King; Sippi Wallace with Bonnie Raitt;
Luther Allison & His Band; Mojo Boogie Band

Sunday Night
Miles Davis; Otis Rush; Leo Smith with Marion Brown; Lightnin'
Slim; Boogie Woogie Red with the Boogie Brothers

1973

@ Otis Spann Memorial Field
Friday Night
Freddie King; Leon Thomas; Count Basie & his Orchestra
Featuring Jimmy Ricks;
J.B. Hutto & the Hawks; Roosevelt Sykes; The Revolutionary
Ensemble

Saturday Afternoon - Music of Detroit
CJQ; John Lee Hooker; Yusef Lateef; Dr. Ross; Little Mack; Little
Junior; Arthur Gunter; Baby Boy Warren; Johnnie Mae Matthews;
One String Sam; Eddie Burns; Bobo Jenkins; Mr. Bo; Boogie
Woogie Red; Lightnin' Slim; Washboard Willie

Saturday Night
The Ray Charles Show; Charles Mingus; Jimmy Reed;
Big Walter Horton Blues Band

Sunday Afternoon
The Johnny Otis Show; Ornette Coleman Quartet; Victoria Spivey;
Infinite Sound; Joe Willie Wilkins & the King Biscuit Boys
Featuring
Houston Stackhouse

Sunday Night
Luther Allison; Sun Ra & His Intergalactic Discipline Arkestra; Otis Rush;
Homesick James; Lucille Spann; Mighty Joe Young Blues Band with Eddie Taylor and Carey Bell; Hound Dog Taylor & the House Rockers

The Festival continued 1974-2004. Source
http://www.a2bluesjazz.org/history/lineup

"Music, then can be thought of as a type of perceptual illusion in which our brains imposes structure and order on a sequence of sounds." <u>This is your brain on music: The science of a human obsession</u> by D.J. Levitin

The last century of our fascination and obsession with this 'perceptual illusion' from 1910 to 2010 is as dynamic a period in music history as any and it may be the most dynamic period in music. By 1910 the world renowned operatic tenor Enrico Caruso (1837-1921) had been responsible in no small way for the sale of a lot of phonographs. Caruso was the most influential tenor of his time aided certainly by recordings of his vocal ability. Carusos' version of "Vesti la guibba" from "I Pagliacci" by Leoncavallo and its sale by gramophone recording made the record a serious medium for the spreading of music. If you could not see Caruso, you could hear him.

Music is multifaceted and multidimensional. Music is in serious trouble from a potential for its continued dissemination and enjoyment. There is a problem with music creation, appreciation and dissemination. Technology has certainly played a part in creating the quantity of music available and now it is part of the problem in terms of it affecting the quality as well.

In acknowledging the change in the way in which music is enjoyed from a personal perspective, i.e. we have moved from early recorded cylinders to vinyl, radio, transistor radios, CD's and now I-PODS vs. listening to music "Live" in performance. In this new current musical landscape music has a shelf life under this system of music performance, reproduction for mass audience and its dissemination. Choice is being limited.

The music industry, record companies, promoters, record producers have harnessed the magic of music and reduced it to a lowest common denominator by artificially creating categories that reduce music from art to commodity. This process is very trend oriented and co-opts the artistic aspects of the music and its creativity. Music stores are in sharp decline. The music that is available through the radio, the internet, your cable systems music channels has reduced the potential for a more expansive and inspirational aspect of the music for young people. There are so many young musicians and artists being held back by the current system in place.

The music industry uses the same commoditization /gratification equation that is used in selling us food, which has gone from sustenance to gratification as a pleasurable experience, i.e. eating a 'Big Mac'.

Choice is subjective in music listening. Under the current music commoditization modality we are creating a sheep mentality with food and music both. Music is now very self-serve, but it is co-opted. Does the music have a real cultural value or is it so much wall paper? Are "live" performances really providing the broadest opportunities for music that is not filtered by the current system in place? Under the current system there is more money in society for opera a centuries old musical form than

there is money for jazz. Jazz is Americas' contemporary classic music developed in the modern era. Rock and hip hop are turned into commodities diminishing their artistic value. It is unfortunately the American Idolization of music.

American Idol and its international imitators created by one Simon Cowell and others are very subversive. True musical ability is minimized to who can get the most number of people to call a phone number and then we crown the next *"American Idol"*. After Jennifer Hudson's elimination from the program, she went on to win great acclaim and a Best Performance by an Actress in a Supporting Role Academy Award with her performance and vocal styling in **Dream Girls** (2006). Cowell was particularly acerbic in his critique of her performances on Idol. Cowell as a personality has become emblematic and imitated so that all other so called talent shows has some judge who copies Cowells' acerbic, caustic and ultimately derisive demeanor. He is reinventing his callousness in something called **The X Factor.** The television series **Glee** (American Idol School of music) has a character that is a carbon copy of Cowell and is one of their most popular characters. Cowell is an acknowledged music impresario, but he has largely been responsible for dumbing down music world wide with the *'American Idolization'* of music, this is a very bad thing for virtuoso musicians who we never see on these programs.

Virtuoso musicians are musicians who have mastered their art and have a unique and original sound. Artist/musicians who have mastered their art and are composers with singular ability and overcame the commoditization of music include some personal favorites like Jimi Hendrix; Miles Davis; "Toots" Thielemans; Chick Corea; Edgar Winter; Carlos Santana to name a few.

Rock, gospel, country, Rhythm & Blues, jazz, new age, rap, pop, alternative, hard rock, urban/alternative, electronic dance, bluegrass, Latin jazz, Latin pop, Latin rock, Latin urban, Tropical Latin, regional Mexican, Tejano, Norteno, Traditional folk, Contemporary folk, Native American, Hawaiian, Zydeco/Cajun, reggae, Traditional world music, Contemporary world music, polka, rock or rap gospel, pop/contemporary gospel, southern country bluegrass gospel, classical, opera, chamber, classical crossover - are just some of the categories in which a **Grammy** is awarded.

The Grammy's are the gold standard for artistic achievement in the American music industry. What has this categorization game that is so market driven done to a true artist who does not fit into a neat category? We need real heroes and sheroes in music not one more copy of what we heard five minutes ago.

VH1 the companion music channel to **MTV** which is designed for the older audience demographic (over 30 years of age), did a Poll of The 100 Greatest Artists of All Time. Upon close scrutiny the poll covers the period from the 1950's to today. Baby-boomers. On their list, artists I have seen perform "Live" are - #5 Rolling Stones, #6 Jimi Hendrix, #9 James Brown, #11 Bob Marley, #18 Pink Floyd, #25 Chuck Berry, #27 Aretha Franklin, #34 Tina Turner albeit with Ike & Revue, #43 Ray Charles, #83 Earth, Wind & Fire, #94 Mariah Carey.

What has the commoditization modality done here? Where is Loretta Lynn the **Coal Miner's Daughter** (1980) her life was made into a successful Academy Award winning film to name only one glaring omission? Johnny Cash comes in at #35. Surely her contributions to country music radio and its rise

★ 349

outstrip KISS at #56 in comparing contributions to American Music. Where are Santana? Santana won nine Grammy's for the album *Supernatural* (1999) still a record for one artist/group for one album. Santana has a multi-decade long career and musically outweighs Madonna at #16.

The Eras of Popular music in America: A Timeline

1910 - 1930	- Tin Pan Alley and the American Song Book & the rise of "race" records
1930 - 1945	- Jazz as Americas popular music
1945 - 1970	- Rise of radio and Rock N' Roll
1970 - 1990	- Electronics and world music
1990 - Today	- Hip Hop & Spoken Word

Music has shifted over the last hundred years from having a functionality i.e. work songs, blues, gospel/sacred music to being an accessory to our lives, like a nice pair of shoes. Also the audience for the music European vs. people of color, the two groups encounter and respond to the music in different ways. Black audiences are more musically oriented than white audiences. In the black home music is as much a part of black life as soul food. Currently however blues is no longer favored in the majority of the black community. Blues is supported by as eclectic a group of listeners as you are to find. The hip blacks of the Woodstock generation still enjoy the blues however, people like myself. Most of the bands at Woodstock played blues derived/influenced rock. Most of the artists who performed at Woodstock consciously acknowledged as much.

Rock music, movies and world music seem to be the new standards for Broadway productions and more. The rock band **Green Day** has had their 2004 album **American Idiot** which won a Grammy for Best Album made into a Broadway musical. Billy Joe Armstrong their leader and primary composer was 22 when the band ascended to pop iconography. Their 1994 album Dookie won a Best Alternative Rock - Grammy. His influences include **The Ramones** and punk music. **Wal-Mart** is currently selling a Green Day Rock Band video game. **Billy Elliott** (2000) was a movie now it is an award winning Broadway musical with words and music by **Sir Elton John**. **Tommy** was a rock opera in an album format by **The Who** then it was made into a movie (1975) now it is also a Broadway musical. There was a successful off-Broadway musical on the life and music of the Nigerian titan of music **Fela Ransome-Kuti** (1938-1997) titled **Fela**. **Fela** is a blend of jazz, funk and African rhythms and harmonies. The musical explores Kuti's controversial life as artist, political activist and revolutionary musician. The show was produced by hip-hop mogul Shawn "Jay-Z" Carter and film actor/producers Will and Jada Pinkett-Smith.

Music can also be used to subvert dissent. In China a totalitarian and state controlled capitalist economy, the government supported the Midi Music Festival. Rock, punk, funk, and electronic music were the genres of choice of the musicians who performed for their young audiences. In 2008 there were five multi-day music festivals all in Beijing. In 2010 there have been more than 60 music festivals all over China. The Communist Party spent over two million dollars to turn cornfields into a venue for more than eighty thousand people to attend a music event. Musicians express anti-government sentiments and vendors sold t-shirts with anti-government slogans. The

government uses these events to sell commercial goods by American companies such as Converse which sponsored the Modern Sky Music Festival in Beijing. One musician expressed the real intent of the government in letting their young people express themselves with their music and festivals, *"The government used to see us as dangerous, now they see us as a market."* (1)

Some artists have gone international and are not bound by borders or genres. Two excellent examples are musicians Andy Narell and Billy Cobham. Narell has made the steel drums a more renowned instrument because of his ability, eclecticism and international collaborations. In 1999 when performing in South Africa Narell discovered his music influenced the Andy Narell Jazz Club in Soweto, South Africa to be named in his honor. The clubs "...primary purpose is to enlighten members and guests on the latest releases by various jazz artists." They play Narells' music at their club which meets the first Sunday of the month during "...*the period usually between 1800h and 1900h — is exclusively for Narell's music. Party time!*" http://andynarell.net/

Billy Cobham is an extraordinary percussionist playing in bands of several countries and as many different genres of music. Cobham's touring itinerary posted on his website illustrates his international audience – NY City, Greece, Turkey, Germany, Hungary and Israel before the end of this year. In addition whenever he appears in a city he does clinics, workshops and master classes. http://www.billycobham.com/

REEL TALK:
A CINEMOIR OF IMAGES,
PEOPLE AND IDEAS

Soundtrack

Alice Coltrane
John Coltrane
Miles Davis
Duke Ellington
Bill Evans
Herbie Hancock
Jimi Hendrix
Billie Holiday
Antonio Carlos Jobim
"B.B." King
Rasaan Roland Kirk
Fela Ransome-Kuti

Abbey Lincoln
Charles Lloyd
Bob Marley
John McLaughlin
Charles Mingus
Charlie Parker
Sonny Rollins
Sun Ra
Santana
Ravi Shankar
Art Tatum
Sarah Vaughan
Frank Zappa

Soundtrack Available Everywhere you normally find music.
So, if you can't find or hear an artist listed here - Why not?

Some of the artists who are listed I saw perform so I enjoyed the air they breathed and the music they made. Their special musical gifts enriched my ears, heart and soul as it journeys through the course of life and moves to an inexorable beat. Great music is a gift. Silence falls compared to great music especially when performed with an audience. Music students you will be well served by listening to and study the music of the artists listed on the Soundtrack. I did not choose a tune or album to recommend. Go through the significant body of music available by each artist for the joy of discovery. As long as there are people there will always be good music just finding it is the issue.

MUSIC BIBLIOGRAPHY

Books

Collins, John
The Story of Chess Records
Bloomsbury, NY & London, 1998

Coryell, Julie & Laura Friedman
Jazz Rock Fusion
Delta, 1978

R. Crumb's Heroes of Blues, Jazz & Country
Abrams, N.Y., 2006, abramsbooks.com, inc. a 21 track CD

Crumpacker, Bunny & Chick
Jazz Legends
Peregrine Smith, Layton, Utah, 1995 – inc. a music CD

Dance, Stanley
The World of Earl Hines
Scribner's & Sons, NY, 1977

Guralnick, Peter
Sweet Soul Music: Rhythm and blues and the Southern Dream of Freedom
Harper & Row, NY, 1986

Hentoff, Nat & Albert J. McCarthy, eds.
Jazz: New Perspectives on The History of Jazz
Da Capo Press, 1975

Levitin, Daniel J.
This is your brain on music: The science of a human obsession
Penguin, N.Y., 2007

McDermott, John with Billy Cox and Eddie Kramer
Jimi Hendrix Sessions: The Complete Recording Sessions, 1963-1970
Little, Brown and Co., N.Y., 1995

Moon, Tom
1,000 Recordings to Hear Before You Die: a Listener's Life List
Workman Publishing, NY, 2008

Moore, Carlos
Fela: This bitch of a life
Lawrence Hill Books, Chicago, IL, 2009

Ramsey Jr., Frederick & Charles Edward Smith, eds.
Jazzmen
Harvest Books, 1967

Robertson, John
The Complete Guide to The Music of The Beatles
Omnibus Press, U.K., 1994

Rockwell, John
All American Music: Composition in the Late 20th Century
Knopf, 1983

Tingen, Paul
Miles Beyond: The Electric Explorations of Miles Davis, 1967-1991
Billboard Books, 2001

Articles

(1) "In China Music Festivals, Hip Rock and the States Blessing",
Andrew Jacobs, N.Y. Times 10/24/10

"Children fight off Israel with music", Eva Bartlett,
Inter-Press Service, 5/13/10

"Interview with Gerald Early" by Ethan Iverson, Do The Math Blog,
5/10

"Mountaintop mobilizes coalfields musicians", Vicki Smith,
Associated Press, 5/4/10

"The return of the one man band", John Wray,
N.Y. Times Magazine, 5/18/08

Other

Fresh Air with Terry Gross: Interview with Billy Joe Armstrong
5/10, **PBS Radio**

RESOURCES

A list of places to find the films in this book and other cinema related resources.

African American Short Films is a one hour quarterly first run series of television specials that enters its eighth year in 2011. Shows range from comedy to drama and all shades in between. The films in these specials are the voices and images of contemporary life in the African American community. The web site features current films in syndication and an archive of previously run programs.

http://www.badamitv.com/aasf.htm

Contact information – shortfilms@badamitv.com & info@badamitv.com

http://www.africandiasporavideo.com/

It is a web site where you can buy some of the best and most popular films from Africa and the African Diaspora

http://www.buy.com/

Anything, anytime, anywhere including ordering by phone 800-800-0800 - Excellent DVD section

http://www.newsreel.org/

California Newsreel

Film and video for social change since 1968

http://store01.prostores.com/servlet/criterionco/StoreFront
The ***Criterion Collection*** Storefront
The Criterion Collection, a continuing series of important classic and contemporary films, is dedicated to gathering the greatest films from around the world and publishing them in editions that offer the highest technical quality and award-winning, original supplements.

http://www.docurama.com/
Founded in 1999 by parent company New Video Group Inc., Docurama is the only label dedicated exclusively to bringing critically acclaimed and cutting-edge documentary films to the home entertainment marketplace.

http://www.facets.org/
Facets Multimedia Media
Facets Multi-Media, located in Chicago, Illinois and founded in 1975, is a non-profit media arts organization which provides an extraordinary range of film and video programs. Facets Video, a division of Facets Multi-Media, is one of the nation's largest distributors of foreign, classic, cult, art, and hard-to-find videos. We search the world for artistically important film on video - bypassing many mainstream releases to focus on the rare and the unusual. As a result, Facets' 60,000 (and growing!) title inventory is an astounding video collection unlike any in the world, famous for its breadth and diversity.

http://www.imdb.com/
The **Internet Movie Database** - Earth's Biggest Movie Database

http://www.movielink.com
Movielink.com

http://www.moviesunlimited.com/
Movies Unlimited
The movie collector's website

The **Corporation for Public Broadcasting** funds five Minority Consortia that develop, acquire and distribute to public television programming of interest to racial and ethnic minorities including African Americans, Asian Americans, Latinos, Native Americans, and Pacific Islanders. CPB funds are used by the organizations to cover their administrative and programming costs. They make grants to producers and public broadcasting stations. CPB does not control the organizations' program or production decisions.

Center for Asian American Media (formerly NAATA)
Founded in 1980 the San Francisco-based Center for Asian American Media, formerly known the National Asian American Telecommunications Association (NAATA), has grown into the largest organization dedicated to the advancement of Asian Americans in independent media, specifically the areas of television and filmmaking. http://asianamericanmedia.org

National Black Programming Consortium
The National Black Programming Consortium (NBPC) was founded in 1979 and is dedicated to developing black digital authorship and distributing unique stories of the black experience in the new media age. Since 1991 NBPC has invested over $7 million dollars in iconic documentary productions for public television; trained, mentored, and supported a diverse array of producers who create content about contemporary black experiences; and emerged as a leader in the evolving next-media landscape through its annual New Media Institute and New

★ 361

Media Institute: Africa programs. NBPC also distributes engaging content online through its social media portal Blackpublicmedia.Org, an online home for enlightening black digital content and engagement. http://www.nbpc.tv/

Native American Public Communications
NAPT shares Native stories with the world through support of the creation, promotion and distribution of Native media.
http://www.nativetelecom.org/

Latino Public Broadcasting supports the development, production, acquisition and distribution of non-commercial educational and cultural television that is representative of Latino people, or addresses issues of particular interest to Latino Americans. These programs are produced for dissemination to the public broadcasting stations and other public telecommunication entities. By acting as minority consortium, LPB provides a voice to the diverse Latino community throughout the United States. http://www.lpbp.org/

Pacific Islanders in Communication
The mission of (PIC) is to support, advance, and develop Pacific Island media content and talent that results in a deeper understanding of Pacific Island history, culture, and contemporary challenges. http://www.piccom.org/

New Yorker Films
For over a quarter of a century, New Yorker Films has been America's leading source for the films that matter on the cutting edge of world cinema.
http://www.newyorkerfilms.com/

Senses of cinema - an on-line journal devoted to the serious and eclectic discussion of cinema
http://www.sensesofcinema.com/

Third World Newsreel (TWN) is an alternative media arts organization that fosters the creation, appreciation and dissemination of independent film and video by and about people of color and social justice issues.

It supports the innovative work of diverse forms and genres made by artists who are intimately connected to their subjects through common bonds of ethnic/cultural heritage, class position, gender, sexual orientation and political identification. TWN promotes the self-representation of traditionally marginalized groups as well as the negotiated representation of those groups by artists who work in solidarity with them.

Ultimately, whether documentary, experimental, narrative, traditional or non-traditional, the importance of the media promoted by the organization is its ability to effect social change, to encourage people to think critically about their lives and the lives of others, and to propel people into action.
http://www.twn.org/

Third World Newsreel   Phone 212.947.9277
545 Eighth Avenue, 10th Floor   Fax   212.594.6417
New York, New York 10018

We are located on 8th Avenue between 37th and 38th Streets
Our hours are by appointment

The **Artist Conference Network** is a nationwide network of ongoing groups of people doing creative work in any field. The practice of **ACN** coaching results in breakthroughs in focus, momentum and empowerment in creative work.

For more information about the **Artist Conference Network** and individual groups,
go to http://www.artistconference.net/

OR

ACN Office
Jean Anderson,
President of Possibilities,
P.O. Box 357,
Weed California 96094
Phone 530-938-4731

Reel Talk A Cinemoir

BIBLIOGRAPHY – BOOKS

American Federation of Arts
A History of the Avante-Garde Cinema
American Federation of Arts, N.Y, 1976

Angelou, Maya
Even The Stars Look Lonesome
Random House, NY, 1997

Anger, Kenneth
Hollywood Babylon, one
Hollywood Babylon, two
New American Library, N.Y., 1959 & 1984

Aranda, Francisco
Luis Bunuel: A Critical Biography
DaCapo Press, N.Y., 1976

Armes, Roy
French Cinema: Since 1946, Vols. 1 & 2
A.S. Barnes. & Co., N.Y., 1970

Arnheim, Rudolph
Film as Art
University of California Press, Berkeley, CA, 1971

Bailey, Alice A. and Djwhal Khul
Ponder on this: a compilation
Lucis Publishing Company, N.Y., 1971

Baldwin, James
The evidence of things not seen
Holt, Reinhart & Winston, NY, 1985

Baer, Ulrich, edit. & trans. By
The wisdom of Rilke
Modern Library, NYC, 2005

Bauerlein, Mark
The dumbest Generation: how the digital age stupefies young Americans and jeopardizes our future or don't trust anyone under thirty Penguin, N.Y., 2008

Baxter, John
The Gangster Film
A.S. Barnes & Co., N.Y., 1970

Beckwourth, James P. as told to Thomas D. Bonner
The Life and Adventures of James P. Beckwourth
University of Nebraska Press, Lincoln NE, 1972

Bergan, Ronald
Film
DK Books, London, 2006

Berry, S. Torriano & Venise T. Berry
The 50 Most Influential Black Films
Kensington Publishing, N.Y, 2001

Bogle, Donald
Blacks in American Films and Television: An Illustrated Encyclopedia
Simon & Schuster, N.Y., 1988

Brown Sugar: Americas Black Female Superstars
Harmony Books, N.Y. 1980

Brown, David & Clive Webb
Race in the American South: From Slavery to Civil Rights
University of Florida Press, Gainesville, FL, 2007

Brezsny, Rob
Pronoia is the antidote for paranoia
North Atlantic Books, Berkeley, CA, 2009

Bunuel, Luis
My Last Sigh
Vintage Books, N.Y., 1984

Cawkwell, Tim and John M. Smith, eds.
The World Encyclopedia of the Film
World Publishing, N.Y., 1972

Cham, Mbye and Claire Andrade-Watkins, eds.
Black Frames: Critical perspectives on Black Independent Cinema
MIT Press, Cambridge, MA, 1988

Chopra, Deepak
The Book of Secrets: Unlocking the hidden dimensions of your mind
Harmony Books, N.Y., 2004

Cocteau, Jean
The Art of Cinema
Marion Boyars Publishing Ltd., London, 2001

Collins, Carol C.,
Black Progress: Reality or Illusion
Facts on File, NY, 1985

Copeland, Brian
Not a genuine black man, my life as an outsider, a true story
Hyperion, NY, 2006

Cowan, Tom, PhD & Jack Maguire
Timelines of African American History
Berkley Publish Group, NY, NY, 1994

Cripps, Thomas
Making Movies Black: The Hollywood Message Movie from World War II to the Civil Rights Era
Oxford University Press, 1993

Slow Fade to Black: the Negro in American Film, 1900-1942
Oxford University Press, N.Y. 1993

Black Film as Genre
Indiana University Press, Bloomington, IN, 1979

Das-Gupta, Chidananda, ed.
Satyajit Ray
Directorate of Film Festivals, Ministry of Information and
Broadcasting, New Delhi, India, 1981

Das, Lama Surya
Buddha is as Buddha Does
Harper Collins, San Francisco, CA, 2007

Dates, Jannette L.& William Barlow, edited by
Split Image: African Americans in the Mass Media
Howard University Press, Washington, D.C., 1990

Diawara, Manthia
African Cinema: Politics & Culture
Indiana University Press, Indiana, 1992

Diawara, Manthia edited by
Black American Cinema
American Film institute, N.Y., 1993

Feeney, F.X.
Welles: Movie Icons
Taschen, Los Angeles, London, 2008

Gadjigo, Samba, R.H. Faulkingham, T. Cassirer & R. Sander,
Edited by *Ousmane Sembene: Dialogues with critic and writers*
University Massachusetts Press, Amherst, MA, 1993

Gandhi, M.K.
An autobiography or the story of my experiments with truth
Navajivan Publishing House, Ahmedabad, India, 1996

★ 369

Garnham, Nicholas
Samuel Fuller
Viking Press, N.Y., 1971

Georgakas, Dan and Lenny Rubenstein, eds.
The Cineaste Interviews: On the Art and Politics of the Cinema
Lake View Press, Chicago, IL, 1982

Gitlin, Todd, ed.
Watching Television
Pantheon Books, NY, 1987

Grund, Bernard
The Timetables of History: A Horizontal Linkage of People and Events
Simon and Schuster, N.Y, 1963

Guerrero, Ed
Framing Blackness: The African American Image in Film
Temple University Press, 1993

Halberstam, David
The powers that be
Knopf, NY, 1979

Hall, Manly P.
Lectures on ancient philosophy
Penguin, NY, 2005

Hampden-Turner, Charles
Maps of the Mind: Charts and concepts of the mind and its labyrinths
Collier Books, N.Y., 1982

Harris, Sheldon
Blues Who's Who: A Biographical Dictionary of Blues Singers
DaCapo Press, N.Y., 1991

Herskovits, Melville
The myth of the Negroes past
Beacon Press, 1941

Hessel, Stephen
Time for Outrage: Indiginez-vous
Hachette Book Co, NYC, 2010

Higham, Charles
The films of Orson Welles
University of California Press, Berkeley, CA, 1971

Hill, George and Spencer Moon
Blacks in Hollywood: Five Favorable Years, 1987-1991
Daystar Press, Los Angeles, CA, 1992

Hurley, Neil P.
Toward a film humanism
Delta, N.Y., 1970

Hyatt, Marshall
The Afro-American Cinematic Experience: An annotated Bibliography and Filmography
Scholarly Resources, Inc., Wilmington, DE, 1983

Ingram, Robert
Francois Truffaut
Taschen, Koln, Germany, 2005

Jodorowsky, Alexjandro
A book of the film El Topo
Douglas Links, NY, 1971

Katz, Ephraim
The Film Encyclopedia
Harper Collins, N.Y., 1994

Katz, William Loren
The Black West
Open Hand Publishing, Inc. Seattle, WA, 1987

Kemble, Francis Ann
Journal of a residence on a Georgia plantation, 1838-39
Knopf, 1961

Key, Wilson Bryan, PhD
Subliminal Seduction, 1973

Media Sexploitation, 1976

The clam-plate orgy and other subliminal techniques for manipulating your behavior, 1981
All published by Signet, New American Library, NY

Keyser, L.J. & A.H. Ruszkowski
The Cinema of Sidney Poitier: The Black Mans' Changing Role in American Cinema
A.S. Barnes & Co. Inc., San Diego, CA, 1980

Klotman, Phyllis Rauch, ed.
Screenplays of the African American Experience
Indian University Press, Bloomington, IN, 1991

Klotman, Phyllis R.
Frame by Frame I: A Black Filmography
Indiana University Press, Bloomington, IN, 1997

Klotman, Phyliss R. & Gloria J. Gibson
Frame by Frame II:
A Filmography of the African American Image, 1978-1994
Indiana University Press, Bloomington, IN, 1997

Krohn, Bill
Luis Bunuel: The Complete Films
Taschen, Koln, Germany, 2005

Kurosawa, Akira
Something like an autobiography
Knopf, N.Y., 1982

Leab, Daniel J.
From Sambo to Superspade: The Black Experience in Motion Pictures
Houghton Mifflin, N.Y., 1975

Leaming, Barbara
Orson Welles: A biography
Viking, NY, 1985

Lee, Bruce
Wisdom for The Way
Black Belt Books, Inc., 2009

Lee, Spike
Five for Five: The films of Spike Lee
Stewart, Tabori & Chang, N.Y., 1991

Lewis, Peter and Corinne Pearlman
Media and Power: From Marconi to Murdoch, A graphic guide
Camden Press, London, U.K., 1986

Maccabe, Julien, Isaac & Colin
The Diary of a Young Soul Rebel
British Film Institute, London, 1991

Mapp, Edward & John Kisch
A Separate Cinema: Fifty Years of Black Cast Posters
Farrar, Straus & Giroux, N.Y., 1992

McBride, James
The Color of Water: A Black Man's Tribute to His White Mother
Riverhead Books, NY, NY, 1996

McLuhan, Marshall
Understanding Media: The Extensions of Man
McGraw-Hill, N.Y. 1965

Mellon, Joan
Voices from the Japanese Cinema
Liveright, N.Y., 1975

Moon, Spencer
Reel Black Talk: A Sourcebook of Fifty American Filmmakers
Greenwood Publishing, Westport, CT, 1997

Murray, James
To Find an Image: Black Films from Uncle Tom to Superfly
Bobbs-Merrill Co., N.Y., 1973

Murray, Pauli
Proud Shoes: The story of an American family
Harper & Row, NY, 1978

Nelson, Jill
Volunteer Slavery: My Authentic Negro Experience
The Noble Press Inc., Chicago, 1993

Newman, Richard
African American Quotations
Facts on File, N.Y., 2000

Nichols, Nichelle
Beyond Uhura: Star Trek and other memories
G.P. Putnam's Sons, N.Y., 1994

Null, Gary
Black Hollywood: From 1970 to Today
Citadel Press, N.Y., 1993

Ogletree, Charles
The Presumption of Guilt: The arrest of Henry Louis Gates Jr.
and Race and Class, and Crime in America
Palgrave Macmillian, NY, 2010

Oshana, Maryann
Women of Color: A Filmography of Minority and Third World
Women
Garland Publishing, Inc., N.Y., 1985

Oumano, Ellen
Thirty-Five Top Filmmakers discuss their craft
St. Martins' Press, N.Y., 1985

Parks, Gordon
A choice of weapons
Falcon Books, N.Y., 1966

Half Past Autumn: A Retrospective
Little, Brown & Co, N.Y., 1997

Parrish, James Robert & George Hill
Black Action Films
McFarland & Co. Publishers, Jefferson NC, 1989

Patterson, Lindsay edited with an introduction by
Black Films & Filmmakers: a Comprehensive Anthology from
Stereotype to Superhero,
Dodd Mead & Co., N.Y., 1975

Peyton, Patricia, ed.
Reel Change: A Guide to Social Issue Films
San Francisco, CA, The Film Fund, 1979

Poitier, Sidney
This Life
Knopf Publishing, NY, 1981

The Measure of a Man: a Spiritual Autobiography
Harper, San Francisco, CA, 2000

Powers, Anne, compiled and edited by
Blacks in American Movies: a Selected Bibliography
Scarecrow Press, N.J., 1974

Reed, Ishmael
Mixing it up: Taking on the Media Bullies and other Reflections
Da Capo Press, Philadelphia, PA, 2008

Another Day At The Front: Dispatches from the Race War
Basic Books, NY, 2004

Reid, Mark
Redefining Black Film
University of California Press, Berkeley, CA, 1993

Rhines, Jesse Algeron
Black Film/White Money
Rutgers University Press, New Brunswick, NJ, 1996

Rideau, Wilbert
In The Place Of Justice: A Story of Punishment and Deliverance
Knopf, NY, 2010

Rogers, J.A.
Sex and Race, Vol.2: The New World
H.M. Rogers, St. Petersburgh, FL, 2000

Rosenthal, Alan
The New Documentary in Action
University of California Press, Berkeley, CA, 1971

Rotha, Paul, Sinclair Road & Richard Griffith
Documentary Film: The use of the film medium to interpret creatively and in social terms the life of people as it exists in reality
Farber & Farber Ltd., London, 1956

Sampson, Henry T.
Blacks in Black and White: A Source Book on Black Films
Scarecrow Press, N.J., 1995

Sarris, Andrew
The American Cinema: Directors and Directions 1929-1968
Dutton, N.Y., 1968

Satin, Mark
New Age Politics: The emerging new alternatives to Liberalism and Marxism
Fairweather Press, Vancouver, B.C., Canada, 1976

Sterne, Emma Gelders
The Story of the Amistad
Dover Publications, Mineola, NY, 2001

Tagore, Rabindranath
Of Myself: Atamaparichay
Anvil Press Poetry, London, UK, 2006

Toms, Coons, Mulattoes, Mammies and Bucks
Continuum Publishing, N.Y., 1989

Tyler, Parker
The Shadow of an Airplane Climbs the Empire State building: A World Theory of Film
Doubleday, NY, 1972

Magic and Myth of the Movies
Simon and Schuster, NY, 1970

Ukadike, Nwachukwa Frank
Questioning African Cinema: Conversations with filmmakers
University of Minnesota Press, Minneapolis, MN, 2002

Valade III, Roger M.
The Essential Black Literature Guide
Visible Ink, Detroit, 1996

Venture, Michael
Cassavetes Directs: John Cassavetes and the making of Love Streams
Kamera Books, U.K., 2007

Vogel, Amos
Film as a subversive art
Random House, NY, 1974

Wakeman, John, ed.
World Film Directors: Volume One, 1890-1945
World Film Directors: Volume Two, 1945-1985
H.W. Wilson Company, NY, 1987 & 1988

Watts, Jill
Hattie McDaniel: Black Ambition, White Hollywood
Harper Collins, NY, 2005

Welles, Orson:
The Rise and Fall of an American Genius
St. Martins' Press, N.Y., 1985

Wise, Tim
Colorblind: The rise of post-racial politics and the retreat from racial equality
City Lights/Open Media Series, San Francisco, CA, 2010

Woods, Paula L. & Felix H. Lidell
I, Too, Sing America: The African American Book of Days
Workman Publishing, NY, NY, 1992

X, Malcolm
On Afro-American History
Pathfinder Press, N.Y., 1970

Yearwood, Gladstone L.
Black Cinema Aesthetics: Issues in Independent Black Filmmaking
Ohio University, Athens, OH, 1982

MAGAZINES, NEWSPAPERS AND OTHER SOURCES

PEOPLE AND GENERES

Black Film Review
Washington, D.C., 1980-91

Black Film Bulletin, British Film Institute: African & Caribbean Unit 1985- 92, U.K.

Black Scholar: Black film & culture
Vol.33, No.1, Spring, 2003, Oakland, CA

Blacks in the West **The Untold Story: The Black West (**1993), 60 min. Narrated by Danny Glover, produced and directed by Nina Rosenbaum, 60 min.

Blaxploitation
Baadasssss Cinema (2002), documentary, 56 min., color, dir. by Isaac Julien

Hell Up in Hollywood: Soul cinema in the 1970's (2003), documentary, 46 min.,
color, Prod. & dir. by Kevin Burns

Badasssss! (2004), 108 min. color, Prod.& dir. by Mario Van Peebles. A son's homage to his father, Black images, breaking down barriers and courage.

Luis Bunuel
http://www.luisbunuel.com/

Nat King Cole
Documentaries
The Unforgettable Nat King Cole (1988) BBC Production, 58 min., color.

The World of Nat King Cole (2004), PBS, 54 min., color
Performance

The Incomparable Nat King Cole (1991), 100 min., b/w, 47 songs from his television program featuring an assortment of guests. http://www.kultur.com

An Evening with Nat King Cole (1995), 47 min., color, performance from 1961 in the U.K. Recorded by the BBC. http://www.image-entertainment.com

Internet Movie Database, http://www.imdb.com/

Welles, Orson
The Economist, "*The truth about rosebud*", October 19, 1985, pages 108-110
Levin, Eric with Sebastian Cody, Joe Pilcher & Frank Sanello

"*At his final exit, Orson Welles leaves a legend and a debate as large as the man himself*", *People,* pages 46-50, 1985

Young, Ian, "*Orson Welles*", *Lambda Philatelic Journal,* June 2001, pages 5-6

Wim Wenders
http://archive.sensesofcinema.com/contents/directors/03/wenders.html
http://www.wim-wenders.com/

SUBJECTS

Bernstein, Dennis and Laurel Sydell, text
Art by Bill Sienkiewicz
Friendly Dictators Trading Cards:
featuring 36 of America's most embarrassing allies
Eclipse Enterprises, Forestville, CA, 1989

Ford, Richard Thompson
A primer on racism: the many uses of the word and how legit
they are
www.slate.com, 9/30/09

Foster, Mary
Interracial couple denied marriage license in LA.
Associated Press, 10/16/09

Goldstein, Patrick
Oscars pass over people of color
Miami herald, 1/25/11

Moore, Curtis
Actual facts about the Henry Louis Gates case
www.theblacklist.com , 7/24/09

Saldana, Dave
Mega-mega-merger: meet the new media monopoly
Commondreams.org, 1/24/11

Trujillo, Melissa
Black scholars arrest raises profiling questions
Associated Press, 7/20/09